The Quest for a Divided Welfare State

John Lapidus

The Quest for a Divided Welfare State

Sweden in the Era of Privatization

palgrave
macmillan

John Lapidus
Department of Economy and Society
University of Gothenburg
Gothenburg, Sweden

ISBN 978-3-030-24783-6 ISBN 978-3-030-24784-3 (eBook)
https://doi.org/10.1007/978-3-030-24784-3

This Palgrave Macmillan imprint is published by the registered company Springer Nature Switzerland AG
The registered company address is: Gewerbestrasse 11, 6330 Cham, Switzerland

Preface

I am 46 years old. Thus, I have lived with the Swedish welfare model long enough to see it change in many ways. Or did I really see it? Transformation is not overnight, and we may all have a lagging self-image of our countries and their development.

Gradually, we move towards a divided welfare state with all its characteristics. Increased inequality. Increased invisibility. And ever-more actors who push for further division, often with anti-intellectual arguments where the most stupid one is that division is perfectly in line with the principles of a universal welfare state.

The twisted debate arises when the advocates of a divided welfare state realize that universalism is still popular in people's minds, and that it must therefore be referred to even when proposals go in the opposite direction. For how long will such tactics be necessary? The wind of change blows hard and it modifies not only the model itself, but also our perception of welfare as a civil right.

There is a strong quest for a divided welfare state and a weak defence for universalism. Development is not set in stone, however, and above all, it is not economically justified. As a result of relative and inevitable price increase in all kinds of welfare services—public as well as private and semi-private—all models are associated with increased relative costs, and the divided welfare state tends to be the most expensive of them all.

Hence, it is about politics rather than economics. It is a political choice between completely different welfare models, a choice that basically revolves around our view of society and ourselves.

I want to thank those who, in different ways, have inspired me to write this book: Jesper Hamark, Birgit Karlsson, Bengt-Olof Andersson, Ingo Schmidt, Jenny Andersson, Brian Shaev, Olav Fumarola Unsgaard, Ann Ighe, Stefan Öberg, Erik Bengtsson, Stig Montin, Jacob Hacker, Daniel Suhonen, Niels Stöber, Enna Gerin, Jesper Weithz, Nathalie Morel, Mio Fredriksson, Beatriz González López-Valcárcel, Bo Rothstein, Erich Chavarría Urbina, Robert Lapidus, Daniel Lapidus and last but most of all Olle, Lisa and Agneta. I also want to thank the Torsten Söderberg foundation for funding my research.

Gothenburg, Sweden John Lapidus

Contents

1
The Divided Welfare State

The Swedish welfare model is gradually losing its characteristics, noticed not least by the extensive privatization of *provision* that began in the early 1990s. But *funding* has also been privatized to a certain extent, primarily through new supplementary services in healthcare, education and elderly care. Rather than full privatization, however, it is about semi-private welfare solutions, where the consumer has been able to reduce the private cost through different types of tax breaks, and where private providers have been able to freeride on an infrastructure built up with public funds.

The clearest example is the rapid growth of private health insurance, which is today signed by every tenth Swede in working age. With a private health insurance, the policyholder is guaranteed quick access to care, normally at a privately run healthcare facility that also receives publicly funded patients in accordance with the slower course of events regulated by the public care guarantee. The insurance also includes a number of other services, including a healthcare coordinator who is responsible for booking patients with the private providers.

The emergence of a parallel healthcare system is fully in line with what has been called *the hidden welfare state* (Howard 1999). It is a type

J. Lapidus, *The Quest for a Divided Welfare State*,
https://doi.org/10.1007/978-3-030-24784-3_1

of welfare that is partly publicly funded but rarely included in the statistics on public expenditure; a welfare that more people want to take part of but few want to recognize as welfare; a welfare that is difficult to investigate due to business secrecy and secret agreements, for example between insurance companies and private healthcare providers; a welfare based on political decisions that go under the radar, decisions that can be so complicated that legislative politicians do not themselves understand what they mean.

The hidden welfare state and the *visible* welfare state together form *the divided welfare state* (Hacker 2002). What is a divided welfare state? The short answer is that it is two very different welfare states within one and the same nation, one welfare state that is aimed at some groups and one that is aimed at other groups. Moreover, in the divided welfare state, between the two welfare states, there is often a gap where many people tend to fall down.

The classic example of a divided welfare state, consisting of a visible welfare state and a hidden welfare state and the gap right between them, is the United States. In terms of healthcare, the visible welfare state in the United States is the means-tested systems directed to those who can prove themselves sufficiently poor (Medicaid) or old (Medicare). We call it the visible welfare state just because it is visible. It is about direct government expenditures that are neatly set up in the state budget and tangible in the welfare debate. It is the visible welfare that US-Americans refer to when talking about welfare. It is thus said *He is on welfare* and *She is on welfare* about people who qualify for the visible welfare state (Bowman 2013). Thus, people are pointed out in the very stigmatizing way (Moffitt 1983; Besley and Coate 1992) that is normally avoided in universal welfare states, this by creating welfare services on equal terms for all citizens.

The word *welfare* gets a completely different meaning in a divided welfare state. The word does not refer to a collective social right, but to a means-tested welfare service that is directed at the most vulnerable groups. It is the recipients of the visible welfare that comes into focus for those who consider the welfare costs to be too high. In the United States, there are countless examples of bumper stickers with texts like *You have to work harder: millions on welfare depend on you.*[1] At the same time, there is often a lot of confusion not only on the hidden welfare state but also on the visible one. In a country that is so much semi-privatized, it may even happen that recipients of the visible, means-tested, state-funded public welfare actually think it is private, why expressions such as *Take your government hands of my Medicare!* are quite common.[2]

But—a big but!—those who get their healthcare through private health insurance also receive state support for their welfare consumption, mainly through different types of tax breaks and tax deductions which are a major cost for the state in the form of lost tax revenue. The more they earn, the greater the support. So, the rich are also *on welfare* even if they would never express it that way. Hence, private health insurance policies are not as private as the name suggests.

Titmuss (1958) was one of the first to note the phenomenon. He considered it misleading to focus only at direct spending on welfare, but instead one must study the "social division of welfare" which included, among other things, the indirect expenditures (in Titmuss' terminology *fiscal welfare*) associated with the hidden welfare state. The phenomenon was also noticed by another of the nestors of welfare state research, who argued that this type of tax breaks is particularly evident in liberal welfare models, where "one of the fastest growing components of public expenditure is tax subsidies for so-called private 'welfare plans'" (Esping-Andersen 1990).

As Esping-Andersen claims, the cost for tax subsidies grew quickly. When summing up the visible welfare state and the hidden welfare state, it turns out that the US-American welfare state is not as small as it often appears. In fact, public welfare spending is approaching northern European levels (Adema et al. 2014) and "Suddenly, the American welfare state did not look so small anymore" (Howard 2008). The state expenditures for universal and divided welfare models are thus more similar than what they seem to be at first glance, even though the models are very different in other aspects.

What do the visible and the hidden welfare states have to do with Sweden? Here, we still have one and the same tax-funded healthcare system aimed at all the nation's citizens? Yes and no. It is not that we suddenly got a divided welfare state like the US-American, but it is obvious that we are moving in that direction. It is obvious not least in the healthcare sector. In a short time, just in lines with the principles of the divided welfare state, we have created a parallel healthcare system where 650,000 people buy quick access to healthcare via their *private* health insurance policies.

The hidden welfare is growing rapidly in Sweden. On the other hand, apparently, nothing has yet happened to the visible welfare state. You do not have to prove that you are sufficiently poor or old in order to utilize the public health system. It is not that we contemptuously say *They are on welfare* about people who see a doctor within the publicly funded system. And it is not that people generally look down on the one who lacks a private health insurance policy, even if there are probably some circles where people would blame you for not having one.

However, appearances are deceiving. In reality, the hidden welfare gradually erodes the visible, public and former universal welfare on every conceivable level. There are a large number of erosive factors that physically weaken the public welfare sector, but there is also a psychological level where our values tend to change over time. The trust in the state-funded healthcare system is reduced when a parallel healthcare system is created with direct support of the state, a parallel system which is obviously more efficient and better in many ways. The tax willingness decreases among those who buy private health insurance and, at the same time, pay tax for a healthcare that they no longer use to the same extent. The most vocal societal groups disappear as opinion formers for a functioning public health system when they, by signing private health insurance, are no longer part of the system and no longer have a self-interest in making sure that the public healthcare works in the best possible way.

There are many more examples of the erosive effects of the hidden welfare, but in the most obvious way, it is about the direct and indirect freeriding on the public sector. In Sweden, the emerging hidden welfare revolves around a confusion of public and private, where the public, in different ways, directly and indirectly, sponsors the private so much that we should talk about semi-private or pseudo-private or half-private health insurance rather than private health insurance.

On the one hand, an indirect state sponsorship, in which the policyholders in various ways freeride on the public by attending private healthcare providers who have agreements with the public sector, agreements in which the public already covers much of the costs. Examples of this are that private hospitals' rents are often paid for by the public and that policyholders thus do not pay a penny to stay there, which means that insurance companies can keep prices down and sell even more insurance. Another example is the doctors' further education and specialization, which is often financed by the public, although during this training period the doctors can be active in the private and semi-private welfare sector.

On the other hand, a direct and statutory state sponsorship via the new options for healthcare, school and elderly care, mainly used by the well-off layers of the population. Here we find the so-called Rut deduction for home care and elderly homes, the so-called homework assistance deduction for education and, not least, the disputed gross salary deduction which has been the driving force behind the rapid growth of private health insurance.

Some of these state sponsorship methods within the framework of the hidden welfare state have come and gone and come again. Some have been politically disputed. But on the whole, they have strengthened their position in the new welfare market as well as in the labour market (the employment tax deduction) and in the housing market (the interest deduction), where we also find tax expenditures targeted at certain groups of the population.

Just as in the United States, the hidden welfare in Sweden revolves around a kind of reverse means-testing, one that is primarily aimed at the more well-off layers of the population. These groups receive state aid—directly and indirectly—to consume a certain kind of welfare, while the less well-off is informally and sometimes even formally excluded from the state support measures.

Some groups are informally excluded since they cannot afford the state-subsidized services. How can that be? Well, even though the state helps with a large part of the payment, it is still relatively expensive to buy *private* home care or *private* homework assistance or *private* health insurance.

Other groups are formally excluded because they do not have the formal right to utilize the tax breaks. The ability to make tax breaks is based on the payment of taxes and most preferably tax payments from a high income. Parents with maintenance support did not even have the formal right to get their children's private homework assistance sponsored by the state. Many pensioners, because of their low incomes—and thus small tax payments—do not even have the formal right to use the entire Rut deduction for home care and elderly homes.

When it comes to *private* health insurance, you may also need an employer willing to help you with the tax break. Those who are unemployed or have unwilling employers, such as everyone who today has different types of temporary employment, have therefore been formally excluded from the possibility of having the private health insurance sponsored by the state.

In a divided welfare state, people become more dependent on their employers, who are suddenly the ones who offer a certain kind of welfare solution. The employer appreciates the goodwill obtained from being the one who, instead of the state, but at the expense of the state, can offer these services, and the employer appreciates the power it gives to link the service to continued and loyal employment. At the same time, the employee is tied to the employer through the new welfare relationship. If you get rid of the job, you risk getting rid of your *private* health insurance. If you are married to a person who, through his or her employer, takes out insurance for the whole family, then you risk getting rid of your insurance if you separate.

The welfare relation between employer and employee is another factor that distinguishes the divided welfare state from the kind of welfare model we have traditionally had in Sweden. The Scandinavian welfare model relied on a relationship between the state and the citizen, but in a divided welfare state, the employee's relation to the employer becomes much more important.

On another level, the emergence of semi-private *funding* within the framework of the hidden welfare state is based on the privatization of *provision* (in Sweden, known and debated as *profits in welfare*) which started in Sweden in the early 1990s. In short, it can be said that the emerging insurance market requires privately provided healthcare, since the publicly run care does not lend itself to policyholders. If there was not a nationwide network of privately provided healthcare at all care levels, then the insurance companies would have nowhere to send their hundreds of thousands of customers. The insurance companies are thus dependent on private healthcare providers for their business, but at the same time, the private providers tend to become increasingly dependent on the insurance companies.

First, it is about spreading risk, where the profit-driven companies are happy to seek agreements with more actors than just the county councils. Second, insurance companies pay more than county councils per patient. This is partly because the insurance companies cannot guarantee the same flow of patients, and partly because the insurance companies require a quicker treatment for their customers. The insurance patients are thus more profitable than the county council patients, a circumstance which, by extension, can have major consequences. In some US states, the differences in ability to pay have made it difficult for publicly funded patients (Medicaid and Medicare) to find caregivers who want to receive them.

The mutual dependency between private provision and funding of welfare services is an under-researched area. The same goes for a lot of what is dealt with in this book, including the erosive mechanisms and the indirect state sponsorship in the form of a healthcare infrastructure and publicly funded further education that is made available to the hidden welfare state.

Overall, the divided welfare state is surprisingly under-researched, given the increasingly important role it plays in many countries. So, for example, it is claimed (Morel et al. 2019) that "social tax expenditures (STEs) – or fiscal welfare – has remained a blind spot in much of the welfare state literature", while Branco and Costa (2018) believe that "We (still) know little about this 'hidden welfare state' as it has been under-researched and under-theorized by the literature on welfare protection". This is also addressed by Konishi and Miyazato (2018), as well as by Sinfield (2018) who at the same time summarizes what the hidden welfare is all about:

> Arguments rage about the welfare state – who gets what, to what effect, and at whose cost? But there is still little attention to an alternative, expensive, and largely hidden 'tax welfare state'. This also conveys

> considerable benefits on many, reinforcing their efforts to achieve social and economic security, encouraging and supporting particular activities such as saving for retirement, bringing up children, or buying a home, while leaving others, generally on lower incomes, with higher taxes and fewer services. Like the public welfare state, the tax system is not only government controlled and organised but its workings also effectively shift resources among different groups in society. However, who benefits from these tax benefits and who pays for them can differ dramatically from public welfare benefits, and it has very different visibility and accountability.

Here, I would like to add that the hidden welfare is a whole system of state sponsorship that is much larger than just lost tax revenue through statutory tax breaks. These other sorts of sponsorship are even more under-researched than the under-researched *fiscal welfare* state (Titmuss 1958) or *social tax expenditures* (Morel et al. 2019) or *private social benefits* (Hacker 2002) or whatever we like to call it. Taken together, this whole system has a great and mainly negative impact on the public welfare sector. Since it develops gradually and under the radar for the political debate, we move towards a divided welfare state without even noticing it.

To shed some more light on this system, three general questions are asked: What characterizes the emerging divided welfare state in Sweden? How has it emerged? Why has it emerged?

In order to tackle the first question, I start from one of the most exhaustive books on the divided welfare state (Hacker 2002), where three characteristics of the US-American divided welfare state are emphasized, characteristics which also seem to fit quite well into the Swedish and European case: (1) Inequality, (2) Invisibility, and (3) The emergence of new actors in the welfare arena, actors which all have an interest in continued privatization or semi-privatization.

First, speaking about inequality, there is a fact that stands above all others: a parallel healthcare system where some people get faster access to care than others at the very same hospital and health centre is by definition more unequal than a universal system. It also challenges the main paragraphs in the Swedish Healthcare Act, that is, healthcare must be given due to needs and on equal terms for all citizens.

Second, private but government-subsidized welfare solutions are more difficult to control and less transparent than public direct-spending programs, something that makes them less contested than they would otherwise have been. In fact, most Americans

> do not recognize the extent to which private benefits are encouraged by government, and even many policymakers admit that they have only a sketchy understanding of the subterranean political processes and public policies that shape private social provision. (Hacker 2002)

Here, there is a direct correspondence with the Swedish case where much of the hidden welfare remains shrouded in obscurity, something that I have experienced in my fruitless efforts to come across materials protected by business secrecy. The new invisibility also seems to affect public officials, who for various reasons are increasingly unwilling to answer questions about public–private partnerships.

Third, private but government-subsidized welfare solutions create a number of new actors in the welfare sector, such as insurance companies and private providers. They are proactive in making the system even more private or semi-private and conservative politicians and employers often join in the chorus. The employers

> praise the flexibility of the private benefit system, prizing the goodwill and productivity that employer-based benefits purchase, all the more so because credit for the provision of benefits goes to them rather than to government. (Hacker 2002)

The new facts on the ground are hard to resist even for many of those who previously advocated universal and public solutions to welfare problems. That is the case with the employees who benefit from the new system. The same goes for their unions, which reluctantly accept the new rules as a strategic response to the state's failure to extend social protection. One example is the Swedish white-collar union TCO, which decided to offer their members private health insurance while arguing that it was a moral problem to go against the Swedish welfare model. This was in 2012. Today, seven years later, it seems like TCO does not have this moral problem any longer. Today's leaders of TCO support the tax subsidies of private health insurance, and they firmly resist any intention to curb the development in this area.

They are far from alone. There are many actors in the new welfare market and moreover, in the absence of sound arguments, they often create a kind of newspeak for the welfare issues, that is anti-intellectual arguments such as claiming that two queues to healthcare are not at all two queues or that the removal of benefit taxation would mean a kind of compulsory taxation or even a triple taxation for some people. The most remarkable of all these arguments is perhaps that the demands for a divided welfare state are fully in line with the traditional Swedish welfare model, even though they are its absolute opposite.

The last of these arguments lead us into the how-question, that is, how did the divided welfare state start to emerge in Sweden. Since the traditional Swedish welfare model continues to be preferred by large segments of the population (Svallfors 2011), the "advocates of change" (Pierson 1996) need to make a sort of gradual and almost invisible changes that are so typical of the hidden welfare state. Further, because of the popular resistance to privatization, politicians and others feel obligated to refer to the Swedish model even when their policy recommendations are the exact opposite of that model.

Cox (2004) has captured this behaviour in the useful term *Path dependency of an idea*, i.e. that the Scandinavian welfare model rests on values (universalism, solidarity, decommodification) so important to so many that "scholars and policy-makers are compelled to justify their observations and proposals for reform by making reference to those values". Hence, the values are allegedly shared even by those who have a completely different agenda. There is thus a political-tactical dimension aiming to change the system not by an open attack but instead by various forms of incremental and hidden means, something which can be much more rewarding way to fundamentally change popular institutions (Hacker 2004).

The above has implied a striking discrepancy between political rhetoric and practice. Ultimately, this kind of political manoeuvring to change the welfare model raises questions about the status of democracy and makes the term postdemocracy (Crouch 2004) worth discussing.

The changes must not be implemented by conservative politicians. At a time when social democratic parties have undergone ideological reversal (Kitschelt 1994; Ryner 2004; Callinicos 2001), it may actually be less complicated for them to make the decisions. This is because Social Democrats are not believed to have such intentions, all in lines with the Nixon-goes-to-China-argument according to which an anti-Communist like Nixon could go to China without being suspected of selling out American interests (Ross 2000).

To answer the question more concretely, it is fruitful to look at the graduality and invisibility that characterizes one part of the divided welfare state: the hidden welfare state. A way to understand how these gradual and invisible changes occur is to look for decisions and non-decisions below the top policy level, i.e. what scholars (Streeck and Thelen 2005; Mahoney and Thelen 2010) within a "more flexible, agent-centered version" (Bell 2011) of Historical Institutionalism have termed layering, drift and conversion.

Layering is defined as the introduction of new rules on top of or alongside (amendments, revisions, additions) existing ones, something that gradually can change the original rules/institutions and give "institutional challengers" the victory over "defenders of status quo" (Mahoney and Thelen 2010). One example cited is that Social Democrats across Europe formally have managed to defend public pension schemes. The Conservatives, however, have succeeded in creating voluntary supplemental pensions alongside the public system, which they "hope will tilt the balance toward the latter over the longer run".

The second term, drift, refers to the phenomenon that institutions are not updated in line with economic development or changes in the external environment. It gradually devalues and erodes the institution, which in turn creates a demand for additional institutions. One example is the Swedish elderly care, which has not been updated to meet the needs of a growing population above the age of 80 (e.g. Meagher and Szebehely 2013).

The third term, conversion, implies that rules remain the same but are interpreted and enacted in new ways by actors who "actively exploit the inherent ambiguities of the institution and convert it to new goals, functions, or purposes". One example of conversion is the rise of the

Swedish market for private homework assistance, which was originally created when homework assistance companies started to claim that parents could make tax deductions within the framework of government-subsidized babysitting.

The final question raised above is the why-question, that is why we have seen the emergence of a divided welfare state in Sweden. The why-question has many answers and is indeed multi-layered, but the most obvious answer is that welfare development has gone hand in hand with the neoliberal development on all other social levels of society. This applies not least to the increased income and wealth inequality, which has a number of driving factors, including the abolition of almost all taxes for the rich such as wealth tax, property tax, inheritance and gift tax (Therborn 2018; Almqvist 2016; Lundberg and Waldenström 2018), as well as lowering of the marginal tax rate for high-income earners decided in the so-called January agreement 2019.[3]

A relatively even distribution of income is in fact a prerequisite for providing welfare services on equal terms for the entire population. With an uneven distribution, it becomes difficult to keep the model together partly because new economic opportunities are created for some groups to demand private and semi-private welfare services, while at the same time they have more reasons for wanting to minimize their tax payments to the common.

In 1980, Sweden held the record in economic equality among the OECD-countries. Since then, we have seen a growing inequality and along with that inequality, the Swedish welfare model has changed in many ways.

The general neoliberal development in Sweden was inspired and initiated by the employers' well-documented break-up (Boréus 1994; Elmbrant 1993) from the general mode of compromise which had characterized the Swedish model and which enabled a large number of reforms in the welfare area.

Could the labour movement have opposed the offensive from the employers, or were there really no options for political parties such as Social Democracy? Ryner (2002) has argued that there were indeed new economic structures to relate to, but that these new structures were open to more than just one idea:

> There is nothing inherently neo-liberal about the technological forces behind contemporary 'post-Fordist' capitalist restructuring and globalisation, and these forces could be mobilised to address contemporary social problems in a manner that is compatible with the norms of social democracy and democratic socialism.

According to Ryner, there were feasible alternatives to the neoliberal development, alternatives related not least to the proposal on wage-earner funds which was in line with traditional social democratic thinking on economic democracy. This and other initiatives were abandoned not due to any predetermined structural logic, but instead due to the inability of the labour movement to withstand the power of external and internal ideas and actors.

On the one hand, there was the newly awakened offensive by the employers which was canalized for example through influential think tanks (Boréus 1994; Blyth 2002). The prime example of this offensive was precisely the resistance to the wage-earner funds, and most conspicuous the large demonstration in Stockholm in 1983 to which 75,000 people were bussed to rally against the funds (Blyth 2002; Elmbrant 1993).

Above all, however, it was the Social Democrats themselves who blocked the alternative pathways. Most importantly, the labour movement was surprised by the employer's counter-attack and was unable to stand up against it, partly because it was "assumed that the issue could be resolved through the normal tripartite channels of mediation and compromise" (Ryner 2002).

For Social Democracy and the trade union movement, which were accustomed to constant compromises with the employers, it was a kind of trauma that the latter no longer acknowledged the reforms and the corporative spirit that built the Swedish welfare model.

It is a trauma that still characterizes parts of the labour movement. It is a labour movement that still strives to negotiate with the opposing side, but now with a counterpart who does not want to make any concessions. The attitude of the labour movement is personalized by the social democratic trade union man and Prime Minister Stefan Löfven, a man of negotiation who sometimes seems to negotiate for the mere sake of it.

In short, the labour movement has been paralysed for decades. No wonder, then, that it has turned to the Third Way (Giddens 1998), which can be understood as "a sophisticated political intervention in support of the argument that 'there is no alternative' to all-out capitalism" (Cammack 2018).

The above, however, gives importance to ideas and actions. It implies that the labour movement had and still has a certain room for manoeuvre and "could have acted otherwise", as it is put in one of the most cited works dealing with the relation between structures and actors (Giddens 1979). In turn, this implies that the labour movement can choose to fight against the advocates of a divided welfare state and for the basic principles of the Swedish welfare model.

The essence of the above is that nothing is set in stone. Structures do not determine everything, and history has not come to an end. The future of the Swedish welfare model is not economically determined, but instead it is a political choice between different alternatives. However, the divided welfare state tends to strengthen itself when it emerges, and at the same time it weakens the universal welfare state as well as its defenders.

Notes

1. https://www.amazon.com/Harder-Millions-Welfare-Depend-Sticker-x/dp/B00MDNTTAO.
2. *The Huffington Post*, 9 May 2009. https://www.huffpost.com/entry/get-your-goddamn-governme_b_252326.
3. *SVT*, 11 January 2019. https://www.svt.se/nyheter/inrikes/detta-vet-vi-om-s-mp-l-och-c-uppgorelsen.

References

Adema, W., Fron, P., & Ladaique, M. (2014). How much do OECD countries spend on social protection and how redistributive are their tax/benefit systems? *International Social Security Review, 67*(1), 1–25.

Almqvist, A. (2016). *Den ekonomiska ojämlikheten i Sverige*. Stockholm: Bantorget Grafiska AB.

Bell, S. (2011). Do we really need a new "constructivist institutionalism" to explain institutional change? *British Journal of Political Science, 41*, 883–906.

Besley, T., & Coate, S. (1992). Understanding welfare stigma: Taxpayer resentment and statistical discrimination. *Journal of Public Economics, 48*(2), 165–183.

Blyth, M. (2002). *Great transformations: Economic ideas and institutional change in the twentieth century*. Cambridge: Cambridge University Press.

Boréus, K. (1994). *Högervåg: Nyliberalismen och kampen om språket i svensk debatt 1969–1989*. Stockholm: Tiden.

Bowman, J. R. (2013). *Capitalisms compared: Welfare, work, and business*. Thousand Oaks: CQ Press.

Branco, R., & Costa, E. (2018). The golden age of tax expenditures: Fiscal welfare and inequality in Portugal (1989–2011). *New Political Economy*. https://www-tandfonline-com.ezproxy.ub.gu.se/doi/pdf/10.1080/13563467.2018.1526264%3FneedAccess=true.

Callinicos, A. (2001). *Against the third way: An anti-capitalist critique*. Cambridge: Polity Press.

Cammack, P. (2018). Gidden's way with words. In *The third way and beyond*. Manchester: Manchester University Press.

Cox, R. (2004). The path-dependency of an idea: Why Scandinavian welfare states remain distinct. *Social Policy & Administration, 38*(2), 204–219.

Crouch, C. (2004). *Post-democracy*. Cambridge: Polity.

Elmbrant, B. (1993). *Så föll den svenska modellen*. Stockholm: T. Fischer.

Esping-Andersen, G. (1990). *The three worlds of welfare capitalism*. Cambridge: Polity Press.

Giddens, A. (1979). *Central problems in social theory: Action, structure and contradiction in social analysis*. London: Macmillan.

Giddens, A. (1998). *The third way: The renewal of social democracy*. Cambridge: Polity Press.

Hacker, J. S. (2002). *The divided welfare state: The battle over public and private social benefits in the United States*. Cambridge: Cambridge University Press.

Hacker, J. S. (2004). Privatizing risk without privatizing the welfare state: The hidden politics of social policy retrenchment in the United States. *American Political Science Review, 98*(2), 243–260.

Howard, C. (1999). *The hidden welfare state: Tax expenditures and social policy in the United States*. Princeton: Princeton University Press.

Howard, C. (2008). *The welfare state nobody knows: Debunking myths about US social policy*. Princeton: Princeton University Press.
Kitschelt, H. (1994). *The transformation of European social democracy*. Cambridge: Cambridge University Press.
Konishi, H., & Miyazato, N. (2018). *Distributive impacts of social protection systems in OECD countries: Public-private mix and hidden welfare states* (No. 1804).
Lundberg, J., & Waldenström, D. (2018). Wealth inequality in Sweden: What can we learn from capitalized income tax data? *Review of Income and Wealth, 64*(3), 517–541.
Mahoney, J., & Thelen, K. (2010). *Explaining institutional change: Ambiguity, agency, and power*. Cambridge: Cambridge University Press.
Meagher, G., & Szebehely, M. (2013). Long-term care in Sweden: Trends, actors and consequences. In C. Ranci & E. Pavolini (Eds.), *Reforms in long-term care policies in Europe*. New York: Springer.
Moffitt, R. (1983). An economic model of welfare stigma. *American Economic Review, 73*(5), 1023–1035.
Morel, N., Touzet, C., & Zemmour, M. (2019). From the hidden welfare state to the hidden part of welfare state reform: Analyzing the uses and effects of fiscal welfare in France. *Social Policy & Administration, 53*(1), 34–48.
Pierson, P. (1996). The new politics of the welfare state. *World Politics, 48*(2), 143–179.
Ross, F. (2000). "Beyond left and right": The new partisan politics of welfare. *Governance, 13*, 155–183.
Ryner, M. (2002). *Capitalist restructuring, globalization and the third way: Lessons from the Swedish model*. London: Routledge.
Ryner, M. (2004). Neoliberalization of social democracy: The Swedish case. *Comparative European Politics, 2*(4), 97–119.
Sinfield, A. (2018). Fiscal welfare. In *Routledge handbook of the welfare state* (pp. 45–55). London: Routledge.
Streeck, W., & Thelen, K. (Eds.). (2005). *Beyond continuity: Institutional change in advanced political economies*. New York: Oxford University Press.
Svallfors, S. (2011). A bedrock of support? Trends in welfare state attitudes in Sweden, 1981–2010. *Social Policy & Administration, 45*(7), 806–825.
Therborn, G. (2018). *Kapitalet, överheten och alla vi andra: klassamhället i Sverige - det rådande och det kommande*. Stockholm: Arkiv förlag.
Titmuss, R. (1958). *Essays on the welfare state*. London: George Allen and Unwin.

2

To Buy Ahead

Are you a lemon or a peach? To find the correct answer, the insurance company Skandia wants you to complete a health declaration that begins with the question whether you are fully employed or not. It is followed by questions about length and weight, HIV test, smoking, drug addiction as well as which health centre and doctor you usually go to. Then follow 23 questions about disease states that also have several subgroups (hearing impairment, rheumatism, diabetes, mental problems, allergies, stomach problems, tumours, eczema, etc.), then one question about the use of drugs, one question whether you have been on sick leave or had reduced work capacity, wholly or partly, more than 14 consecutive days, one question whether you have been examined or treated in a hospital, health centre or other healthcare facility or if you have just seen doctor or other healthcare practitioners during the last 5 years (including chiropractor, naprapath, psychologist, psychotherapist or similar), as well as one question whether it is planned or recommended any form of medical visit, examination, treatment or surgery.[1]

Before the declaration is signed, it must be certified that you are aware that incorrect or incomplete information may invalidate the insurance policy. You must also certify that you are aware that Skandia

J. Lapidus, *The Quest for a Divided Welfare State*,
https://doi.org/10.1007/978-3-030-24784-3_2

files the information, regardless of whether the application is approved or not.

Why is a health declaration so important? Well, in a private healthcare system, some have to be excluded. It is about peaches and lemons. If an insurance company welcomes sick individuals (lemons), the premium will rise. Then healthy individuals (peaches) do not want to be involved anymore, and the insurance company is stuck with sick and expensive people.

This is well-known insurance logic. Lemons create *adverse selection* that acidifies the market for private health insurance. The only way to avoid acidification is to reduce the number of lemons. Therefore, you must prove that you are a peach before signing up for private health insurance.

The Nobel laureate George Akerlof (see also Cutler and Zeckhauser 2000; Barrett and Conlon 2003; Jacobs and Sommers 2015) described the phenomenon based on the trade-in used cars (Akerlof 1978). Adverse selection has long been an established concept, but it is not common to hear insurance industry's own representatives speak openly about it. Thus, it was interesting to hear Skandia's CEO Frans Lindelöw during a panel discussion in the 2017 yearly Politician's Week in Almedalen.

I had to listen to my recording an extra time to make sure that Lindelöw said what I thought he was saying. The moderator asked about the exclusion mechanisms, and Lindelöw replied:

> Yes, but it is the whole idea of the insurance. It is a collective that comes together, and if you would bring in someone with a severe form of cancer [a lemon] it might cost a lot for that collective… /… / It would be deeply immoral [towards the peaches] if we brought in someone who had a severe cancer that may cost 10 million. /… / Then you have to create a collective with only severe cancer disease [lemons only], and then the premiums will be very high.[2]

Frans Lindelöw spells it out: for the insurance companies, it is a matter of survival to sort out lemons and store peaches. The companies would not make it if they did not weed out the sick from the healthy. Even in state-regulated systems, intended to be non-discriminatory and equal for all, it has proved difficult to prevent insurance companies from taking measures to sort out lemons. Jacobs and Sommers (2015) show that "insurers are resorting to other tactics to dissuade high-cost patients from enrolling" even within the US-American Affordable Care Act (ACA), which is set up just to get away from this behaviour. One of the tactics is to place all HIV medications in the highest cost category so as to "discourage people with human immunodeficiency virus (HIV) infection from selecting their plans".

In an interview with Eva Erlandsson, economist at the industry organization Insurance Sweden, I get the same baskets of peaches and lemons when I ask about her view on the fact that the insurance is much more expensive for those who are old, sick or unemployed:

> Yes of course, but it is about private business and no solidarity funding. The solidarity that exists is within this insurance group. And if someone enters who is 68 years old and a little diseased, then the premium for the whole group increases. /... / Then those who are healthy will not want the insurance anymore, and then the insurance is dead. So, it's simple logic. You contribute with a risk when you enter a collective and it must be paid in some way. The public sector has the advantage that the entire population shares the risk. But you can never compare a public insurance with a private insurance, it will be the death of the private insurance. You will only have the bad risks if you raise the cost. So, redistribution, we have it in the public system... And to some extent in the private sector, because it is still a collective that shares risks. But it is not shared risks between sick people and healthy people, it is not as far-reaching as in the public sector.[3]

Hence, something that unites all private insurance companies is the inherent desire to sort out lemons, but the insurance companies offer different kinds of insurance policies in different countries. Three of the most common insurance policies are substitutive, complementary and supplementary ones (Mossialos and Thompson 2009; Mossialos et al. 2016). The substitute insurance is for the patient who is not offered care by the publicly funded healthcare system. In Germany, for example, people with high incomes can refrain from entering the public system and instead arrange their care entirely through private insurance (Hullegie and Klein 2010). The complementary insurance covers healthcare services that are not included in the public commitment, and it also covers costs (patient fees and the like) for public care. This type of insurance is common in France (Franc and Pierre 2015; Nay et al. 2016) and Denmark (Kiil and Arendt 2017) where such things as dental care, psychotherapy and chiropractic are covered by private insurance. Finally, the supplementary insurance, which in particular offers faster access to the healthcare services already included in the public commitment. This type of insurance can be found in, for example, Spain (Pons-Pons and Vilar-Rodríguez 2019) and Sweden.

It should also be added that there are not always sharp boundaries between different types of insurance and, moreover, they can have very different ranges in different countries. In Denmark, for example, there is not only the complementary insurance but also the supplementary one that we find in Sweden (Tynkkynen et al. 2018). In Spain, for example, the insurance also covers emergency care, which is (yet) not the case in Sweden. In MUFACE's (the Spanish public organization responsible for social security for civil servants) manual, civil servants are taught not to call 112 in case of emergency, but instead to learn the various private insurance companies' telephone numbers.[4]

With the Swedish version of private health insurance, the supplementary one, the policyholder thus buys faster access to care. More and more health centres and hospitals have two queues for their nursing departments, a quick queue for those who have insurance and a slow for those who do not.

On the healthcare providers' websites, you will find out how to behave if you are an insurance patient or a county council patient. If you are an insurance patient, you call the care coordinator who schedules you quickly at the care provider. If you are a county council patient, just like a large majority of the Swedes, completely different rules apply.

The Swedish version of healthcare insurance thus provides quick access to healthcare. The insurance companies guarantee treatment within a couple of weeks while the state, through the *Public care guarantee*, promises the same thing within six months. Or, to be more precise, within 183 days: 3 days before you get to meet a general practitioner, 90 days before you get to meet a specialist, another 90 days before the treatment must be started.

There is thus a big difference between the waiting times in the public and the semi-private healthcare. Then it should also be said that the public may not always keep the above promise, which is why you have to wait considerably longer than half a year. It can also be a longer wait without breaking the public care guarantee. This is because, for example, any return visits in primary or specialist care are not included in the public care guarantee. There are additional factors that make the waiting time much longer than the promised 187 days, something that the Authority for health and care analysis has shown in their reports (Myndigheten för vård- och omsorgsanalys 2017).

In contrast, the insurance companies' customers are guaranteed initiated treatment within two weeks. If for some reason the insurance company would not keep that promise, the customer is entitled to compensation for each day that goes after the agreed time.

The main reason for taking out a private health insurance in Sweden is to buy ahead the queue in the public system. There are also a number of other reasons to take out private health insurance, but first of all let us focus on the disputed issue of the two queues for healthcare.

Yes, the question is disputed. It is a bit strange as it is an undeniable fact that many private caregivers have a fast queue and a slow queue to their nursing departments. This is possible due to the agreements with the county council on the one hand, and the agreements with the insurance companies on the other. The caregivers undertake to receive county council patients in accordance with the waiting times of the public care guarantee, and the same provider commits to receiving insurance patients in accordance with the short waiting times that the insurance companies have promised their customers.

As we shall see, there are hundreds of private healthcare providers in Sweden who have double agreements, one with county councils and another with insurance companies. One example is Lundby Hospital in Gothenburg, which has a quick queue for certain patient groups and a slow queue for other patient groups. If you have insurance, you are in the fast queue. It is the main purpose of an insurance to be in that queue, and Lundby Hospital is concerned that you as an insurance patient have understood this. Therefore, they write on the website:

> Contact your insurance company directly and they can book an appointment for you at Capio Lundby Hospital.[5]

Although it is clear that the private caregivers have two different queues, there are plenty of opposite statements in the debate on private health insurance. So, for example, previously mentioned Eva Erlandsson and Anna Pettersson Westerberg, also economist at the industry organization Swedish Insurance, claim that "Patients who have a private health insurance do not buy ahead the queue in the public sector".[6] Representatives of the insurance company IF and Skandia agree: "Our policyholders do not buy ahead",[7] says Carin Gyris, head of the insurance company IF's healthcare planning, while Skandia's CEO Frans Lindelöw and health strategist Kristina Hagström believe that "no patients buy ahead in any queue".[8] The editorial pages of the centre-right-wing newspapers have also been frequent users of this argument. So, for example, the one of them says that "People who use private health insurance do not buy ahead some queues, which the critics claim".[9]

It is strange. Buying ahead the public health queue is after all the main purpose of the insurance, and spontaneously it does not seem particularly clever to argue as absurdly as do the advocates of the divided welfare state. But the arguments stick. The arguments are presented everywhere, and they are further used by anyone who wants to legitimize both the purchase and sale of private insurance. The arguments prevent any serious discussion on the issue, and they compel the comparatively few critics to devote time to trying to crack down on myths that get much attention in the media even though they do not deserve any attention at all.

The above (two queues are not two queues) is but one of several examples of the newspeak that characterizes the Swedish welfare debate, a debate where lobbyists have managed to frame not only certain aspects but even the language used to address them (e.g. McGrath 2007).

At the same time as the insurance companies' representatives argue that no one buys ahead, their own marketing is based on the fact that the customers should buy ahead and get faster treatment than they would have received as *regular* patients. The title of Skandia's product brochure is "Private health insurance - care when you need it" and already in the first sentence it is stated that you get access to fast care and do not have to wait. It is interesting to see how Skandia compares with the public healthcare system. Among other things, Skandia states that "often we can read about people who have had to wait unreasonably long for their diagnoses and treatments".

For the retailers of private health insurance, it is important to emphasize their own excellence, while it is not damaging for business if the public sector is discredited. In short, it is in the interest of profit to talk badly about the public sector and, in different ways, exaggerate the crisis in a Swedish healthcare system which actually performs quite well in international comparison (e.g. Barber et al. 2017). The constant and recurring trash talk of the public can in turn have fatal consequences for our way of looking at public welfare.

Private caregivers are also informative about the double queues. You can look up any privately owned health centre or any privately owned hospital online, and you will get a description of how you should behave if you are a publicly and privately funded patient. The insurance patients are asked to call their care coordinator to get help as soon as possible. Another typical writing can be found on the home page of Capio Health Center Axess in Gothenburg:

> To book an appointment with us, turn to your insurance company's healthcare coordinator. All companies that we have agreements with have access to a selection of "earmarked" hours at our nursing departments.[10]

The private caregivers can let the staff work with both the patients of the fast queue and the slow queue, or they can set aside staff who only work with the fast queue. Gunnel Anderzzon, operations manager at Capio Health Center Axess in Gothenburg, tells me that:

> One can choose to have a small private part [of the health center] and then have someone staffed for this, to take a day or two days a week for insurance patients. /… / Or, for example, you have seven doctors employed, and a certain percentage of the time they just see insurance patients, other time to everyone else.[11]

The system of two queues is found at all private healthcare providers who have agreements with both county councils and with the insurance companies. That is, all healthcare providers who receive both publicly and *privately* funded patients. From a political point of view, attempts have been made, or at least alleged attempts, to force the private caregivers to choose between public and privately funded patients (Lapidus 2017), but for the moment they are free to receive different patient groups on different conditions.

So, which are these dual-agreement healthcare units? As mentioned above, a simple Internet search is enough to see that it applies to most private health centres and hospitals. But to get a clearer picture of which private healthcare providers have two different queues, I decided to focus on individual insurance companies and their partners among the private healthcare providers. My idea was to find out which private healthcare providers the insurance companies cooperate with, and then find out if these private healthcare providers also had agreements with the county councils.

The problem was that the insurance companies did not want to give out their healthcare provider networks. One example is the company Länsförsäkringar, one of the largest actors in the market. They work with more than 900 healthcare providers in Sweden, but they did not want to disclose information about which these 900 caregivers are. I called and emailed without results. In vain, I spent a few working days on this, and the difficulty—the impossibility—for a researcher to get this simple information out is but one of many examples of the invisibility that characterizes the hidden welfare state.

After several contacts with managers at Länsförsäkringar, I finally got an email saying: "We have now discussed this internally and we are not able to send the entire list on all suppliers".

However, it was so that Länsförsäkringar, on its website, presented a list of 115 of the more than 900 caregivers. By studying these 115 geographically dispersed care providers, I could get an idea of what kind of healthcare provider Länsförsäkringar cooperates with. I reviewed the websites and other information pages for 108 of these 115 caregivers, and it turned out to be a motley collection; everything from hospitals, health centres and clinics down to private practitioners such as physiotherapist, naprapaths and medical doctors.

Common to all 108 healthcare providers was that they were privately run. Here I wanted to look more closely at the caregivers who welcome both insurance patients and publicly funded patients. Of the total of 108 caregivers, it was 62 who explicitly stated that they also received publicly funded patients in accordance with the rules that apply to these patients.

Thus, 62 of 108 caregivers had two queues. The other 46 healthcare providers focused solely on insurance patients and patients who pay out of pocket. Most of these other caregivers provided care that is not included in the public commitment, such as occupational health, naprapathy and various forms of SPA treatments.

The 62 healthcare providers with two queues show great differences in terms of focus, size and activity. Here we find, for example, the non-profit hospital Ersta in Stockholm. At Ersta hospital, insurance patients are asked to contact their health coordinator, who in turn contacts a special officer at Ersta Hospital. A procedure described on the website:

> As a private insurance patient, you indicate to your health care coordinator that you want to come to Ersta Hospital. At Ersta Hospital, insurance patients have their own administrator who will help your health care coordinator and yourself to access fast care.[12]

In this context, I received a more vivid description of the relationship between health care coordinator, administrators and healthcare staff. It was one that was given me during an interview with Ingrid Thulin, former CEO of the profit-driven Capio Lundby hospital in Gothenburg:

> One needs to have a nurse who is only engaged in guiding the insurance patients, it must be one who can flirt and perhaps tell the reluctant doctor that he gets 100 bucks extra for the trouble. She gets to squeeze in the patients, there is no schedule that does not allow you to squeeze in an extra. /… / In the beginning it was a lot of fuss about no profits in healthcare among the staff… /… / There were doctors who opposed insurance patients but as a manager you have to say that it will be interesting when we talk salary this that you oppose certain patients or schedule changes, then we must lower your salary.[13]

Among the 62 healthcare providers with two queues, all levels of care are represented. In addition to hospitals, there are health centres and clinics such as Hansa Health in Visby, the Health Center in Karlskrona, Capio Läkargruppen in Örebro and many others. These health centres and clinics also explain on their websites that they have an agreement with the county councils, while receiving insurance patients via collaborations with the insurance companies.

Fully private alternatives, i.e. privately run healthcare providers with privately funded customers, have always existed in Sweden. But they have been very few and only able to establish themselves where there was a sufficiently large customer base to run them (Dahlgren 1994; Norén 2008). With mixed funding and dual agreements and queues, completely new opportunities are opened up for private healthcare providers around the country. It is about private healthcare providers who build the bulk of their business in publicly financed care and see the insurance patients as a bonus, but a bonus that is increasing and thus increasingly important the more people who sign private health insurance.

The market for private health insurance is growing rapidly. In the 1990s, private health insurance was still something of a CEO's insurance (Skoglund 2012), but in the past decade, insurance companies have targeted entirely new and large population groups. As recently as 2000, approximately 100,000 people were insured and in 2019 the estimated figure is slightly more than 650,000.[14] The number of caregivers who are open to policyholders has also increased significantly, as have the number of insurance companies and banks that offer employers, organizations and individuals to buy insurance.

The main reason for signing up for insurance is, of course, to buy ahead and get quick access to care. But the more the insurance market grows, the more the insurance companies tend to include in their insurance policies.

If we look into the insurance company Länsförsäkringar, the insurance also covers part of the care that is usually not included in the public undertaking, such as naprapathy, chiropractic, speech therapy and dietician care. Furthermore, you get access to aftercare and rehabilitation measures of various kinds, as well as so-called home service after the operation.

Something that is almost always included in the insurance is a so-called second opinion, that is, the right to renewed medical assessment. The insurance also provides access to treatment for addiction, as well as compensation for certain trips and accommodation in connection with all types of treatment.

Furthermore, most insurances provide access to healthcare counselling around the clock and, of course, quick time booking and care planning. Most insurance companies also have supplementary packages (e.g. insurance plus, insurance gold, insurance extra, insurance large, insurance max, insurance top) which include such things as costs for public care and medicines up to the high-cost ceiling, vaccinations, health checks, foreign care, dental care and much more.

Let us return to the insurance company Skandia's website. Anyone who needs surgery or other treatment is guaranteed, within 20 working days, to be enrolled in a hospital in Skandia's network of private healthcare providers. If Skandia does not succeed in this, the policyholder is guaranteed a compensation of SEK 300 per weekday until the day of enrolment for surgery or hospital care.

There are companies that are more generous with delay premiums or promise even faster care than Skandia does. Examples are IF and Bliwa, which guarantees initiated treatment within 14 days. An insurance company with higher delay premiums is Länsförsäkringar, which promises SEK 1000 per day if they do not fulfil the promise of initiated treatment within 20 working days.

There is a lot to consider when signing up for private health insurance. An important factor is the extent of the companies' healthcare information and care planning for the customers. Here, Skandia has a healthcare information that is open 24 hours a day and a coordinating group of registered nurses who help the policyholder to get access to a suitable provider within a network of 1000 doctors, 850 physiotherapists, naprapaths and chiropractors and 250 psychologists.

The coordinators are an important link in the chain between customer and provider. The policyholders must call the coordinator when they need care. However, it is important that the policyholder knows whether the insurance applies with or without a referral from the public system. Often, you can choose to buy your insurance with or without a claim for referral. On Skandia's website, you are told that insurance with a referral claim is less expensive, but that the policyholder with such an insurance must start by turning to a doctor in the public primary care. It is only when you have referral from the primary care that the insurance enters into force, and it is only the specialist care that is covered by the insurance.

The websites provide information about all levels and price classes offered by the insurance companies. A company like Bliwa offers health insurance Basic, Premium and Premium Extra, while Euro Accident offers Bronze, Silver and Gold insurance. Skandia has four levels of insurance, namely Basic, Access, Plus and Excellent. Or even six levels considered that Basic and Access can be purchased with or without referral requirements.

In order to find out what the insurance costs, we must do more than decide which insurance company we should hire and which insurance level we should choose. For example, we must consult the insurance companies' age-groups, where we find out what our age costs to insure. The premium increases with the policyholder's age. Most insurance companies do not sell insurance to anyone over the age of 65. One of the exceptions is Skandia, which offers healthcare insurance to 85-year-olds, this at a cost of SEK 32,258 (Bas) or SEK 39,997 (Access) or SEK 41,862 (Plus) or SEK 42,404 (Excellent).

The market for private health insurance is growing and the industry organization Swedish Insurance is one of several actors who actively promote the development, and regularly presents figures about how the policyholders increase in number. Swedish Insurance Economist Eva Erlandsson is herself a proud proprietor of private health insurance:

> I think it is a great insurance, I love it, I have it myself as you hear... I save an incredible amount of time, I avoid the turn through the primary health center which rarely gives any outcome, unfortunately, I am quite critical of the primary health centers overall...[15]

Erlandsson is very pleased with her insurance, and she is not alone. Besides, the satisfaction is often about more than just quick access to care. Let me exemplify with the engineer Anders, one of many policyholders whom I have interviewed within the framework of my research. He points to the quick access but there are other things he wants to emphasize:

> As a patient I enter with more self-confidence, because I feel that I have somehow an insurance company behind me... Yes, I am more confident as a patient and see it more as a meeting between two equal parties... And then prescribing becomes easier to ask for and almost like I presume that if I go there with a cold, I will get penicillin. In the public healthcare I am in another situation and I take what I get, or I have to fight more maybe... /... / I have had problems with my eyes, a pressure in the eyes right where you get cataract, it is hereditary and there I got in contact with the healthcare system through my private insurance. And right away I got to come to a specialist, so I passed the primary care step where they would refer me to a specialist, I went directly to an eye specialist, and got enrolled with her and now she handles everything... Every third year I come back... A great thing for me as a patient. And practical as well. No worries about taking renewed contact with primary care. The frames are set, and I feel comfortable. /... / You get a little cockier as a patient. If, for example, I was to be discouraged by the doctor, which has never happened, then I always have my care coordinator to complain to, and then the care coordinator will probably call back to the doctor...[16]

Given the customers' satisfaction, it is no wonder that *private* health insurance policies have experienced explosive growth in Sweden. Eva Erlandsson mentions several reasons why they are so beneficial, and according to her, one should always ask for one when looking for new employment.

Shouldn't everybody have a health insurance then, I ask, if it's so good? Erlandsson has more difficulty answering that question. It is so complicated that we save it to future chapters, where we examine the seemingly logical arguments of the advocates of a divided welfare state.

Notes

1. https://www.skandia.se/forsakra/halsodeklaration/fullstandig-halsodeklaration/?group=Webbhalsa&form=vuxen.
2. Franz Lindelöf, 6 July 2017.
3. Interview, 5 October 2017.
4. https://www.muface.es/muface_Home/Prestaciones/asistencia-sanitaria-nacional/atencion-urgencia.html.
5. https://capio.se/sjukhus/vastra-gotaland/capio-lundby-narsjukhus/vardutbud/privat-vard/.
6. *Dagens industri*, 9 March 2017. https://www.di.se/nyheter/regeringen-missuppfattar-de-privata-sjukvardsforsakringarna/.
7. *Svenska Dagbladet*, 9 October 2012. https://www.svd.se/vanligt-med-privat-sjukforsakring.
8. *Svenska Dagbladet*, 29 June, 2017. https://www.svd.se/feltankt-ny-skatt-kommer-att-oka-vardkoerna.
9. *Göteborgs-Posten*, 26 July 2013. http://www.gp.se/ledare/f%C3%B6rs%C3%A4kringar-%C3%A4r-inte-hot-mot-v%C3%A4lf%C3%A4rden-1.566441.
10. https://capio.se/narsjukvard/vastra-gotaland/goteborg-axess-vardcentral/.
11. Interview, 5 December 2017.
12. https://www.erstadiakoni.se/sv/sjukhus/Patient/Sa-soker-du-vart/.
13. Interview, 20 May 2013.
14. Swedish Insurance, 15 April 2019. https://www.svenskforsakring.se/aktuellt/press/pressarkiv/2019/fortsatt-upp-for-sjukvardsforsakringar-/.
15. Interview, 5 October 2017.
16. Interview, 3 July 2017.

References

Akerlof, G. A. (1978). The market for "lemons": Quality uncertainty and the market mechanism. In *Uncertainty in economics* (pp. 235–251). Cambridge: Academic Press.

Barber, R. M., Fullman, N., Sorensen, R. J., Bollyky, T., McKee, M., Nolte, E., et al. (2017). Healthcare Access and Quality Index based on mortality from causes amenable to personal health care in 195 countries and territories, 1990–2015: A novel analysis from the Global Burden of Disease Study 2015. *The Lancet, 390*(10091), 231–266.

Barrett, G. F., & Conlon, R. (2003). Adverse selection and the decline in private health insurance coverage in Australia: 1989–95. *Economic Record, 79*(246), 279–296.

Cutler, D. M., & Zeckhauser, R. J. (2000). The anatomy of health insurance. In *Handbook of health economics* (Vol. 1, pp. 563–643). Amsterdam: Elsevier.

Dahlgren, G. (1994). *Framtidens sjukvårdsmarknader*. Stockholm: Natur och kultur i samarbete med Institutet för framtidsstudier.

Franc, C., & Pierre, A. (2015). Compulsory private complementary health insurance offered by employers in France: Implications and current debate. *Health Policy, 119*(2), 111–116.

Hullegie, P., & Klein, T. J. (2010). The effect of private health insurance on medical care utilization and self-assessed health in Germany. *Health Economics, 19*(9), 1048–1062.

Jacobs, D. B., & Sommers, B. D. (2015). Using drugs to discriminate—Adverse selection in the insurance marketplace. *New England Journal of Medicine, 372*(5), 399–402.

Kiil, A., & Nielsen Arendt, J. (2017). The effect of complementary private health insurance on the use of health care services. *International Journal of Health Economics and Management, 17*(1), 1–27.

Lapidus, J. (2017). Private health insurance in Sweden: Fast-track lanes and the alleged attempts to stop them. *Health Policy, 121*(4), 442–449.

McGrath, C. (2007). Framing lobbying messages: Defining and communicating political issues persuasively. *Journal of Public Affairs: An International Journal, 7*(3), 269–280.

Mossialos, E., Wenzl, M., Osborn, R., & Sarnak, D. (2016). *2015 International profiles of health care systems*. Ottawa: Canadian Agency for Drugs and Technologies in Health.

Myndigheten för vård- och omsorgsanalys. (2017). *Löftesfri garanti?: en uppföljning av den nationella vårdgarantin*. Stockholm: Vårdanalys.
Nay, O., Béjean, S., Benamouzig, D., Bergeron, H., Castel, P., & Ventelou, B. (2016). Achieving universal health coverage in France: Policy reforms and the challenge of inequalities. *The Lancet, 387*(10034), 2236–2249.
Norén, L. (2008). Att göra patienter till kunder – om sjukvårdsförsäkringar och entreprenörskap. In A. Lundström & E. Sundin (Eds.), *Perspektiv på förnyelse och entreprenörskap i offentlig verksamhet*. Örebro: Forum för småföretagarforskning.
Pons-Pons, J., & Vilar-Rodríguez, M. (2019). The genesis, growth and organisational changes of private health insurance companies in Spain (1915–2015). *Business History, 61*(3), 558–579.
Skoglund, C. (2012). Privata sjukvårdsförsäkringar i Sverige–omfattning och utveckling. *Rapport till SKL*, 2–49.
Thomson, S., & Mossialos, E. (2009). *Private health insurance in the European Union*. European Commission, 320–323.
Tynkkynen, L. K., Alexandersen, N., Kaarbøe, O., Anell, A., Lehto, J., & Vrangbæk, K. (2018). Development of voluntary private health insurance in Nordic countries—An exploratory study on country-specific contextual factors. *Health Policy, 122*(5), 485–492.

3

Private Provision and Private Funding

Initially, since the early 1990s, there was a privatization of *provision*, a gradual increase in the number of schools, health centres, hospitals, retirement homes and home care providers in the private sector. The process has been going on since then and has created a large-scale welfare industry, an industry that makes profits in welfare.

The politicians asserted that it was not important who ran and owned the operations, because all of this would still be funded with taxes within the framework of the universal welfare state.

The politicians were wrong. They claimed that welfare provision was decoupled from welfare funding, but it now turns out that welfare funding is also being split into two parts. They claimed that the admission of *profits in welfare* would not affect the principles of the universal welfare state, but now we have two welfare states entirely in accordance with the principles of the divided welfare state.

The clearest example: we have suddenly received a parallel healthcare system where 650,000 people, one-tenth of the adult population, are buying themselves ahead with private health insurance.

What has private provision—in the general Swedish debate called *profits in welfare*—of central welfare services to do with the rapid emergence

J. Lapidus, *The Quest for a Divided Welfare State*,
https://doi.org/10.1007/978-3-030-24784-3_3

of private health insurance? This chapter examines the mutual relationship between provision and funding, that is, how profits in welfare make the rapid rise of private health insurance possible and how the insurance industry, in turn, becomes increasingly important for the profit-driven welfare companies. Private provision of welfare services thus lay the foundation for a new welfare model, a divided welfare state. It is an aspect that, although it can be the most important, has completely been missed in the decade-long Swedish debate on profits in welfare.

But first of all: what is actually provision and funding? The fact that there are decisive differences of meaning between them should really be quite obvious, but the concepts have often been mixed together despite the fact that researchers have long tried to bring order to the mess (e.g. Donahue 1989; Starr 1988).

In short, the one responsible for provision is the one who owns and runs the performance of the welfare services. Thus, a health centre can be run by the public sector (by a county council) or privately (by a profit-making or non-profit company). The question of profits in welfare thus revolves around the provision of the welfare services, that is, who own and perform the same.

The funding of a welfare service, such as healthcare, can also be public or private. If it is public, it is funded via taxes, if it is private, it is funded via own payments (out of pocket) or via private health insurance, where insurance companies and banks are intermediaries between producers and consumers of welfare.

Consequently, provision and funding come in four different combinations. First, something can be publicly run and publicly funded. Second, something can be privately run and privately funded. Third, privately run and publicly funded. And, fourthly, publicly run and privately funded (in the latter case, for example, one can imagine publicly run national parks, where private entry covers a large part of the costs).

Here it should be pointed out that these four are found in additional variants. Something, for example a health centre, can be privately run but both publicly and privately funded. As stated in the previous chapter, it is a common combination in today's Swedish healthcare, where private healthcare providers have agreements with both county councils and with insurance companies. Besides, it should be said that what is publicly run and publicly funded is rarely publicly financed at a hundred per cent, but elements of private funding also exist there. One example is the publicly funded healthcare, where the majority of costs is funded through taxes but where a smaller proportion of self-fees are charged up to the high-cost ceiling.

Does privatization of provision lead to increased private funding? The issue has been largely absent from the political agenda ever since privatizations began in the early 1990s. If the politicians ever touched on the issue, then it has been to deny such a connection between provision and funding. The crucial thing is that welfare services are publicly funded and provided on equal terms to all citizens, they have argued, and it does not matter whether these services are performed on a public or private basis. There is no connection between provision and funding. The issue of provision is separate from the issue of funding.

In 1985, however, the social democratic Prime Minister Olof Palme warned of the consequences of privatizing the provision of the welfare services (Antman and Schori 1996), and something that for a long time characterized the Swedish welfare model was that the publicly funded welfare services were provided through public operating monopolies which tended to strengthen their position over time (e.g. Tilton 1990). One example is healthcare. Through various reforms in the 1970s and early 1980s, the public sector increasingly took responsibility for Swedish healthcare. At the same time, the doctors' opportunities to conduct private care were restricted and these were incorporated, not without resistance, into the publicly funded and operated healthcare system (Heidenheimer and Elvander 1980; Immergut 1990).

But then the trend turned. The public operating monopoly on welfare services had been one of the cornerstones of the Swedish model, but in the late 1980s there were suddenly no political obstacles to start privatize the provision of healthcare, school and elderly care. The employers and the centre-right-wing political parties had long advocated such privatization. Now, the Social Democrats were on the same train. From having previously considered the public sector's expansion as a kind of democratization process (Premfors 1991), Social Democracy came to accept and, in some cases, lead the development towards increased marketization of welfare. Now,

> during the years of Social Democratic governance (1986–90), decentralization and deregulation measures were undertaken whereby much of the administrative and regulatory controls of the central state agencies within the education, health-care and social services sectors were dismantled. (Blomqvist 2004)

With such a consensus, it was not surprising that the public operating monopoly in healthcare, school and elderly care was broken up with new laws and regulations. With the 1992 free school reform, it was possible for private companies to run publicly funded schools, this through a voucher system where each student brought in a certain amount of money to the school that the student chose. Similar publicly funded voucher systems have subsequently been introduced for healthcare and elderly care through the Act on Freedom of Choice (LOV), a law that states that any approved supplier should be able to offer certain types of healthcare and elderly care. In other cases, the Public Procurement Act (LOU) provides that municipalities and county councils must purchase health and care services from those who can offer these at the best price.

The result has become an increasing proportion of private provision in healthcare, school and elderly care. As far as the school sector is concerned, the development has been most noticeable in the high school, where a quarter of all pupils attended private schools during the school year 2017/18. The same trend can be seen in primary school. In the mid-1990s, just over 17,000 primary school pupils went to a private school, for the academic year 2017/18 this figure was 156,000. In the healthcare sector, it has largely been about privatization of primary care. More than 40% of the country's health centres were thus run privately in 2016. For the capital Stockholm, the corresponding figure was 67%. Elderly care has also been privatized to an increasing extent. In 2016, 88,000 people lived in retirement homes and 228,000 people had been granted home care. 23% of the home care hours were carried out privately during this year. Here, too, there are big differences within the country. In Stockholm, 62% of the home care hours were carried out privately, while in the county of Norrbotten the corresponding figure was 2%.[1]

Is it possible to privatize provision to the extent mentioned above, without affecting the funding in any way? In theory, of course, it can work that way. We have seen how provision and funding can occur in four different combinations, one of which is private provision and public funding.

But theory is one thing and practice is another. In practice, private provision creates pressure against increased private funding, which in turn creates pressure on further privatization of provision. Thus, there is a mutual relationship and dependence between provision and funding, where, for example, private healthcare providers (provision) and insurance companies (funding) reinforce each other in different ways.

What does the mutual relationship look like? Let us begin with the dependence of private funding on private provision. In this book, private health insurance is used as an example of private—or at least semi-private—funding of welfare, and here it can easily be stated that a mass scope of private health insurance is not possible without a prior privatization of provision on a large scale.

This is primarily due to the fact that publicly delivered healthcare does not welcome patients with private health insurance on the terms set by insurance companies. You cannot go into the publicly run Sahlgrenska hospital in Gothenburg and wave your insurance, and you cannot get your private care coordinator to make an appointment at a publicly run health centre.

It is therefore no coincidence that the 62 privately run healthcare providers who had agreements with both the insurance company Länsförsäkringar and with the county councils (see previous chapter) were just privately run. The publicly run healthcare providers simply do not have the right to conclude agreements with the insurance companies.

The private health insurance in Sweden is thus based on the fact that there are private providers who receive the person who has signed such insurance. Publicly run care has not yet been opened up for insurance companies. Although the system has been loosened up[2] and although some want to see a change,[3] there is a continuing political resistance to allowing public-run healthcare to receive insurance patients. At the same time, there is a pressure from several actors to open up the publicly run care for insurance customers, something which makes The Swedish Association of Local Authorities and Regions (SKL) write that it must be made clear in a "future bill that the public-run healthcare cannot receive private insurance patients nor patients who pay out of pocket".[4]

In some countries, private insurance can also be used in publicly run healthcare facilities. One example is Australia (Colombo and Tapay 2003; Seah et al. 2013; Willis et al. 2016) where policyholders have to choose whether they want to go to public hospitals as insurance clients or as public patients, something that appears to be a headache for all parties: the patients themselves, who in each case must take a position on which of the two choices is the best and cheapest. The hospitals, who are glad to send the invoice to the insurance companies but who get less paid than the private hospitals, and who have to meet the insurance customers' demands for better rooms and other things. The insurance companies, who prefer that their clients go to the public hospitals as publicly funded Medicare patients, which means that insurance companies are free-riders on the public system and still collect money from premiums. Keleher (2016) expresses the latter in the following way:

> One of the major threats to the public hospital system from PHI [private health insurance] is the use of public hospitals by privately insured patients. While there is no legal reason to prevent this from occurring, the practice does compromise one of the objectives of subsidising PHI in the first place. The Commonwealth and states have an agreement that people can choose to be a private patient in a public hospital and that the public hospitals can charge for these private patients at a fee set by each state, but there is no requirement for people to declare their PHI status. So even though PHI companies collect insurance premiums from their members, when those members enter a public hospital and do not declare their PHI status, the insurance companies are not charged and therefor avoid any responsibility for such treatment in public hospitals.

In order to use your private insurance in Sweden, however, you need a private healthcare provider. Or more precisely, because the insurance company must have somewhere to send you, the insurance company needs to have agreements with private healthcare providers. The more agreements the better. In order for you not to have to travel all over the country, the insurance company needs a national network of healthcare providers at its disposal. In order for you to be able to receive different types of care, the insurance company needs care providers at all levels of care. As stated earlier, Länsförsäkringar had 900 such private healthcare providers to send their customers to, and the same applies to the vast majority of insurance companies.

Without extensive privatization of provision, the insurance companies had not been able to fulfil their obligations to the 650,000 customers. This is a fact that is generally agreed upon. For example, it came up in my interview with Eva Erlandsson at Swedish Insurance. I pointed out that the insurance industry is dependent on private caregivers and she replied:

> Yes absolutely. Oh yes, otherwise there would have been excess capacity and very slack accessibility for private insurance companies. It had been pretty tough.[5]

It is self-evident that private health insurance is dependent on privately delivered care as long as the publicly run care does not receive insurance patients. This is something that has been highlighted also by other researchers. One of them is Norén, who in 2008 writes that:

> The insurance companies' opportunity to expand is therefore dependent on the expansion of private healthcare in Sweden. This expansion is currently rapid, which should benefit private insurance.

Another is Dahlgren, who in 1994 pointed out that the supply of private healthcare providers was still insufficient to achieve a rapid expansion of private health insurance:

> One limiting factor, however, is that the private healthcare supply is still too limited to offer a comprehensive range of care services to people with private health insurance. With the increased supply of publicly funded but privately delivered healthcare that characterizes the development

> – and the healthcare policy of right-wing political parties – the market for private health insurance is of course also increasing.

In the quote above, Dahlgren points to another important factor in this context. It is not the case that private provision alone is sufficient for the rapid growth of private health insurance, but the healthcare providers must also be publicly funded to a considerable extent. With mixed funding, the private healthcare providers can build the bulk of their business on publicly funded care, and see the insurance patients as a bonus. Here's what the former CEO of Capio Lundby Hospital, Ingrid Thulin, said about this when I interviewed her:

> If you get a patient extra every hour this is when you start making money. The policyholders are very important for the profit, we budget for the publicly funded care and the insurance patients become a bonus.[6]

Without extensive privatization of provision, the insurance companies could not have fulfilled their obligations to the 650,000 customers. The same applies not only to healthcare, but also to elderly care, which we look into later on. It can thus be stated that the connection between provision and funding is very clear in one direction, namely that private funding is dependent on private provision.

And in the other direction? Is it also possible to state that the private provision of welfare services strengthens its position thanks to the increased private funding? Yes, to a great extent.

First of all, it must be said that the private caregivers are usually profit-driven companies who, as such, seek as large income as possible from as many directions as possible. At the same time, it is a question of spreading risk. A private healthcare provider who has concluded an agreement for publicly funded patients with the county council has the income secured for some time to come, but only for a certain time. The success of having won a procurement can, a couple of years later, be replaced by the defeat of not being procured by the public, this because the agreements according to the Public Procurement Act (LOU) must be reviewed regularly.

Trusting only the public can thus be risky for a private healthcare provider. From this point of view, it is important for the private providers to have more than one buyer in the healthcare market. However, it is still the case that most private providers have the county council and the publicly funded patients as their main source of income. In these cases, the privately funded patients, as we recently saw, become a welcome bonus that raises the profit margins.

With regard to the increased dependence of private provision on private funding, there is another important factor that we should dwell on. It is based on the fact that private providers charge more money per patient from insurance companies than from county councils. This is partly due to the fact that the insurance companies cannot guarantee as large patient volumes as the county councils, and partly because the insurance companies have greater demands on the private care providers. The insurance companies require fast access to care for their customers, and it is therefore reasonable that they also have to pay more than the county councils.

Why is it important to find out if the insurance companies pay more? What are the consequences? Let us start with a debate in the Swedish newspaper Svenska Dagbladet where Anders Morin, welfare manager at the employers' organization The Confederation of Swedish Enterprise, confirms that insurance companies have to pay more for their customers:

> At one point, Lapidus is actually right. The private providers are generally slightly more paid by the insurance companies than by the county councils. However, it has the effect that the private providers can work with lower compensation from the county council than would otherwise have been the case. Because of this, the tax-financed money thus endures for more care than would otherwise have been the case.[7]

On closer inspection, it is a twisted argument from Morin's side. The higher reimbursements from the insurance companies can, for the private providers, just as well be a viable bargaining argument to get the county councils to pay more per patient. But above all, there are other and greater risks connected with the fact that insurance companies are more willing to pay than county councils.

In countries where insurance patients are in the majority, private healthcare providers can simply refuse to accept the compensation that the public offers and thus say no to receiving publicly funded patients, precisely because insurance companies pay so much more for each patient. In the United States, it has been a notable problem that doctors refused to receive publicly funded Medicaid patients, since Medicaid paid too little compared to the insurance companies. In some states and disciplines, the percentage of doctors who have denied Medicaid patients has been so large that these patients have had difficulty getting any care at all (e.g. Decker 2012; Yudkowsky et al. 1990; Moffitt and Moffitt 2003). According to a study from 2019 (Anderson et al. 2019), the difference between private and public payments to providers is now bigger than ever before:

> In 2000 the price differential between what public and private insurers paid was approximately 10 percent. The Medicare Payment Advisory Commission recently estimated that private insurers pay prices that are 50 percent higher than what Medicare pays. Increased attention needs to be paid to the prices paid in the private sector.

But is it really true that insurance companies pay more? And if so, how much more? To find out, I did a large number of interviews with representatives of insurance companies, county councils and private healthcare providers. I finally got the general hypothesis confirmed from several directions, but at the same time I gained insight into the lack of transparency that characterizes the hidden welfare. First, there were many who did not want to answer at all. Second, the agreements between insurance companies and private healthcare providers are subject to business secrecy, which is why it has been impossible for me to obtain any exact figures.

At first, I tried with the county councils and insurance companies, but then it struck me that it was better to turn to the private caregivers as they get paid both from the insurance companies and from the county councils. The private providers should know best who pays the best.

The first one to confirm that insurance companies pay more was Henrik Brehmer, one of seven people in the management group of

Capio, where he holds the position of Senior Vice President Group Communication & Public Affairs. In a longer telephone interview, he tells me that:

> Insurance prices are generally a little higher than the prices that apply in the publicly funded choice of care and procurement. /… / It is about volumes and it is another administration around that type of patients which operate slightly different prices.[8]

This is also confirmed in telephone interviews with managers at local level, for example by the operations manager Gunnel Anderzzon at Capio Health Center Axess in Gothenburg and by the operations manager Anna Berglund Melin at Capio Health Center Hovås/Billdal. The latter says that "You would be stupid if you say that it is not so that insurance companies have to pay more than county councils".[9] Another person I spoke to is Maria Kajson, insurance coordinator at the Capio healthcare group. She says that:

> If it means that it will be more expensive for insurance companies to buy care from us than it is for county councils, this is what you are looking for? Yes, of course it will.[10]

Although the above is obvious, a lot of work was required to get this information. And, as I have said, some precise information is impossible to get. Here, they refer at best to each other, for example, Kajson refers to the above-mentioned Henrik Brehmer, who in turn refers to me to the insurance companies, who in turn refer me back to the healthcare group Capio. Here's how the conversation between me and Brehmer went on this point:

> I: Is there any possibility for me to obtain some figures about this? /… / Or is everything very classified or how does it work…
> Brehmer: Classified sounds so dramatic… No, but it is clear that we… Yes, the insurance companies will have to answer if they want to disclose that kind of information, I do not feel that…
> I: They say the same don't you think, *Capio must answer…*
> Brehmer: Yes, I understand that, I understand…

In summary, it can thus be said that there is a clear and mutual dependence between private provision and private funding of healthcare. From this perspective, it is interesting that advocates of private provision argue that provision and funding do not have to do with each other, an argument that has been used to calm those who worry about what will happen with public funding when private healthcare providers are allowed to establish themselves on an ever-increasing scale.

Alongside the denial, there is pure negation of this relationship. Lots of books and articles have been written about Swedish privatization of provision, but they have always focused on other things than how this type of privatization triggers private funding and drives a divided welfare state. A typical example is one of the most noticed books on Swedish welfare privatization (Hartman 2011), which addresses a variety of aspects of privatization of various welfare services. When it comes to healthcare, the book brings up differences in quality, productivity, cost-effectiveness, accessibility, administrative costs and patient satisfaction between public and private-run hospitals, opportunities for new innovations and forms of collaboration, forms of compensation for the private providers, different aspects of continuity and freedom of choice, i.e. basically everything you can imagine except the emergence of an insurance market based on semi-private funding of welfare.

From a political point of view, it has been both denial and neglect. Prime Minister Olof Palme's warnings of the consequences of privatization were forgotten during the course of the 1980s, and instead the Social Democrats came to accept the incipient privatization of provision. Although several of the new laws were founded during the centre-right-wing government period 1991–1994, the Social Democrats had already laid the foundation for opening up the public sector to private actors. An example is the new Competition Act of 1993, instituted by a centre-right-wing government but largely prepared by the Social Democrats in the late 1980s.

It is interesting to study the role of the Social Democrats in the comprehensive and ongoing privatization of Swedish welfare. The Social Democrats were the historical bearer of the Swedish welfare model and thus had great weight and confidence in these issues. For employers and for all advocates of a divided welfare state, the social democratic ideological shift was very much longed for.

This social democratic ideological shift from the 1980s onwards is well documented (Kitschelt 1994; Ryner 2002). Among other things, the Social Democrats embraced a new view of competition policy and a new view of the relationship between equality and efficiency. Now, growth and social security had become "deeply contradictory ideological goals" which meant that "a way of looking at social policy as an investment, as something that releases resources and contributes to growth, has thus been replaced by a view of social policy as a cost, something that takes up resources" (Andersson 2003, 11). Further, the social policy ideas from the 1960s and 1970s, including elements such as a "broadening of the social security systems, an expanded responsibility for the state vis-à-vis the individual's welfare and social rights, as well as solidarity with vulnerable people", were now replaced with increased emphasis on the individual's own responsibility and duty vis-à-vis society (Junestav 2007, 41).

On a more direct level, the Social Democrats' new approach was made possible by the fact that the party began to question the public sector from two directions: on the one hand the Ministry of Civil Affairs' criticism of bureaucracy and centralization, and on the other hand the Ministry of Finance's criticism of inefficiency and unproductivity. Those who made the first mentioned criticism did not see privatization as the solution to the problem, but instead the public sector would be made more democratic by raising the level of service and creating increased co-determination (Montin 1992, 38; Antman 1994).

But it was the Social Democrats at the Ministry of Finance, and their economic criticism of the public sector as ineffective and unproductive, which became key in the debate. In this context, a number of influential social democratic economists are often mentioned. They belonged to a corps which had now been given expert status when it came to welfare sector efficiency, and they often defined the public sector as "constituting a problem" (Hugemark 1994; Blyth 2001). For various reasons they made the most important decisions and, accordingly, "the shift towards a social democratic compensatory neo-liberalism in the mid-1980s, /…/ although it had profound effects on Swedish society, was never established as policy through the procedures of mass politics" (Ryner 2002).

Notably, both types of criticism of the public sector also came from political scientists. An example of this is one of the most well-known interpreters of the Swedish welfare model, Bo Rothstein, who went to attack against the public monopolies which he considered to be "unfair in terms of distribution, politically unmanageable, ineffective and unjust" why one should "shut down as much as possible of them" (Rothstein 1988).

Rothstein's article is interesting also in other ways. Here and elsewhere, he argues that privatization of provision does not affect the funding of welfare through taxes. Provision has nothing to do with funding. One can privatize the entire welfare provision, but still let it be publicly funded to the same degree as before.

Rothstein was wrong. On the contrary, there is a mutual link between private provision and private funding. Or is it really about private funding? In the next chapters, we will talk about the state's crucial role in the emergence of *private* health insurance and a divided welfare state.

Notes

1. https://www.ekonomifakta.se/.
2. The county council of Stockholm decided that public providers in some cases may welcome policyholders. LS 0805-0480.
3. In referral answers to the so-called Stop law, many respondents—among them the Swedish Medical Association—demanded that publicly provided health facilities would also be allowed to welcome policyholders.
4. https://skl.se/download/18.58b0262215876529e6011e7/1479474484327/SKL-16-04412-YTTR-Sjukvardsforsakringar.pdf.
5. Interview, 5 October 2017.
6. Interview, 20 May 2013.
7. *Svenska Dagbladet*, 19 October 2016. https://www.svd.se/privata-forsakringar-forstarker-sjukvarden
8. Interview, 5 October 2017.

9. Interview, 5 December 2017.
10. Interview, 5 December 2017.

References

Andersson, J. (2003). *Mellan tillväxt och trygghet: Idéer om produktiv socialpolitik i socialdemokratisk socialpolitisk ideologi under efterkrigstiden*. Uppsala: Acta Universitatis Upsaliensis.

Anderson, G. F., Hussey, P., & Petrosyan, V. (2019). It's still the prices, Stupid: Why the US spends so much on health care, and a tribute to Uwe Reinhardt. *Health Affairs, 38*(1), 87–95.

Antman. (1994). Vägen till systemskiftet – den offentliga sektorn i politiken 1970–1992. In R. Gustafsson (Ed.), *Köp och sälj, var god svälj? Vårdens nya ekonomistyrningssystem i ett arbetsmiljöperspektiv*. Stockholm: Arbetsmiljöfonden.

Antman, P., & Schori, P. (1996). *Olof Palme: den gränslöse reformisten*. Stockholm: Tiden.

Blomqvist, P. (2004). The choice revolution: Privatization of Swedish welfare services in the 1990s. *Social Policy & Administration, 38*(2), 139–155.

Blyth, M. (2001). The transformation of the Swedish model: Economic ideas, distributional conflict, and institutional change. *World Politics, 54*(1), 1–26.

Colombo, F., & Tapay, N. (2003). *Private health insurance in Australia: A case study*, 2213.

Dahlgren, G. (1994). *Framtidens sjukvårdsmarknader*. Stockholm: Natur och kultur i samarbete med Institutet för framtidsstudier.

Decker, S. L. (2012). In 2011 nearly one-third of physicians said they would not accept new Medicaid patients, but rising fees may help. *Health Affairs, 31*(8), 1673–1679.

Donahue, J. (1989). *The privatization decision: Public ends, private means*. New York: Basic Books.

Hartman, L. (Ed.). (2011). *Konkurrensens konsekvenser: Vad händer med svensk välfärd?* Stockholm: SNS förlag.

Heidenheimer, A. J., & Elvander, N. (Eds.). (1980). *The shaping of the Swedish health system*. London: Croom Helm.

Hugemark, A. (1994). *Den fängslande marknaden: Ekonomiska experter om välfärdsstaten*. Lund: Arkiv.

Immergut, E. M. (1990). Institutions, veto points, and policy results: A comparative analysis of health care. *Journal of Public Policy, 10*(4), 391–416.
Junestav, M. (2007). *Socialförsäkringssystemet och arbetsmarknaden: Politiska idéer, sociala normer och institutionell förändring - en historik.* Uppsala: Institutet för arbetsmarknadspolitisk utvärdering.
Keleher, H. (2016). The private health sector and private health insurance. In *Understanding the Australian health care system* (p. 35). Australia: Elsevier.
Kitschelt, H. (1994). *The transformation of European social democracy.* Cambridge: Cambridge University Press.
Moffitt, R. A., & Moffitt, R. (Eds.). (2003). *Means-tested transfer programs in the United States* (pp. 291–363). Chicago: University of Chicago Press.
Montin, S. (1992). Privatiseringsprocesser i kommunerna – teoretiska utgångspunkter och empiriska exempel. *Statsvetenskaplig Tidskrift, 95*(1), 31–57.
Norén, L. (2008). Att göra patienter till kunder – om sjukvårdsförsäkringar och entreprenörskap. In A. Lundström & E. Sundin (Eds.), *Perspektiv på förnyelse och entreprenörskap i offentlig verksamhet.* Örebro: Forum för småföretagarforskning.
Premfors, R. (1991). The "Swedish model" and public sector reform. *West European Politics, 14*(3), 83–95.
Rothstein, B. (1988). Socialdemokratin och välfärdens institutioner. *Tiden, 88*(8), 467–474.
Ryner, M. (2002). *Capitalist restructuring, globalization and the third way: Lessons from the Swedish model.* London: Routledge.
Seah, D. S., Cheong, T. Z., & Anstey, M. H. (2013). The hidden cost of private health insurance in Australia. *Australian Health Review, 37*(1), 1–3.
Starr, P. (1988). The meaning of privatization. *Yale Law & Policy Review, 6*(1), 6–41.
Tilton, T. A. (1990). *The political theory of Swedish social democracy: Through the welfare state to socialism.* Oxford, USA: Oxford University Press.
Willis, E., Reynolds, L., & Keleher, H., (Eds.). (2016). *Understanding the Australian health care system.* Australia: Elsevier Health Sciences.
Yudkowsky, B. K., Cartland, J. D., & Flint, S. S. (1990). Pediatrician participation in Medicaid: 1978 to 1989. *Pediatrics, 85*(4), 567–577.

4

State as Sponsor

Private provision is associated with private funding. Profits in welfare are associated with private health insurance. But without the state as a sponsor, it would not have been much of privatization whatsoever. In this chapter, and the following three, we will see how the new welfare model and the associated welfare industry—sometimes referred to as the welfare industrial complex (Svallfors 2014)—are dependent on state capital in three phases which partly overlap.

First, state capital as initial capital and venture capital. Second, state capital as a source of income. And third, directly linked to the emergence of the divided welfare state, the dependence on state capital as a co-financier of new, semi-private welfare services offered within the frame of the private welfare industry.

First, state capital is thus discussed as start-up capital and risk capital for the emerging welfare industry. Here it is interesting to see how state capital has run in and out of the companies in a way that has been of great importance to the companies' funding and political legitimacy. It turns out that state capital played a crucial role in the foundation of three of the largest welfare companies: the education company Academedia, the caring company Attendo and the healthcare company

J. Lapidus, *The Quest for a Divided Welfare State*,
https://doi.org/10.1007/978-3-030-24784-3_4

Capio (which in 2018 was sold to the French company Ramsay). Subsequently, the role of state capital in the continued development is discussed up to the recent stock exchange listings. Here it is interesting to study the state pension funds' (the AP Funds) willingness to create legitimacy for the welfare industrial complex in times of political turmoil.

Second, state capital is discussed as a source of income and profit. In a welfare sector that is publicly funded for the most part, it has been necessary for the welfare companies to have tax resources as the primary source of income and profit. A basic condition has thus been a legislation that gives the welfare companies increasingly access to state capital. Equally important has been to dispute all forms of restrictions in this legislation, something that has been particularly relevant during the recent years' debate on profits in welfare. In this decade-long social debate, the welfare industrial complex has had the public opinion against it, but received an unequivocal support from all advocates of the divided welfare state: the centre-right wing political parties including the far-right Sweden Democrats, leading media, lobbyists, employers' organizations and also certain trade unions and non-profit organizations that vacillate in their view of profits in welfare. Among the vacillating actors, we also find the Social Democratic Party, which has never taken an unambiguous position on the issue but instead been very dependent on how the political winds blow.

Third, the role of state capital as a co-financier of the new, pseudo-private welfare services within the framework of the welfare industrial complex. It is a matter of state subsidies (direct subsidies in the form of legally established tax deductions, indirect subsidies in the form of public infrastructure, education, etc.) to those who choose to top their welfare with the private providers. Here too, the basic premise is a legislation that releases state capital for the benefit of the welfare industrial complex. In this phase emerges the divided welfare state, something that would not have been possible without the previous phases.

These three types of state sponsorship are thus three important and partly overlapping phases in the development of the new welfare model and the new welfare industry. In the first phase, the welfare industry is built up, followed by consolidation in the form of ownership and legal status, which makes the welfare industrial complex more robust against political turmoil. In the second phase, the private welfare industry will have access to state capital and the welfare model will be reshaped on the supply side through an increased number of private providers in the new welfare market. In the third phase, the private welfare industry gets direct or indirect access to state capital through various tax deductions, and the welfare model changes on the demand side through the topping up opportunities offered by the private providers.

In all the three phases mentioned above, it is also possible to distinguish social actors who have been driving forces and social actors who have willingly or reluctantly adapted to the prevailing order. The process has to some extent been self-reinforcing. It is typical of this kind of privatization process that they change reality in a way that strengthens the original advocates of privatization, while other community actors abandon approaches and positions that were previously obvious to them (e.g. Pierson 1996; Hacker 2002).

Even at the individual level, important shifts can occur from the "marketization of welfare" (Petersen and Hjelmar 2014) and the subsequent shift of risks from the collective to the individual, for example through phenomenons like asset-based welfare and the urge for financialization and financial literacy (Finlayson 2009; Watson 2009), where everyone is supposed to invest in the best pension fund (Palme and Sundén 2004) and choose the right insurance policy (Schram and Sonnemans 2011) for their private health insurance. It forces everyone to think more about their private situation and less about welfare as a civil right. The word welfare may thus change its connotation from a "positive term that signified a broad spectrum of public benefits" (Soss and Schram 2007) to something where some people "are on welfare" (Bowman 2013), producing a "meagre endorsement of provision for needy social minorities /…/ who are often seen as morally undeserving" (Taylor-Gooby 1988).

Let us start by looking at the state's role as start and risk capital for the welfare industrial complex. An examination of three of the largest welfare companies Capio (healthcare), Attendo (elderly care) and

Academedia (education) shows that state start-up and risk capital played a major role in the creation and further development of the private welfare industry up to today's date. Capital from state-owned companies and authorities has, in short, run into and out of the welfare companies in a way that has contributed to, or even enabled, their increasingly strong position in the Swedish welfare market.

One example is the importance of the state pension funds (the AP Funds)[1] for the growth and development of the welfare industrial complex. As early as early 2015, Capio, Attendo and Academedia were owned by three different venture capital companies, in turn, Nordic Capital, Industri Kapital and EQT.

Now, these venture capital companies wanted to sell large parts of their holdings. It is certainly the case that venture capital companies have a company only for a number of years and then sell to other companies, often other venture capital companies (e.g. Black and Gilson 1998; Akhmejanova et al. 2015). But because of the political situation (partly the ongoing investigation into profits in welfare and partly the fact that advanced tax avoidance had received increasing attention in the media), they were now unusually keen on such a sale, while it was unusually difficult to find any kind of buyers.

In this situation, another *exit* for the venture capital companies was to try to introduce the welfare companies to the stock exchange. For several reasons, it would be a good solution from the point of view of the venture capital firms.

First, it would create legitimacy if the welfare companies were owned by more—preferably many more—than just the questioned venture capital companies. Particularly legitimizing would be institutional investors and parts of the public, perhaps even the employees of the welfare companies concerned.

Second, the criticism of lack of transparency would be less relevant as the stock market exchange places greater demands on information for both the public and the media.

Third, the venture capital companies would only have to sell a portion of the holding at the discounted introductory price, while the rest of the ownership could be maintained in anticipation of rising stock prices.

But even an Initial Public Offering (IPO) requires buyers. Here, it has become increasingly common to try to find trusted investors who pre-bind themselves for a certain proportion of the shares in the new listed company. These so-called anchor investors (e.g. Espenlaub et al. 2016) are both a guarantee that a certain number of shares will actually be bought and a form of quality stamp that can attract other stock buyers to join the company.

It was the venture capital company Nordic Capital that first found heavy anchor investors for its company Capio, which meant that this healthcare group was introduced into the stock market in July 2015.

One of these anchor investors was the Fourth AP Fund. In the negotiations with Nordic Capital, the Fourth AP Fund went on to buy 5.5% of the shares in Capio, an investment of SEK 375 million. Other anchor investors—such as Handelsbanken and Swedbank—were also important in this context, but it was extremely important to get a state investor such as the AP Fund on board.

The main reason why the Fourth AP Fund was a particularly important anchor investor was the uncertain political situation, manifested in the ongoing Welfare investigation[2] into profits in welfare. In the 2014 annual report, Capio states that "the single biggest risk for the Group is political decisions that change the market's conditions", and the report dwells on the fact that the new social democratic government and the Left Party have agreed to initiate one or more investigations that will highlight possible changes of current regulations for welfare services such as healthcare, elderly care and education.

The Fourth AP Fund's decision to enter as an anchor investor was, under current political circumstances, important for Capio and for the entire private welfare industry. It can be assumed that a government agency like the AP Fund made a careful consideration before it agreed to make such an investment, partly because another part of the state apparatus was carrying out a related investigation and partly because a state investor would be particularly hard-criticized if it risked the pensioner's money on a company that was later forbidden to make a profit.

Getting a state actor like the Fourth AP Fund on board was the closest Nordic Capital, and Capio could get to a guarantee that profits in welfare would not be banned, and at the same time, a go-ahead for other investors to enter the new listed company.

A state actor such as the Fourth AP Fund was the best possible investor for the profit-driven welfare companies and for everyone who wanted to see a continued permissible regulatory framework for profits in welfare. One of them is the business economist Sophie Nachemson-Ekwall, who wrote that she had "wished for the sake of the Swedish people that the AP Funds would buy large stakes in the healthcare provider Capio",[3] among other things to save the legitimacy of the profit-driven company and pave the way for more welfare companies on the stock exchange.

The Fourth AP Fund's decision to enter as an anchor investor was perhaps the single most important factor in enabling stock exchange listing of Capio and, in the long run, also of other welfare companies.

But how did it come about that this government authority, in the midst of an ongoing investigation into profits in welfare, in an uncertain political position, chose to enable the venture capital companies' exit via stock exchange listing?

In addition to a number of ethical guidelines established by the AP Funds Ethics Council,[4] there are no special rules that limit what is the AP Funds' main task, namely to have managed assets grow from year to year. Thus, there are no formal obstacles for the AP Funds to invest in profit-driven welfare companies. However, like other profit-maximizing actors, the AP Funds must make various forms of risk assessments, where any political risks are included as a natural part of such an assessment.

The political risk had diminished just as the AP Funds decided to enter as Capio's anchor investor. The single most important reason for the reduced political risk was that the political majority passed over in favour of a permissive regulatory framework for profits in welfare, which can partly be explained by intensive lobbying against the far-right political party, the Sweden Democrats, who had previously been critically opposed to profits in welfare.

Without the Sweden Democrats' rapid turnaround in the question of profits in welfare, it would have been difficult to get the AP Funds as anchor investor and difficult to introduce Capio on the stock market.

According to Capio's CEO, it was important that "the uncertainty was displaced",[5] while the Fourth AP Fund's share manager believed that the political risks were reduced when the Sweden Democrats changed sides on the question of profits in welfare.

One who criticized the actions of the AP Funds was the Left Party leader Jonas Sjöstedt. He thought it was unethical for the AP Funds to buy into Capio, and he added that it would be a bad deal for the small shareholders.[6] In turn, Sjöstedt was criticized by economist Claes Hemberg, who considered Sjöstedt's opinion to be an "infringement on our democracy". A more interesting and balanced remark from Hemberg was that he believed the AP Funds' decision to be based on considerations, and that it was a sign that profits in welfare were completely unthreatened:

> One of the new owners will be the fourth AP Fund, which is an important base in our pension savings. Many small savers can see it as a quality brand. We can also interpret it as signal that a ban on profit in welfare never becomes relevant. It must be the AP Fund's analysis. And they usually do analyse well. All of this have made the Lefty Party leader burst out into clichés.[7]

With the AP Funds and a few other anchor investors firmly anchored, Capio could thus be listed on 30 June 2015. The venture capital companies Nordic Capital and Apax had succeeded with their desired exit, but could still retain a large part of the healthcare group Capio in the form of just over 50% of shares.

In the press release announcing the IPO,[8] Capio's CEO says that "long-term ownership is achieved through the stock exchange listing with four industrial and financial anchor investors who have a long-term perspective on Capio's development". He is supported by the chairman of the board who believes that "We are very pleased that four experienced anchor investors have undertaken to support Capio's continued development".

The next venture capital company to aim at the stock exchange was Industri Kapital, who wanted the same exit with its caring company Attendo and its 20,000 employees. Industri Kapital also managed to find some anchor investors, including Swedbank and Nordstjernan. The AP Funds did not enter as an anchor investor this time, but two of them (Second and Third AP Funds) are today among the twenty largest owners.

Attendo was listed on the stock exchange on 30 November 2015. Over 30,000 people have since then bought shares in the care company, including 1000 of Attendo's own employees. Even though the venture capital company retains a great deal of ownership, Attendo appears to have become something of a common people's low-denomination share, which can be seen as another obstacle to a legislation designed to stop the welfare industrial complex's continued expansion. So, for example, the financial journalist Patricia Hedelius talked about Attendo's IPO as "The nail in the coffin" for a more restrictive attitude towards profits in welfare, an issue that was already disarmed "as the Fourth AP Fund and state pension money became a major owner" in Capio six months earlier.[9]

The only one of the three aforementioned welfare companies that had not yet been listed on the stock exchange was the educational company Academedia, owned by the venture capital company EQT. The stated goal, however, was that Academedia would also be introduced to the stock exchange. So, in 2013, representatives of EQT and Academedia believed that a stock exchange listing was imminent, and they continued to make similar statements.

There are various reasons why Academedia's IPO took some time. One is that school companies have been particularly politically sensitive to run—not least after highlighted bankruptcies, especially the JB group—and that no stakeholders were prepared to be anchor investors. Another explanation is that the question of profits in welfare had already been disarmed as above, and that it was no longer as urgent with a corresponding exit for the venture capital company EQT. Like other welfare companies, Academedia adheres to the political development, and one of its annual report's states that "Proposals that limit Academedia's ability to distribute profits to shareholders can have major adverse effects on Academedia's share and market value".[10]

A third reason why the IPO was delayed is that Academedia already had a couple of heavy and trustworthy investors in the form of the

Fourth and Sixth AP Funds. Academedia was owned by EQT's fifth fund (EQT V), where both the Fourth and Sixth AP Funds were large investors. It is clear from the Fourth AP Fund's annual report 2015 that EQT V, based in Guernsey, tops the list of the five largest holdings in Other Shares & Shares, foreign unlisted companies.[11] In the Sixth AP Fund's annual report for the same year, there is a report on the long-term cooperation between the pension fund and the venture capital company.[12]

Academedia, Sweden's largest educational company, was listed on 15 June 2016. In the end, all three companies, with the help of the state-owned AP Funds, had finally saved themselves into the stock market in a time of political turbulence.

In short, state capital has been around ever since the three welfare giants were founded. For Attendo's part, it began with state-owned Procordia laying the foundations for Svensk Hemservice AB, a company that according to the government's letter would market itself towards the municipalities. In his own historiography, Attendo refers to Procordia and the unusually cold winter of 1985. At that time, "a kind of ice age also existed for private welfare",[13] it is noted, an ice age where almost all elderly care and healthcare were handled by public monopolies and where hardly anyone considered that private actors could be part of the Swedish welfare model.

For Capio's and Academedia's part, ironically, it began when large sums of money from the liquidated *wage-earner funds* (the politically disputed funds aimed at strengthening the employees' influence over the private sector) gave rise to Bure, a partly state-owned company that was at the forefront of investments in private healthcare and private education.

In the early stages of the privatization wave of the 1990s, the private providers were seen with scepticism by the municipalities and county councils that were expected to hire their services. The phenomenon was still new and there was doubt about the fact that private actors were allowed to enter the welfare market at all.

According to Bure's then CEO Per Båtelson, there was a "massive historical resistance to private healthcare" which meant that the company initially concentrated on investments in healthcare activities that were less politically charged, such as laundries and laboratories.[14] For the forerunner of Academedia and Attendo, it was initially difficult, for the same reason, to translate the welfare legislation into practical policy and actual privatization on a larger scale.

However, between 1994 and 1996, the turnover in Bure's healthcare increased from SEK 90 million to SEK 1000 million, according to its own annual reports, primarily via "takeover of county council-owned administrations and acquisitions of private healthcare companies".[15]

At the same time, the criticism of private-provided healthcare was a factor that Bure still had to count on, for example in 1998, a year which according to the annual report was marked by "very limited expansion opportunities for private providers because of the political elections".[16]

The fact that Bure nevertheless dared to provide private healthcare was partly due to the fact that municipality and county council politicians saw it as a mitigating factor that Bure had the state as a co-owner and that the company was built up by money from the wage-earner funds. So, for example, Bure's then CEO meant that it facilitated the negotiations with the politicians all over the country, an image confirmed by a county council director: "The heritage from the wage funds was an important reason for our cooperation with Bure".[17]

The same goes for with Bure's investments in education. With the positive experience from the healthcare area, the company began to make major investments in private schools, among other things through the purchase of Vittra Förskolor & Skolor AB in 1998. In connection with the acquisition, the person responsible for Bure's new business area meant that it was "Bure's unique political legitimacy" that did it possible to enter the school business to a greater extent than anyone had previously managed.[18]

The annual report for 1999 states that Bure Education has developed very strongly in its two areas, business education and schools, and that Bure has a leading position in both of these markets. In the same annual report, however, there are concerns over the political debate on free schools and the privatization of healthcare, a debate that is said to have affected the value of the Bure share.[19]

At the same time, it is stated that the good cooperation with the public sector continues, a collaboration where Bure seems to have continued to benefit from the state ownership and the historical connection to the wage-earner funds.

Thus, in a company like Bure, the state had two functions with regard to the original build-up, partly as capital and partly as a legitimacy builder for an industry that was strongly questioned.

Bure emerged from the liquidated wage-earner funds. It is a historical irony that the wage-earner funds, which aimed to strengthen the influence of wage earners over private business, were instead used to open up markets that private business did not have any control over.

The opening of new markets leads us to the second of the three phases, namely state capital as a source of income for the welfare companies in the form of the allowance of *profits in welfare*. In this context, it is usually said that the 1990s legislation opened up the public sector to competition from private actors. Another way of expressing this is that new legislation allowed private actors to use state capital as a source of income for their activities.

The Swedish welfare was and still is publicly funded for the most part, that is, it is tax money that pays for healthcare, school and elderly care. In order to enter this market and to take part of the tax money, it was necessary to have a legislation that allowed private companies to have state resources as a source of income.

The dependence on state capital as a source of income applies to all three companies studied in this chapter, i.e. the healthcare group Capio, the educational company Academedia and the care company Attendo.

For example, the educational company Academedia's business is dependent on the free school reform (1992) stipulating that private school companies can use state capital as a source of income via the school voucher. As stated, the free school reform meant that the Swedish school was organized according to a voucher system where private and publicly run schools received a certain amount of money for each student. Likewise, the healthcare group Capio and the care company Attendo are dependent on state capital either in the form of a similar voucher system regulated in the Act on Freedom of Choice (LOV), or through municipal and county council procurement of services regulated in the Public Procurement Act (LOU).

As we shall see, in all the three welfare companies, there is an obvious awareness that income and profits come from tax money and thus a strong desire that the legislation will continue to allow state capital to be the source of income and profit.

The private welfare industry would prefer all this to become a political non-issue and maybe they are succeeding now that the Social Democrats, in an agreement (the January agreement 2019) with the centre-right wing parties, have decided to talk no more about profits in welfare. Up until now, however, profits in welfare have become increasingly questioned. The debate gained strength when the maladministration by a number of private providers, especially Carema which had to change its name to Vardaga, was given media attention in 2011 and 2012.

In 2014, the newly appointed government (Social Democrats and the Green Party) agreed with the Left Party to appoint an investigation, the so-called Welfare investigation,[20] with the purpose of ensure that public funds are used for precisely the activities for which they are intended and that any surpluses as a general rule must be returned to the activities where they originated.

The Welfare investigation submitted its final report to the government on 9 May 2017 (Statens offentliga utredningar 2017), while what revolves around profits in welfare was already submitted on 8 November 2016 (Statens offentliga utredningar 2016). It is noteworthy that the investigation violated the above-mentioned aim and directive by not proposing that "surplus as a general rule be returned to that activity where they occurred", that is, a ban on profits in welfare. Instead, the investigation proposes a profit limitation where welfare gains may not exceed 7% of the operating capital plus the government borrowing rate.

The proposal is technically complicated and disarms rather than promotes political discussion and opinion on the issue. The proposal is thus an example of the ambiguities that characterizes the social democratic stance on profits in welfare.

At the same time, it must be said that the Welfare investigation, led by the Social Democrat Ilmar Reepalu, was initially politically disputed. In 2015, the centre-right wing political parties and the Sweden Democrats voted for a non-binding so-called announcement, according to which the Welfare investigation was asked to focus on quality and follow-up rather than on profits in welfare. In 2017, when the investigation presented its final report, it was already obvious that the investigation's recommendations would not be supported by a majority in Sweden's parliament.

The private welfare companies have followed developments closely. The educational company Academedia's annual reports always include the section political and legal risks, and the annual report for 2016/17 discusses and problematizes the fact that the company's operations are largely based on publicly funded private schools. It is stated, under the heading *Risks related to school vouchers and economic situation*, that "Most of AcadeMedia's revenues come from public funds". This means that profit restrictions in the welfare area will hit hard on Academedia and its shareholders. Academedia states that "Proposals that limit the company's ability to distribute profits to shareholders can have major negative effects on AcadeMedia's share and market value".

Academedia, however, looks bright on the future. Admittedly, publicly funded independent schools are subject to "significant reviews from authorities and the media, among others". But at the same time, Reepalu's Welfare investigation has met with extensive criticism, and the government will probably not receive support for a proposal based on the findings of the investigation. It would also be difficult from a legal perspective, says Academedia, to implement what the report proposes. In the annual report 2017/18, Academedia draws a sigh of relief and notes that the Welfare investigation was voted down by the Swedish Parliament on 7 June 2018.[21]

The care company Attendo has a similar perspective. Until 2014, it sees a long-term and continuing trend towards an increasingly large proportion of private care, although the pace and focus of this development are dependent on political decisions. However, the annual report for 2014 includes concerns over the Welfare investigation, an agreement that "creates significant uncertainty about the conditions for investments in Swedish welfare".

The annual report for 2015 states that the uncertainty persists, but that a majority in the Swedish Parliament have urged the government to "change the committee directive to focus on quality requirements rather than economic issues and that the same requirements shall be imposed on both public and private actors". In the annual report for 2016 and 2017, Attendo speaks of the results of the Welfare investigation, and it is argued, among other things, that the profit restrictions proposed by the investigation do not have parliamentary support in parliament and that they, "according to investigations", are not compatible with Swedish law nor EU law.[22]

The healthcare group Capio follows the same pattern. Until 2013, it is thus generally stated that "The single biggest risk is political decisions that change the market conditions". The annual report for 2014 mentions the forthcoming Welfare investigation, while the annual report for 2015 emphasizes the fact that "A majority of the opposition parties in parliament have issued announcements that oppose the investigation". The annual report for 2017 emphasizes that the risks are reduced by the fact that "Capio is active in several countries and has a wide range of care at different levels of care and in different specialties".[23]

Awareness of state capital as a source of income and profit, as well as the compact resistance to restrictions in this legislation, is also found in the employer organizations in which the welfare companies are organized. While the trade union's approach to the emergence of the welfare industrial complex has been characterized by some ambivalence (see the Chapter 13), the attitude of the private employers has been clear since they started questioning the public welfare monopoly at the SAF Congress in 1980 or even when Sture Eskilsson presented his *secret PM* in 1971 (Boréus 1994; Elmbrant 1993; Andersson 2000).

The larger the welfare industry has become, the more the employer organizations, of course, have grown in strength. As long as there was no welfare industry, there were no private employers in these industries. The central employer organization SAF therefore, for several decades, had to rely on related organizations such as the think tank Timbro and the publisher SNS.

In recent years, the private employer organizations themselves have taken a greater place in opinion-forming. With the growth of the welfare industry, the healthcare group Capio and other private employers in the healthcare sector have organized themselves in a chain of strong opinion formers at each level, from the employer organization the Confederation of Swedish Enterprise via the employer organization Almega down to the employer organization Vårdföretagarna.

We get the opportunity to return to these actors and to the question of profits in welfare, but let us now focus on the third phase in the fascinating story of how state capital contributes to reshaping the welfare model as we previously knew it.

In the first and second acts, the private welfare industry gained access to state capital as a source of revenue, while state capital contributed to the consolidation of ownership and legal status.

Now, in the third act, state capital plays the role of contributor to those who choose to top their welfare within the framework of the private welfare industry. It is now, through the state as a sponsor of the hidden welfare state, that the welfare model is reshaped on the demand side.

Formally, the prerequisite for supplementary welfare is already created in the first two phases of the private welfare industry's development. With privatization of provision, we get a lot of providers who are not hindered by laws and regulations when, in order to spread risks and increase revenues, they want to sell their welfare services to as many as possible.

But what is the point of creating formal space for these services if hardly anyone can afford to use them? Increased private funding of welfare services, ironically, requires increased state support. By subsidizing consumption of *private* healthcare, school and elderly care, the state creates real space for *private* supplementary welfare services for a certain part of the population. The so-called Rut deduction halves the personal costs of *private* services in elderly care (home care and retirement homes) and in the school sector (homework assistance), while the employee who signs up for private health insurance has escaped taxation at the same time as the employer can deduct certain costs.

If we move outside the welfare sector, we find different types of tax deductions that are also aimed at certain social groups while excluding others. These deductions imply lost tax revenue for the state, but the most striking is that they favour the more affluent social groups much more than the less affluent groups.

The interest deduction for example. It is easy to believe that everyone has great pleasure from this tax deduction because most households have some type of loan, but the fact is that it spreads extremely unevenly over the entire population. Thus, Statistics Sweden's survey showed that the richest tenth got 20 times more money than the poorest tenth.[24] According to the same survey, it was found that as much as 85% of the SEK 30 billion in lost tax revenue went to the richer half of Sweden's households, while only 15% of these 30 billion went to the poorer half.

Here is how Hans Heggemann, investigator at Statistics Sweden's income statistics department, puts it:

> It is a double effect: those with low incomes do not usually own their housing and have no loans, and then you get nothing from the system. If they have loans then it is usually low loans.

The interest deduction is thus a typical tax deduction. Just like the deductions in the welfare sector (gross wage deduction for private health insurance, Rut deduction for elderly care and homework assistance), this means lost tax revenue for the state, while at the same time it primarily benefits those at the top. How has this type of deduction been able to grow ever stronger? How can the state choose to benefit the rich more than the poor?

In general terms, it is about a move towards a liberal welfare model, where this type of tax deductions is legio and where there is a completely different view of the relationship between equality and efficiency. In the traditional Swedish welfare model, equality was desirable, which is expressed in the following way by Esping-Andersen (1989):

> It was not only argued that equality can be combined with efficiency, but also for equality as a means of optimizing efficiency. More equitable distribution of purchasing power is a prerequisite for successful macroeconomic policies; family policy is an investment in the future; fair allocation of resources such as healthcare and education is a basis for optimal labor productivity; the solidaristic wage policy promotes industrial modernization; income security helps overcome the workers' natural resistance to

rationalization; and preventive social policies reduce both the economic costs and the loss of human resources.

Esping-Andersen pointed to three different welfare models—the social democratic, the conservative and the liberal—where the social democratic model is characterized by state playing a major role, and where the liberal model is characterized by the market playing a major role. However, Esping-Andersen discovered some contradictions in the liberal, market-based welfare model. Already in 1990, he stated that one of the fastest-growing public expenditures in this type of model is "tax subsidies for so-called private welfare solutions".

It was the hidden welfare that Esping-Andersen discovered, that is, the type of *private* alternative that characterizes the liberal welfare models. Today, there are several mechanisms that strengthen these *private* alternatives in the Swedish welfare society. One of these mechanisms is that more actors are drawn into the semi-private welfare, not least the strong social groups that are increasingly benefiting from the state sponsorship. To make these groups happy, to avoid that these groups *revolt* against the welfare state, politicians must pledge even more state sponsorship of supplementary services. An example of this is the so-called January agreement (signed in January 2019) where Social Democrats and centre-right wing parties agree to substantially raise the Rut deduction for homecare services.

Here, for some researchers, the only chance to *save the welfare model* is to introduce typically liberal elements in the same. Klitgaard (2007) argues that the Social Democrats, with their support for different types of market solutions, have tried to save the Swedish welfare model. What Klitgaard never asks is whether these *rescue attempts* are creating a completely different type of welfare model.

Another example is Bergh (2008), who argues that a number of necessary and desirable changes have been made within the framework of the "Nordic welfare state". The changes include reduced progressivity in the tax system and an increased incidence of *private* supplementary services, that is, changes that are badly matched with what is usually associated with the Nordic model. At the same time, Bergh believes that the support for the Nordic welfare state, thanks to these changes, remains strong among high-income groups. In order to maintain support for the Nordic welfare state, even more changes should be made in liberal direction, including an even greater scope for *private* welfare consumption.

In order to save the Nordic welfare model, one must therefore destroy it. In order to ensure the continued support of high-income earners, one must create a completely different welfare model. All the world's countries have some form of welfare state, and the interesting thing is what distinguishes these welfare states. But what Andreas Bergh ultimately means by the *Nordic welfare state* is simply the welfare state that exists in the Nordic countries.

Vocal social groups that benefit from the state sponsorship of supplementary welfare services are one of several factors that, in various ways, make the hidden welfare strengthen its position at the expense of the visible welfare. Before we deepen our understanding of these erosive factors, however, we will examine the state sponsorship of "private" welfare services within healthcare, elderly care and education.

Notes

1. http://apfonderna.se/.
2. https://www.regeringen.se/rattsliga-dokument/statens-offentliga-utredningar/2016/11/sou-201678/.
3. *Dagens industri*, 16 June 2016.
4. http://etikradet.se/.
5. *Dagens industri*, 25 September 2015.
6. *Dagens Nyheter*, 9 June 2015.
7. https://blogg.avanza.se/hemberg/2015/06/09/sjostedt-vill-hota-capio/.
8. http://mb.cision.com/Main/277/9788733/389807.pdf.
9. *Svenska Dagbladet*, 30 November 2015. https://www.svd.se/de-ar-vinnarna-pa-vinster-i-valfarden.
10. Academedia, Annual report 2014/15.
11. Forth AP-Fund, Annual report 2015.
12. Sixth AP-Fund, Annual report 2015.
13. http://www.attendo.se/30-år; http://www.attendo.com/sv/content/attendos-historia.

14. *Aftonbladet*, 3 March 1998.
15. Bure, Annual report 1996.
16. Bure, Annual report 1998.
17. *Aftonbladet*, 3 March 1998.
18. *Dagens Industri*, 13 November 1998.
19. Bure, Annual report 1999.
20. https://www.regeringen.se/rattsliga-dokument/statens-offentliga-utredningar/2016/11/sou-201678/.
21. Academedia, Annual reports 2014–2018.
22. Attendo, Annual reports 2014–2018.
23. Capio, Annual reports 2014–2018.
24. *SVT Nyheter*, 24 March 2015. https://www.svt.se/nyheter/ekonomi/rika-far-mest-av-statens-30-miljarder-i-ranteavdrag.

References

Akhmejanova, T. A., Vikulina, V. V., Votchel, L. M., Ivashina, N. S., & Kuznetsova, M. V. (2015). Assessment of efficiency of innovation projects financing through the exit strategies of venture capital investors. *Journal of Advanced Research in Law and Economics, 6*(3 (13)), 463.

Andersson, B. O. (2000). *Den svenska modellens tredje kompromiss. Efterkrigstidens välfärdspolitik med utgångspunkt från industrins kompetenssäkring och skolans reformering*. Göteborg: Ekonomisk-historiska institutionen.

Bergh, A. (2008). Explaining the survival of the Swedish welfare state: Maintaining political support through incremental change. *Financial Theory and Practice, 32*(3), 233–254.

Black, B. S., & Gilson, R. J. (1998). Venture capital and the structure of capital markets: Banks versus stock markets. *Journal of Financial Economics, 47*(3), 243–277.

Boréus, K. (1994). *Högervåg: nyliberalismen och kampen om språket i svensk debatt 1969–1989*. Diss. Tiden.

Bowman, J. R. (2013). *Capitalisms compared: Welfare, work, and business*. Washington: CQ Press.

Elmbrant, B. (1993). *Så föll den svenska modellen*. Stockholm: T. Fischer.

Espenlaub, S., Khurshed, A., Mohamed, A., & Saadouni, B. (2016). Committed anchor investment and IPO survival—The roles of cornerstone and strategic investors. *Journal of Corporate Finance, 41*, 139–155.

Esping-Andersen, G. (1989). Jämlikhet, effektivitet, och makt. Socialdemokratisk välfärdspolitik. In K. Misgeld, K. Molin, & K. Åmark (Eds.), *Socialdemokratins samhälle: SAP och Sverige under 100 år*. Stockholm: Tiden.
Esping-Andersen, G. (1990). *The three worlds of welfare capitalism*. Cambridge: Polity.
Finlayson, A. (2009). Financialisation, financial literacy and asset-based welfare. *The British Journal of Politics and International Relations, 11*(3), 400–421.
Hacker, J. S. (2002). *The divided welfare state: The battle over public and private social benefits in the United States*. Cambridge: Cambridge University Press.
Klitgaard, M. B. (2007). Why are they doing it? Social democracy and market-oriented welfare state reforms. *West European Politics, 30*(1), 172–194.
Palme, M., & Sundén, A. (2004). Premiepensionen i det reformerade pensionssystemet–är det önskvärt att kunna välja mellan 663 fonder. *Ekonomisk Debatt, 32*(3), 6–15.
Petersen, O. H., & Hjelmar, U. (2014). Marketization of welfare services in Scandinavia: A review of Swedish and Danish experiences. *Scandinavian Journal of Public Administration, 17*(4), 3–20.
Pierson, P. (1996). The new politics of the welfare state. *World Politics, 48*(2), 143–179.
Schram, A., & Sonnemans, J. (2011). How individuals choose health insurance: An experimental analysis. *European Economic Review, 55*(6), 799–819.
Soss, J., & Schram, S. (2007). A public transformed? Welfare reform as policy feedback. *The American Political Science Review, 101*(1), 111–127.
Statens offentliga utredningar. (2016). *Ordning och reda i välfärden, SOU 2016:78*. Stockholm: Wolters Kluwer.
Statens offentliga utredningar. (2017). *Kvalitet i välfärden – bättre upphandling och uppföljning*. Stockholm: Wolters Kluwer.
Svallfors, S. (2014). Politik som organiserad kamp: nya spelare och nya spelregler i Sverige. *Arkiv. Tidskrift för samhällsanalys, 3*, 39–64.
Taylor-Gooby, P. (1988). The future of the British welfare state: Public attitudes, citizenship and social policy under the conservative governments of the 1980s. *European Sociological Review, 4*(1), 1–19.
Watson, M. (2009). Planning for a future of asset-based welfare? New labour, financialized economic agency and the housing market. *Planning, Practice & Research, 24*(1), 41–56.

5
Half-Private Healthcare

The hidden welfare has grown stronger in Sweden in recent years. It is about a mix of public and private, where the public in different ways, directly and indirectly, sponsors the private so much that we should talk about semi-private or *private* health insurance rather than private health insurance.

On the one hand, it is an indirect state sponsorship, where insurance patients in various ways sponge on the public and where private healthcare providers can welcome patients with private health insurance to get an extra income for an activity that rests on public funds.

On the other hand, a direct state sponsorship via tax deductions for healthcare, school and elderly care, deductions which is mainly used by the well-off layers of the population. These deductions are gross salary deduction for private health insurance, homework assistance deductions for education and Rut deductions for home care and retirement homes.

In the following chapters, we focus on the direct and statutory tax subsidies that enabled the emergence of semi-private welfare services on a massive scale, tax subsidies that have become common not only in Sweden but also in a large number of countries such as Australia (Stebbing and Spies-Butcher 2010), France (Morel et al. 2019),

J. Lapidus, *The Quest for a Divided Welfare State*,
https://doi.org/10.1007/978-3-030-24784-3_5

Canada (Béland and Koreh 2017), the United States (Hacker 2002; Mettler 2011; Faricy 2011) and England (Orton and Davies 2009), although there are also few examples (e.g. Portugal) where the phenomenon has decreased in importance (Branco and Costa 2018).

What do tax subsidies for private welfare solutions mean in practice? What does the hidden welfare look like?

When it comes to the rapid growth of private health insurance in Sweden, it has been based not least on the possibility of, via the employer, making a so-called gross salary deduction. With the simplest possible example, let us illustrate how this gross salary deduction works when the employee acquires private health insurance:

Suppose you earn SEK 30,000 a month and pay 50% in tax. You thus get 15,000 in net income and then you buy a private health insurance for 5000.

Remaining in the wallet is SEK 10,000.

Now suppose you still earn SEK 30,000 a month but that your employer pays the insurance company 5000. The employer then deducts SEK 5000 from your gross salary and you thus receive a monthly salary of 25,000.

When you have paid tax of 50%, you have 12,500 left in your wallet.

In the first case 10,000 in the wallet, in the second case 12,500 in the wallet.

You have earned 2500 on the gross salary deduction, but who has lost 2500? The state has done so in the form of lost tax revenues.

The above magic was possible thanks to the lack of taxation of benefits of private health insurance policies. It is precisely this type of lost tax revenue that is the state expense for the hidden welfare. It is about a state sponsorship that primarily benefits people in the higher income strata, something that would be unthinkable within the framework of the visible welfare where it had become a ramshackle if every year a lot of healthcare money was distributed to the richest and slightly less healthcare money for middle class and no healthcare money at all for those who earned the least.

When it comes to *private* health insurance, you must also have an employer who is willing to help you with the tax deduction. Those who are unemployed or have unwilling employers, such as everyone who today has different types of temporary employment, are therefore formally excluded from the possibility of having their healthcare insurance sponsored by the state.

For the employer, it implies both goodwill and power (e.g. Dobbin 1992; Hacker 2004) to be the one who—at the expense of the state—offers this kind of benefits. From the employee's horizon, it is the employer who provides the welfare. This creates the welfare relationship that is so typical of the divided welfare state, a relationship between employer and employee rather than between state and citizen.

It was the above gross salary deduction that contributed to the rapid growth of private health insurance in Sweden. In recent years, the gross salary deduction has been questioned from a political perspective (see below), but as long as it was intact, the insurance companies and the banks turned directly to the employers highlighting this type of tax solutions.

So, for example, the insurance company Länsförsäkringar said that "Healthcare insurance should also help you as an entrepreneur to maintain productivity and the employees' health"[1] while Handelsbanken wrote that "Sign a private health insurance with gross salary deduction. At a marginal tax rate of 50 percent, the employee pays only half of the premium".[2]

For employers, these tax exemptions and opportunities were a perfect employee benefit to the employees, that is, a good way to attract new staff and retain the one that they already had. This was something the private healthcare provider GävleDalakirurgin[3] pointed out in its advertising to employers:

> Being able to offer the staff the opportunity to favourably funding an operation or treatment is something that has become a success among large and small firms in Sweden. The Tax Agency offers very favourable deduction rules.

The gross salary deduction could be used when signing insurance, but also when paying operations out of pocket. GävleDalakirurgin stated:

> The gross salary deduction is a simple and very advantageous way of funding your operation. It also means no cost to your employer. Through company funding, your employer pays the operation or treatment and then deducts your gross salary during an agreed period of time. Depending on your tax level, this means that you can save up to 55 percent of the cost of the operation or treatment. As an example, at 54 percent income tax, you can save over SEK 26,000 on an operation that costs SEK 50,000.

GävleDalakirurgin turned to employers but also to the employee to explain how this was possible:

> The Swedish Tax Agency approves that your company helps its employees to finance private healthcare through gross salary deductions. This allows you to save up to 57% on your surgery or treatment.

The employee could thus save up to 57% on his surgery or treatment. Who paid for this? The state did in the form of lost tax revenue. It was thus the taxpayers who lost these 57% and the individual, private customer who saved hat money.

For the employer, however, the whole party was absolutely free, something that GävleDalakirurgin emphasizes:

> With gross salary deductions, you can offer the staff a benefit that gives them the opportunity to get special surgery or treatment that results in increased quality and joy of living – without costing the company anything extra.

Given that the Swedish Tax Agency was so generous with this employee benefit, it was no wonder that many employers mentioned it in the advertisement, such as the consultancy company ÅF who wrote on Facebook that:

> For us, it is important to have happy employees and as an employer we want to support the employees who need help. As a benefit here at ÅF, therefore, part of the treatment is paid via a gross salary deduction, which gives the employee a lower cost through a so-called tax effect.

In this case, the employer's goodwill is something that cannot be underestimated. It is of course good for the employer to be able to offer these benefits at the state's expense, and according to GävleDalakirurgin, it has thus become a success among small and large companies in Sweden.

In its approach to employers, GävleDalakirurgin describes how to "initially invoice the company for the operation or treatment". Then the employer deducts the cost from the employee's gross salary, usually for a period of three to six months.

GävleDalakirurgin adds that the employer determines the time period and, in addition, who is to be offered the benefit. At the same time, it is stated that the person who has a high salary can make even more money on the tax deduction. However, nothing is said about anyone who does not have a willing employer and who, therefore, is excluded from this possibility.

Private health insurance was exempt from taxation of benefits, but the advocates of the divided welfare state were not satisfied. Employer organizations required private health insurance to be deductible also for the companies. For example, the employer organization the Confederation of Swedish Enterprise said that "a deduction option should be introduced for the employer who signs a private health insurance".[4]

We have already mentioned what the absence of benefit taxation means for the employee and for the employer. When it comes to the right of tax deduction for a company, it is a question of whether the company may or may not count the expense as a cost necessary to run the business. Either the company can count the cost of private health insurance as a cost necessary to run the business and, in that case, it may use that cost to reduce the taxable profit and thereby pay less tax. Or, the company may not count the expense as such a cost and cannot reduce the taxable profit by that amount.

Anyone who really wants to promote the emergence of *private* health insurance policies therefore believes that the insurance should be exempt from benefit taxation and also deductible for the employer.

What did it mean that the insurance was not deductible for the employer? Let us look at a calculation made by the insurance company

Bliwa[5] and presented on the website under the heading *Bliwa's health insurance—tax rules for the employer.*

Bliwa begins by explaining how beneficial it is for the employee to get a gross salary deduction from his employer, entirely according to the principles we mentioned in the above example. Bliwa notes that the gross salary deduction reduces the taxable income by the same amount as the deduction, for example: at an annual premium of SEK 1500, the gross salary deduction makes the taxable income decrease by SEK 1500. Bliwa summarizes:

> If the employee has a marginal tax of 50%, the cost of the insurance will be SEK 750 per year for the employee. Savings for the employee: The employee receives an insurance that costs SEK 1500 per year for an actual cost of SEK 750.

This is the same magic mentioned before. The employee pays half the insurance and the rest is paid by the state in the form of lost tax revenues. The employee thus earns money, but is there really no expense for the employer when the insurance premium is not deductible for the companies?

Here, Bliwa and all other insurance companies can give a relieving message to all employers. The cost of health insurance does not at all mean a cost to the employers. On the contrary, it is actually the case that employers earn a few dollars, even if the most important gain is in the goodwill that it gives the employer to, at the expense of the state, be able to offer their employees these favourable gross salary deductions.

How can it be that the employer actually earns money even without deductions? Bliwa explains by comparing the employer's costs for paying wages with the same employer's costs for paying an insurance. In the first case, payroll, the employer must pay salary costs and employer contributions (31%) on these salary costs. In the second case, payment of health insurance, the employer must pay the insurance premium and corporate tax (21.4%) on this premium.

In the case of salary, the cost is thus: payroll costs + employer contributions.

In the case of insurance, the cost is thus: insurance premium + corporate tax.

In a calculation example, Bliwa shows that it becomes cheaper for the employer to pay the insurance than to pay the salary to the employee. The difference between gross pay deductions and payroll payments for an insurance premium of SEK 1500 is shown below.

Employer's cost for gross salary deductions:

Non-deductible annual premium to the insurance company: SEK 1500. Corporate tax (26% on 1500 SEK): 390 SEK. Total cost: 1890 SEK.

Employer's cost for payroll:

Deductible salary cost: 1500 SEK. Employer fees: (31%): SEK 465. Total cost: 1965 SEK.

Total savings for the employer (SEK 1965–SEK 1890): SEK 75.

The employee earns quite a lot from avoiding taxation of benefits, but the employer also earns a little money. The only loser is the state that loses tax revenue.

As we shall now see, the centre-right wing political parties and, above all, the employer organizations wanted to take another step. They were not satisfied with the fact that the private health insurance was exempt from taxation of benefits, but also wanted to make it deductible for the employers. That is, let the companies avoid the corporation tax of 21.4% (the SEK 390 in the example above).

The centre-right wing parties had long wanted to have both freedom from benefit taxation for those who take out insurance and the right to tax deduction for the employers who pay the same. For example, the Centre Party meant in a proposal from 1987 that it was "completely unfounded" to believe that various tax reliefs would contribute to inequalities in healthcare. The Moderate Party, for their part, believed that it was pure discrimination against private healthcare not to allow companies to deduct costs for private health insurance.[6]

Here, it is interesting to see how the Moderate Party criticized the trade union movement for not approving all types of tax relief for private care. In the proposal from 1987, the Moderates believe that trade union goes against its members' interest in gaining fast access to care. Here, parallels can be drawn to today's split, where the union wrestles with the question of whether to follow their ideological beliefs about equal healthcare for all or if they should try to retain and win more members by embracing the divided welfare state.

The centre-right wing parties have continued to raise the issue of making the private health insurance policies both free of benefit taxation and deductible for the companies. In an article, two MPs from the Moderate Party write that

> Tax exemption for individual welfare solutions would open a gigantic new market for insurance companies and healthcare providers.[7]

In this new and divided welfare state, according to Tolgfors and Graf, it would simply be two choices:

> Those who like county councils pay county council tax as today. Those who have greater confidence in insurance companies and individual healthcare providers insure themselves and get the county council tax reduced.

What Tolgfors and Graf propose is thus a regular divided welfare state, a system in which some leave the visible welfare to fully enter into the shadows of the hidden welfare state.

However, it is the employers who most consistently have raised these issues. Time and again, the Confederation of Swedish Enterprise has pledged to make the health insurance deductible for the companies, for example in a report where it is stated that "all employer-financed care should be treated the same in fiscal terms"[8] and in a referral statement it is claimed that "a deduction option should be introduced for that employer who signs a private health insurance".[9]

What are the arguments for companies being able to deduct this type of cost? The question is answered by Kristina Hagström, health strategist at the insurance company Skandia, in a debate article. Hagström believes that:

> The cost of repairing a broken machine is deductible for the company. If the person who handles the machine is ill, the company must pay the

entire cost of the insurance it has signed to get the employee back to work. Is it reasonable?[10]

No, it would not be reasonable if it were the only way to get the person back to work. Of course, the companies may deduct costs that are necessary for the business, but now we have a public health system that is meant to be for all citizens. Should we encourage state sponsoring of the companies to take out private health insurance for their employees? Should we have one kind of healthcare for those who work and another for those who are unemployed? Or one kind of healthcare for those who have secure employment and good employers, and another for those with insecure employment? In this way, should we withdraw tax money from the public healthcare, and let them go to a hidden welfare that grows stronger and stronger?

These are no rhetorical questions. These are questions that must be asked because the advocates of a divided welfare state, with seemingly well-founded indignation, often emphasize that companies must get all possible help to quickly get their employees back to work.

It sounds good. But what it really means is that those who work, or rather those who have safe employment with decent employers, should have a different and better healthcare than those who are unemployed or old or sick or all those who do not have a proper employer. What it really means is that the state should recognize the necessity for the companies' operations to have a parallel healthcare system, and that the state should therefore help the companies to build such a system.

Is that how it should be? Then we must first and foremost re-write the Healthcare Act, which says that care should be given due to needs and on equal terms.

The emergence of private health insurance has been very fast, even though these insurance policies have not been deductible for the companies. The lack of benefit taxation for the policyholders has thus been more than sufficient to promote this development.

For those who say they want to slow down the emergence of *private* health insurance, there is no reason either to sponsor the companies with the right to deduct or to sponsor the employees (and to some extent also the companies) with a lack of benefit taxation.

With regard to the decisions in the 1980s and 1990s, one can thus conclude that a party like the Social Democrats was opposed to the attempts to make the insurance both tax-deductible and exempt from benefit taxation.

On the other hand, the Social Democrats agreed to one of these two tax reliefs for private health insurance, that is, the lack of benefit taxation.

One can ask why the Social Democrats agreed to no benefit taxation. There were referral answers, such as the National Board of Health and Welfare, who were critical of both the right to deduct and lack of benefit taxation. Actually, the Social Democrats themselves argued that no benefit tax would reduce tax revenues, and in a bill from 1995,[11] they made roughly the same calculations as those made by the insurance company Bliwa in the example above. In their own bill, on these fiscal grounds, they raise certain objections to their own proposal:

> An objection to the rules proposed by the government may be that for both the company and its owner as well as for the employee, it is fiscally advantageous to have limitations on tax deductions but no benefit taxation on non-publicly financed care.

Thus, despite these reservations, the Social Democrats suggested that there would be no benefit tax on *private* health insurance. These principally important discussions were not much publicized in the media. The freedom from benefit taxation is a typical example of the fact that important decisions about the hidden welfare state often go under the radar, at least as long as these decisions go in the direction that the advocates of a divided welfare state wish.

When decisions go against them, however, there will be a lot of fuss. One example is precisely the social democratic government's decision to reintroduce benefit taxation on *private* health insurance policies in 2018. Let us take a closer look at how this decision emerged and what kind of resistance it has met from the advocates of a divided welfare state.

Under pressure from the Left Party, the Social Democrats gradually came to change their minds on the question of benefit taxation.

In the debate, the Social Democrats were suddenly unusually explicit. One example is an interpellation debate between Lotta Finstorp (Moderate Party) and Finance Minister Magdalena Andersson (Social Democrats), where Andersson claims that it is "unreasonable that all taxpayers should be involved in financing individual employees' various benefits".[12]

Furthermore, the Minister of Finance points to the fact that many people do not even have the opportunity to make use of the favourable gross deduction, and she therefore notes that private health insurance is "subsidized by taxpayers who have no such benefits from their employer".

The Left Party has been an even more driving force on the matter. In a parliamentary debate in May 2017,[13] Karin Rågsjö, the Left Party's healthcare spokesperson, talked, among other things, about the confusion between public and private that can become so costly for the public welfare system.

I cannot help but mention that Rågsjö, in her introductory speech in the parliamentary debate, quoted large pieces from one of my debate articles on the subject.[14] Among other things, she stated just like I did that:

> There is a limited range of healthcare resources in each country: health centers, hospitals, doctors, nurses and more. If a doctor treats an insurance patient, it by definition means not treating a publicly funded patient, something that the doctor could have done at that very moment.

Rågsjö was supported by the Social Democrats and the Environmental Party in the debate. Social Democrat Anna-Lena Sörenson believed that an increasing proportion of privately funded care risks creating a parallel healthcare system with a VIP lane for those who can afford insurance, while the environmentalist Jan Lindholm argued that everyone's right to care on equal terms is threatened by the rapid growth of private health insurance.

Of course, they were criticized by other party representatives. The Swedish Democrat Per Ramhorn argued that the whole debate was about a "hypothetical problem", while the Christian Democrat Emma Henriksson made a comparison with queuing in a grocery store:

> I think we all recognize the situation when standing in the grocery store and the queue for the checkout is quite long. You sigh a little. But then one sees that another cash desk opens. Sometimes it gets a little hot-blooded. Some want to run forward and stand first in the new checkout. Others are a little more loyal and think that those who stand before me have waited longer; let them go ahead to the new checkout. But regardless of who goes to the new checkout, the consequence for everyone who is queuing is that if there is another desk, it is faster for everyone to come forward.

An interesting but somewhat strange comparison. For example, the newly opened cash desk is open for everyone and not just for those who have signed a grocery store cash desk insurance. Besides, the food store is a private establishment that does just as it wants (still, it does not let people buy ahead the queue), while we talk about a healthcare system which according to the law should be equal for everyone. Third, for a large number of reasons, the healthcare sector is not functioning as smoothly as a market as do a grocery store (Arrow 1978)

In the parliamentary debate, the centre-right wing party representatives insisted that the emergence of private health insurance is the best thing that can happen to the universal welfare model, and that we must therefore subsidize special solutions for the most powerful groups in society.

But the Social Democrats went ahead with the bill. In a memorandum from the Ministry of Finance, published in September 2017, it is said that the amendments are proposed to enter into force in July 2018. Under the heading *Reasons for the proposal for memorandum,* you do not find much of what we have talked about here, namely that it is harmful to the universal welfare model to sponsor the emergence of a semi-private welfare market. Instead, certainly correct, it is claimed that benefit taxation is a basic rule in this type of situations and that it is important to have a certain degree of uniformity and predictability in the tax system.

The Social Democratic Government introduced benefit taxation on private health insurance in July 2018.[15] At the same time, the insurance became deductible for the employer. But even if the advocates of the divided welfare state want both freedom from benefit taxation for the employees and the right of deduction for the employers, the freedom from benefit taxation is the most important. It is fully understandable. The freedom from benefit taxation creates—all according to the principles of the divided welfare state—a bond between employer and employee, where the employer receives goodwill at the expense of the state. The freedom from benefit taxation is something that the employee notices and benefits from. It is therefore a more powerful ideological weapon than the right of deduction for the employers.

The decision on benefit taxation was therefore considered a declaration of war against the advocates of a divided welfare state, who used a lot of the newspeak we talked about earlier. How many times do people really have to pay for their healthcare, asked lobbyists and editorials in centre-right wing newspapers. It is terrible that the Social Democrats force people to pay *three* times for healthcare, they answered the rhetorical question they themselves posed.

This way of arguing is discussed below, but first and foremost, because of all misunderstandings and *misunderstandings* in the tax question, we must sort out the concepts. What is it that you really pay tax for? And how many times do you actually get to pay if you sign a private health insurance?

This is how it is:

Everyone pays tax to the public health service and everyone has the same right to use public health services. Thus, it is not like in Germany that you can opt-out of the public tax system for healthcare (Thomson and Mossialos 2006; Greß 2007). The Swedes pay one (1) time for the healthcare via the taxes.

Anyone who, in addition, chooses to buy a private health insurance pays a price for this insurance, just as you pay a price when you shop at the store. The difference between health insurance and food in the store is that many policyholders (those who had a willing employer) were able to deduct half the cost of the tax. These policyholders have thus paid for half (0.5) healthcare insurance.

The person who signs insurance thus paid one (1) time through the tax and a half (0.5) time via the *private* insurance. Total sum: the person who buys a private health insurance through the employer had to pay one and a half (1.5) times for healthcare.

Thus, the Social Democratic Government legislated in 2018 that the person signing a private health insurance should pay almost the full price (1) for their insurance (I say almost since the insurance is sponsored in many other ways, something that we will investigate later on). Since the person who buys a private health insurance must also pay tax (1) for the public healthcare, the result is that the policyholder now has to pay almost two (2) times for healthcare.

However, deliberate or unconscious miscalculations became very common when the government presented its proposal for benefit taxation. According to the advocates of the divided welfare state, policyholder would now have to pay three times. Three times! In the newspaper Göteborgs-Posten, it was argued that "What the proposal means in practice is that the person who has a private health insurance through the job may pay three (!) times for healthcare", and in another article it was said that "The benefit taxation affects about 430,000 workers who now have to pay a third time for healthcare: First through the tax bill, then for private health insurance (even though it is technically the employer who is responsible for it) and then once again through benefit taxation". In the newspaper Svenska Dagbladet, it was also said that you now have to pay three times for healthcare, and it was added: "Is there any upper limit on how many times you have to pay to see a doctor?" And in the newspaper Östersunds-Posten it was said that: "Only in Sweden you have to pay three times without seeing any improvement of the healthcare system".[16]

At the think tank Timbro, financed by the Confederation of Swedish Enterprise, the same incorrect calculation was made. In the newspaper Expressen, Timbro's responsible for welfare issues claimed that citizens are treated as an "economic Sæhrímnir, who can be taxed both double and triple for one and the same service".[17]

The advocates of a divided welfare state have continued to demand that the benefit taxation be removed. In January 2019, the newspaper Göteborgs-Posten claims that "the health tax" must be removed as it threatens the employers' opportunities to get the workers back to work quickly.[18] The word *health tax* has been used frequently to describe the benefit taxation, and it is another example of a new type of propaganda language. Although it is customary to tax all types of benefits, the expression *health tax* gives it another meaning and makes it sound more draconic than it actually is.

It is a bit contradictory that liberals are pushing for the state to sponsor the private sector in various ways. Here, it is interesting to note that they are criticized by the neo-liberal debater Johan Norberg, who speaks of "socialism for the rich" when it comes to state sponsorship within the framework of the hidden welfare, in this case the interest rate deduction discussed in the previous chapter.[19]

Today, there are many signs indicating that the benefit taxation on private health insurance will again be abolished. There is a parliamentary majority for this to happen, and many other strong actors are pushing in the same direction. The employer organizations demand that it be abolished as soon as possible[20] and Swedish Insurance writes a referral reply to the Tax Agency, criticizing it for the interpretation of the new legislation and trying to get the Tax Agency to modify and lighten the tax rules in this area.[21]

In a response[22] to Swedish Insurance and other actors, the Swedish Tax Agency defends its interpretation of the new law, but in fact, there are a number of loopholes and exceptions in the new legislation. And many actors are willing to explain these loopholes and exceptions for their clients. One such actor is the HR company Tholin & Larsson who explains, quite rightly, that despite the benefit taxation, it can be worthwhile for all parties to continue to take out insurance through the employer.[23] First, insurance companies often give employers a discount on the insurance, partly because the insurance companies know that these policyholders are *able-bodied* and probably less unhealthy than the population on average and partly because the employers often sign many insurance policies at the same time and thus receive a discount. Second, usually benefits of this kind should be valued at market price, but in this case the benefit (advantageously enough) should be valued at the price paid by the employer, that is, a "significantly lower price than what the employees themselves would have to pay for the same insurance". Third, health insurance can include rehabilitation measures and other tax-free items. Tholin & Larsson explains that in spite of benefit taxation, "quite a large part of the premium can actually be tax-free".

Notes

1. https://www.lansforsakringar.se/varmland/om-oss/press-media/nyheter/117920/.
2. https://www.handelsbanken.se/sv/privat/lan/forsakringar/vardforsakring.
3. https://gavledalakirurgin.se.
4. Referral answer to Statens offentliga utredning 2009:49 (2009). *Bättre samverkan: några frågor kring samspelet mellan sjukvård och socialförsäkring*. Stockholm: Fritze.
5. https://www.bliwa.se/.
6. Parliamentary publications, Motion 1987/88:Sk9 and 1987/88:Skl5.
7. *Dagens industri*, 27 August 2001.
8. The Confederation of Swedish Enterprise, *En förändrad sjukförsäkring*.
9. Referral answer to Statens offentliga utredning 2009:49 (2009). *Bättre samverkan: några frågor kring samspelet mellan sjukvård och socialförsäkring*. Stockholm: Fritze.
10. *Dagens industri*, 1 September 2009.
11. Parliamentary publications, Proposition 1994/95:182, *Beskattning av fri hälso- och sjukvård samt vissa andra förmåner*.
12. Parliamentary publications, Interpellation 2016/17:549, *Förmånsbeskattning av privata sjukvårdsförsäkringar*.
13. Parliamentary publications, Protocol 2016/17:117.
14. *Svenska Dagbladet*, 18 October 2016. https://www.svd.se/forskare-privat-forsakring-urholkar-varden.
15. Parliamentary publications, Department of Finance, Fi2017/03709/S1, *Slopad skattefrihet för förmån av hälso- och sjukvård*.
16. *Göteborgs-Posten*, 5 April 2017; *Svenska Dagbladet*, 5 April 2017; *Östersunds-Posten*, 7 April 2017.
17. *Expressen*, 28 August 2017. https://www.expressen.se/debatt/hur-manga-ganger-ska-vi-skatta-for-varden/.

18. *Göteborgs-Posten*, 1 February 2019. http://www.gp.se/ledare/en-opposition-utan-oppositionspolitik-1.12860719.
19. *Metro*, 15 April 2015. https://www.metro.se/artikel/r%C3%A4nteavdraget-%C3%A4r-socialism-f%C3%B6r-rika-xr.
20. https://www.svensktnaringsliv.se/regioner/vastmanland/skatten-pa-sjukvardsforsakringar-bor-slopas_727561.html.
21. https://www.svenskforsakring.se/globalassets/remissvar/2018/48.-stallningstagandet-forman-av-halso--och-sjukvard.pdf.
22. https://www4.skatteverket.se/rattsligvagledning/372021.html.
23. https://www.tholin.se/artiklar/viktigt-att-veta-nar-privat-sjukvard-blir-skattepliktig-1-juli-2018/; https://tholin.se/artiklar/vanliga-fragor-om-forman-av-fri-sjukvardsforsakring/.

References

Arrow, K. J. (1978). Uncertainty and the welfare economics of medical care. In *Uncertainty in economics* (pp. 345–375). Cambridge: Academic Press.

Béland, D., & Koreh, M. (2017). The fiscal side of social policy: State building, payroll contributions, and pension reform in 1960s Canada. *Journal of Policy History, 29*(4), 594–613.

Branco, R., & Costa, E. (2018). The golden age of tax expenditures: Fiscal welfare and inequality in Portugal (1989–2011). *New Political Economy*. https://www-tandfonline-com.ezproxy.ub.gu.se/doi/pdf/10.1080/13563467.2018.1526264%3FneedAccess=true.

Dobbin, F. R. (1992). The origins of private social insurance: Public policy and fringe benefits in America, 1920–1950. *American Journal of Sociology, 97*(5), 1416–1450.

Faricy, C. (2011). The politics of social policy in America: The causes and effects of indirect versus direct social spending. *The Journal of Politics, 73*(1), 74–83.

Greß, S. (2007). Private health insurance in Germany: Consequences of a dual system. *Healthcare Policy, 3*(2), 29.

Hacker, J. S. (2002). *The divided welfare state: The battle over public and private social benefits in the United States*. Cambridge: Cambridge University Press.

Hacker, J. S. (2004). Privatizing risk without privatizing the welfare state: The hidden politics of social policy retrenchment in the United States. *American Political Science Review, 98*(2), 243–260.

Mettler, S. (2011). *The submerged state: How invisible government policies undermine American democracy*. Chicago: University of Chicago Press.
Morel, N., Touzet, C., & Zemmour, M. (2019). From the hidden welfare state to the hidden part of welfare state reform: Analyzing the uses and effects of fiscal welfare in France. *Social Policy & Administration, 53*(1), 34–48.
Orton, M., & Davies, R. (2009). Exploring neglected dimensions of social policy: The SDW, fiscal welfare and the exemplar of local taxation in England. *Social Policy & Administration, 43*(1), 33–53.
Stebbing, A., & Spies-Butcher, B. (2010). Universal welfare by "other means"? Social tax expenditures and the Australian dual welfare state. *Journal of Social Policy, 39*(4), 585–606.
Thomson, S., & Mossialos, E. (2006). Choice of public or private health insurance: Learning from the experience of Germany and the Netherlands. *Journal of European Social Policy, 16*(4), 315–327.

6
Half-Private Elderly Care

"The Rut deduction is appreciated by Swedish pensioners", it is stated in the welfare companies' advertising for services that entitle to tax deductions of 50% of the labour cost. "Yes", one can answer, "at least by those who can afford to take advantage of these state-sponsored domestic services".

By any measures, the Rut deduction is a typical fiscal welfare construction that benefits the rich much more than the poor (e.g. Faricy 2015; Branco and Costa 2018). More money for rich municipalities. More money for rich pensioners. According to Statistics Sweden's figures, every inhabitant of one of Sweden's richest municipalities, Danderyd, received an average of SEK 2000 from the state through Rut deduction. The corresponding figure for Åsele municipality was SEK 40. For pensioners, the pattern is equally clear. In the large retirement group (348,000 persons) who have an income of around SEK 140,000 a year, only one out of nine used the Rut deduction, and those who did so received an average of SEK 3300 on the tax. Of the 10,000 pensioners who earn more than 1 million, almost every third used the deduction, and they received SEK 8600 per person.[1]

J. Lapidus, *The Quest for a Divided Welfare State*,
https://doi.org/10.1007/978-3-030-24784-3_6

Just like *private* health insurance, it is a combination of factors that make the state money go to the rich.

If you are a poor pensioner, you cannot afford to spend money on the myriad of services that the private companies offer. Although the state pays back half the cost, it is still too much money for you to be able to use this benefit. That is the real factor.

The formal factor is that in any case, you do not have the right to make full use of the Rut deduction. You can never make a deduction that is greater than the tax you would have paid into the Tax Agency. Many Swedish pensioners today have such a low pension that they do not pay enough tax to have a formal right to fully utilize the Rut deduction.

One who points out this is the president of the pensioner's organization PRO, Christina Tallberg. In a debate response[2] to representatives of employer organization Almega and another pensioner organization (SPF Seniors), she points to the fact that a monthly income of SEK 18,500 before tax is required in order to be able to make a full Rut deduction. As Swedish women's average pension amounts to SEK 13,700, it is consequently very many who are formally excluded from the possibility of making full Rut deductions.

But above all, Tallberg points to the lack not of formal but of real possibilities. She writes: "With such low pensions it is impossible to buy home services at all".

Tallberg is right. There is a lot of examples that show how little money a large group of Swedish pensioners have after paying rent, food, dental care, clothes, shoes, telephone, consumables, home insurance and more. It goes without saying that these pensioners do not have real opportunities to buy the welfare companies' services and then, as in the municipality Danderyd, make a favourable tax deduction and get half the amount from the state.

In her article, Tallberg touches on another problem with the Rut deduction. She believes that the deduction erodes the public care of the elderly. She points to, among other things, the opinion-related consequences that result from the fact that the most vocal pensioners disappear from the system:

> A divided elderly care also threatens quality. Resourceful older people are needed in the publicly funded elderly care in order to be able to make demands on quality. It keeps up the quality even for those people who do not have the same conditions to make demands. It is also important that resource-rich people think that they get the public welfare they need in order for them to want to pay taxes. In countries with a layered elderly care there are significant quality deficiencies. We do not want to see this development in Sweden.

Thus, from a welfare perspective, semi-private elderly care might have the same consequences as semi-private health insurance. Anyone who buys out of the public system neither knows about nor needs to worry about the crisis in the public elderly care, as that person no longer forms part of the same. In this way, the most vocal pensioner group disappears, the group that has the greatest potential to put pressure on politicians and demand that they update the public elderly care. In this way, the voice and resource-strong group's willingness to pay tax will also decrease as they, just as Tallberg reason, do not feel that they benefit from the public care of the elderly.

What has Tallberg's opponents to say? In her reply,[3] Christina Rogestam (SPF Seniors) does not mention the erosive and inequality-generating effects that Tallberg's article was about. Instead, she claims that Tallberg compares apples and oranges when talking about the Rut deduction in relation to means-tested home care service. Rogestam writes that "PRO seems to have misunderstood the difference between the current Rut deduction and elderly care".

What Rogestam wrongly thinks is that means-tested home service is one thing and that Rut deduction service is something completely different, i.e. that it is two different services that are used for different purposes. It is true that the Rut deduction can be used for more than traditional home service, but it can definitely be used for traditional home care services.

Here is how this is expressed on the website Seniorval.se, which explains how the Rut deduction can be used:

> You may use the Rut deduction for personal care performed in or in close proximity to your home. Most of what is usually included in the public home care service gives the right to a tax reduction.[4]

It is possible that Rogestam misunderstood this. As can be seen from the quotation below, it is a common misconception, but one that was sorted out a long time ago by Henriksson and Önstorp:

> One common misconception is that Rut deduction services only include cleaning or other everyday tasks. It can be seen from the Tax Agency's example of Rut services that virtually all services provided within the municipal home care service can also be obtained through Rut deduction. This means that, for example, laundry, purchasing, clothing care, escorting, cooking, personal hygiene, dressing and feeding are approved Rut deduction services.[5]

If we look more closely at elderly care, we see that private provision has become dominant in some areas. For example, 64% of all home care hours in Stockholm County were carried out by private providers in 2015, while the corresponding figure for Kalmar County was only 3%. In 2007, private providers accounted for 13% of home care hours for people over 65, and in 2015, that figure had increased to 24%. The proportion of people in retirement homes run by private providers has also increased over time.[6]

Publicly funded elderly care occurs in retirement homes or, more commonly, in the individual's home through home care. It always comes with a personal cost for the user. But, like public healthcare service, the services are heavily subsidized, and just as there is a high-cost ceiling in healthcare, there is also a maximum rate in the elderly care (in 2018, this amounted to SEK 2044 per month).

The semi-private funding, via the Rut deduction, is increasing. Meanwhile, there are some new economic mechanisms that allow the Rut deduction to outcompete the publicly funded elderly care, something which makes some pensioner groups leave the public system. Since private elderly care might actually be cheaper than public elderly care, some pensioner groups must now consider in which doses they should mix public and *private* funding.

Leave the publicly funded elderly care? Why? Is it really possible that *private* elderly care can be cheaper than public elderly care?

Yes, it is. The Rut deduction means that certain groups of the elderly, those who have a lower need for home care but a high pension, benefit from leaving the publicly funded system and paying their elderly care with private (albeit state-subsidized) money. How can this happen? It is because many municipalities charge a high hourly rate for the first home care hours, that is, before reaching the maximum rate. For some people, it may be thus worthwhile to buy these hours *privately* and use their right to Rut deduction.

This is as remarkable as fascinating: if the private cost of a certain number of home care hours is lower in the privately funded system than in the publicly funded system, then the privately funded system is actually more publicly funded than the publicly funded system!

Consulting the website Seniorval.se, we find that the above is advised to the pensioners precisely because privately funded elderly care can be cheaper than publicly funded elderly care:

> In addition, home services with Rut deduction can be cheaper than public home help if you do not need so much help. Compare the municipality's prices for home care services with companies that offer household-related services to see what is most beneficial to you.[7]

The phenomenon is also highlighted in the above-mentioned debate article[8] by Henriksson and Önstorp. The headline, "Rut deduction outcompetes the public home care service", is precisely aimed at the fact that many municipalities charge such a high rate for the first hours of home help services that for some groups it can be cheaper to solve this through Rut deductions. As the article authors point out, it is not a solution for all pensioners:

> An injustice is that elderly people with a low pension cannot fully benefit from the Rut deduction because it is designed as a tax deduction. This somewhat strange effect should be eliminated.

As already stated, there is a clear class aspect on the Rut deduction. The class aspect also contains a gender aspect. Studies show that the elderly, regardless of class affiliation, prefer professional help over the help of relatives (e.g. Szebehely and Trydegård 2007). But while those with high incomes can realize this desire by purchasing *private* services, those with low incomes must rely more heavily on their relatives. The relatives are often women of working age. They are often forced to go part-time to help out, and then they fall into the same poverty trap as their parents (e.g. Johansson et al. 2003).

The emergence of a semi-private welfare in elderly care is encouraged in various ways. The Agency for Growth,[9] an authority under the Ministry of Enterprise, recommends the private providers to mix publicly and semi-privately funded services to one and the same consumer. The Agency for Growth recently had the following text on its website:

> For example, if you deliver home services through the municipality's freedom of choice system, you can sell other services parallelly, such as window cleaning, which the customer can pay for himself.

Thus, both consumers and private providers are expected to mix public and *private* funding in appropriate doses. Here, it can be argued that there are signs of a divided welfare state in elderly care, where different pensioner groups receive their elderly care based on completely different rules and conditions.

It was the inequality-generating effects of the Rut deduction that PRO's chairman Christina Tallberg turned to in her article, a response to the employer organization Almega and the SPF Seniors. In their article, they propagated for the so-called home deduction, an Almega product according to which the Rut deduction should be increased both in terms of business areas and the amount of money to deduct from taxes. Almega proposes that all kinds of Rut deductions be baked together into one single, and that the tax deduction at the same time doubles to SEK 100,000 per person and year.

Almega writes in a report that "The goal of our proposal is to create opportunities for a HOME industry to grow".[10]

It is a particular kind of HOME industry that is intended. It is a HOME industry where some societal groups pilgrim to other community groups' homes, usually when people are not at home. Figures from

Statistics Sweden show that 20% of the residents in the well-situated Stockholm district of Karlaplan utilize the Rut deduction, while the corresponding figure for Fittja is 0.3%. The inhabitants of Fittja do no Rut deductions. They do Rut work. They take the metro to the expensive apartments at Karlaplan or to the villas in Danderyd.

Almega wants to develop this commuter traffic by expanding the Rut deduction and also allowing many more services to be included in the same. Almost everything should be included in the deduction:

> The starting point is that all services that are performed in or in connection with the home are entitled to deductions, except when there are direct reasons for the service not to be included. This means that deductions must be allowed for services such as cooking, homework, planning and construction of garden, coarse cleaning, retrieval of recycling, interior decoration of the home, home care during travel, care of animals and home care services to give some examples. The services do not need to be defined in advance from a political point of view, but it is up to buyers and contractors to agree.

For a few years, I worked as an aid worker in Nicaragua. In the mornings, I drove the kids to the international school that was located in one of the areas where the Nicaraguan upper class and the Swedish embassy staff lived. I was accompanied by truck floats filled with maids, gardeners, guards and all sorts of servants who spent their working life polishing and sweeping in the homes and gardens of the rich.

Is it best to invest all this tax money and all this workforce in helping people at Karlaplan and in Danderyd with cooking, homeworking, planning and construction of garden, coarse cleaning, retrieval of recycling, etc., or is it best to invest the tax money and all this labour to cover the needs of the public welfare system?

It is a matter of taste. But it is important that the advocates of the divided welfare state say as it is, namely that they create a tax-subsidized market that the rich in particular can utilize and which the poor cannot take part of other than as labour. It is important that they get questions about the erosive and inequality-generating effects. These were the questions that PRO's Christina Tallberg posed in her debate and these questions that her opponents chose not to answer.

With Almega's home deduction, citizens can make tax deductions of SEK 100,000 per person per year. The centre-right wing political parties have been inspired by the proposal and require, since June 2017, that the Rut deduction be raised to SEK 75,000.

In 2019, Almega and the centre-right wing parties got what they wanted. This happened via the so-called January agreement, where the Social Democrats, in order to stay in power, made a compromise with some of the centre-right wing parties. Among the 73 points in the agreement is one that deals with precisely the Rut deduction, which, according to the agreement, should triple as well as "be extended to laundry, transportation and security services".[11]

Of course, it is remarkable that the Social Democrats accept such changes in a welfare model that they themselves contributed in founding. With a triple Rut deduction, the Social Democrats pave the way for a divided welfare state in the area of elderly care.

But it is not only within the elderly care that the Rut deduction is used. It is just as common for younger people to make use of the deduction, especially for cleaning services in the home, and now they have received a number of new services to use it for.

Subsidized home care services have gained a strong foothold in many European countries. In Britain, there was a resurgence in demand for waged domestic labour already during the 1980s and early 1990s and thus "the consistent growth of a new 'servant' class" (Gregson and Lowe 2005). And in 1991, France introduced a 50% tax reduction for anyone who bought domestic services. The same goes for Belgium and Denmark, and more countries have followed the same track, for example Germany, the Netherlands, Finland and Sweden (Carbonnier 2015; Morel 2015)

Morel (2015) shows how the European Union has been promoting this type of domestic services since the early 1990s. She speaks of a political economy of domestic services, where:

> The delegation of domestic work and the development of domestic services being encouraged and structured through specific political and economic strategies, which have been actively promoted by national governments and national lobby groups, but also by the European Commission since the 1990s.

Morel (2015) tracks the EU's interest in domestic services back to a 1993 White Paper, which is followed up 19 years later by the explicit "Commission staff working document on exploiting the employment potential of the personal and household services". In this paper from 2012, subsidized domestic services in France and Germany are emphasized as a good example for other countries, and there are a multitude of arguments for promoting this kind of domestic services in the report. Mention is made, among other things, of the potential to create simple and white jobs for low-skilled people who otherwise find it difficult to enter the labour market and also to set time free for highly qualified people who do not need to do domestic services. In short, the development of domestic services is "presented as some kind of panacea that responds to both employment and social concerns".

Both the arguments and the enthusiasm for a new *servant class* are more or less the same in the Swedish debate. The Swedish centre-right wing political parties seem to have made a blueprint of the EU document from 2012, and these issues have been successfully highlighted since the end of the 1990s. At that time, there was a Swedish *maid-debate* (Nyberg 2013; Platzer 2006; Bowman and Cole 2009) where the left criticized the plans for subsidized home care services and saw them as a return to an obsolete system of employment filled with subordination, but that idea has long been stamped as hostile towards this kind of jobs. Instead, the centre-right wing parties have moved forward and now, in cooperation with the Social Democrats, tripled the Rut deduction for domestic services.

Just like any other tax deduction for welfare services, these subsidized home care services flourish in a community characterized by increased income and wealth gaps. The subsidized domestic services drive inequality, while gradually changing not only the welfare model but also our way of thinking about welfare. We let Morel (2015) summarize:

> The development of domestic work, as it is structured through these policies, can only prosper in a context of important socio-economic inequalities. Thus, not only do these policies explicitly seek to accentuate income differentials, they also implicitly promote a societal structure based on a distinction between "productive" and "unproductive" workers, where the

more highly skilled productive workers and/or wealthier individuals are encouraged to delegate the more "basic" domestic and caring tasks to the low-skilled.

Notes

1. Own calculations based upon figures provided by Statistics Sweden 2018. https://www.scb.se/.
2. *Dagens industri*, 27 June 2017.
3. *Dagens industri*, 28 June 2017.
4. https://seniorval.se/bra-att-veta/sa-funkar-rut.
5. *Dagens Samhälle*, 5 October 2011.
6. Figures from SKL (https://skl.se/) and Ekonomifakta (https://www.ekonomifakta.se/).
7. https://seniorval.se/bra-att-veta/sa-funkar-rut.
8. *Dagens Samhälle*, 5 October 2011.
9. https://tillvaxtverket.se/.
10. Almega, *Ett HEM-avdrag för alla HEM-tjänster*. https://www.almega.se/2016/10/rapport-ett-hem-avdrag-for-alla-hem-tjanster/.
11. https://www.socialdemokraterna.se/globalassets/aktuellt/utkast-till-sak-politisk-overenskommelse.pdf.

References

Bowman, J. R., & Cole, A. M. (2009). Do working mothers oppress other women? The Swedish "maid debate" and the welfare state politics of gender equality. *Signs: Journal of Women in Culture and Society, 35*(1), 157–184.

Branco, R., & Costa, E. (2018). The golden age of tax expenditures: Fiscal welfare and inequality in Portugal (1989–2011). *New Political Economy*. https://www-tandfonline-com.ezproxy.ub.gu.se/doi/pdf/10.1080/13563467.2018.1526264%3FneedAccess=true.

Carbonnier, C. (2015). *The political economy of household services in Europe*. New York: Springer.

Gregson, N., & Lowe, M. (2005). *Servicing the middle classes: Class, gender and waged domestic work in contemporary Britain*. London: Routledge.

Faricy, C. G. (2015). *Welfare for the wealthy: Parties, social spending, and inequality in the United States*. Cambridge: Cambridge University Press.
Johansson, L., Sundström, G., & Hassing, L. B. (2003). State provision down, offspring's up: The reverse substitution of old-age care in Sweden. *Ageing & Society, 23*(3), 269–280.
Morel, N. (2015). Servants for the knowledge-based economy? The political economy of domestic services in Europe. *Social Politics: International Studies in Gender, State & Society, 22*(2), 170–192.
Nyberg, A. (2013). RUT-avdraget–subventionering av vit sysselsättning eller av höginkomsttagares fritid? *Fronesis,* 42–43, 114–130.
Platzer, E. (2006). From private solutions to public responsibility and back again: The new domestic services in Sweden. *Gender & History, 18*(2), 211–221.
Szebehely, M., & Trydegård, G. B. (2007). Omsorgstjänster för äldre och funktionshindrade: skilda villkor, skilda trender? *Socialvetenskaplig Tidskrift, 14,* 197–219.

7
Half-Private Education

The ban on fees in the Swedish school system is not set in stone and several political parties want to reintroduce the state sponsorship of *private* homework assistance. Let us start by discussing the latter. Private extra education—sponsored or not sponsored by the state—has aptly been named *shadow education*, and it is a growing phenomenon in countries around the world (Baker et al. 2001; Bray 2009; Buchmann et al. 2010). The amount that Greek parents spend on private extra education corresponds to up to 20% of the state school budget. In France, parents can deduct from tax a large part of the cost of extra tuition, something that also recently applied to Sweden.

Through the so-called homework assistance deduction, Swedish parents, up to 2015, had the right to deduct from taxes half the cost of their children's *private* homework assistance. That is, those who had tax to deduct. In a parliamentary debate, it was pointed out that there were 138,000 children whose parents received support payments and did not pay tax.[1] These parents, therefore, did not have a formal opportunity to use the tax deduction. Neither did those who lived in smaller towns or in the countryside, and in the 10 municipalities with poorest school results there were no companies that offered homework assistance.[2]

J. Lapidus, *The Quest for a Divided Welfare State*,
https://doi.org/10.1007/978-3-030-24784-3_7

In addition to the formal factor, there was a much larger group of parents who did not have real opportunities to utilize the deduction. The private cost was significant even with the state subsidy. The largest homework assistance company, My Academy, offered homework assistance in the form of a two-hour session for SEK 300 per hour after the deduction. With such a double lesson a week, the price was SEK 2400 per month, a considerable expense for a large part of Sweden's wage earners.

The Act on Tax Reduction for Homework Assistance came into force in 2013. However, there was a possibility of making such a tax deduction already even when the centre-right-wing government introduced tax relief for household services (the Rut deduction) in 2007. The original Rut deduction included babysitting, something which created application difficulties and a kind of grey zone in relation to deductions for homework assistance. How would the difference between childcare and homework assistance be defined? Would the babysitter refuse to answer if the child asked a question about his/her school work?

The homework assistance companies did not hesitate to use this loophole, and they began to offer homework assistance with tax deductions long before the actual introduction of the explicit law. The Swedish Tax Agency interpreted the law to the benefit of the homework assistance companies. But since this part of the Rut deduction was all about childcare, the deduction was only allowed for children up to the age of 16.

Homework assistance companies wanted the tax deduction to apply also to high school students, and so did the centre-right-wing parties in parliament. Hence, in 2013, they legislated on tax deductions for homework assistance, a legislation in which even high school students were included. In the bill, signed by Prime Minister Fredrik Reinfeldt and the Ministry of Finance's Peter Norman, it says that:

> The bill proposes that homework assistance and other school work assistance for children and young people who are pupils in primary and secondary school and corresponding forms of schooling should be explicitly covered by the tax reduction for domestic work.[3]

Several referral bodies criticized the government's proposal. One example is the Swedish National Agency for Education, who wanted this type of effort to cover all students and who feared that tax deductions for homework assistance would not benefit the pupils who did not have resourceful parents. Other referral bodies, such as the employer organization Almega, expressed their full support. The Interest Association for Domestic Services and the homework assistance company My Academy also belonged to the referral bodies that favoured the proposal. They considered, among other things, that tax deductions for homework assistance would relieve the parents, and thus create an expanded labour supply.

The homework assistance industry grew sharply during this period. My Academy went from sales of SEK 2 million in 2008 to 70 million in 2014, and the company planned for further growth in the future.[4] The hiring of a new CEO marked a "continued ambition to maintain our market-leading position in the homework assistance industry in Sweden".[5] The numbers pointed upwards. In addition, homework assistance companies such as My Academy were helped by the attention in the media, where both negative and positive views on the new phenomenon in the welfare market were presented. In 2013, the homework assistance companies Studybuddy and My Academy were nominated by the magazine Resumé to this year's lobbyist. The justification was that they had successfully propagated for a homework assistance deduction that previously could only be combined with childcare.

At the same time, the growing criticism was a growing concern for the homework assistance industry. Metta Fjelkner, chairman of the National Union of Teachers in Sweden, said that homework assistance must be offered on equal terms for all children. The Swedish Teachers' Union's chairman Eva-Lis Sirén agreed. She said that it was not desirable to let the size of the parents' wallets decide the support to the students, and she claimed that it was better to use the money inside rather than outside the school system. The Swedish National Agency for Education, through its director-general Anna Ekström, also feared that the support would not reach those who did not have economically resourceful parents.[6]

The homework assistance deduction was also criticized from the left-wing political parties. Rossana Dinamarca, the Left Party's parliamentary member of the Education Committee, argued that the homework assistance deduction increased the gaps and that it was "disgusting"[7] to allow private homework assistance to be subsidized by the state. The Social Democrats also criticized private but state-subsidized homework assistance. In a TV debate ahead of the 2014 election, future Prime Minister Stefan Löfven claimed that the deduction should be abolished. He said:

> We shall not have a tax deduction for homework assistance that makes it possible for those whose parents can afford to buy it, but instead it is important to ensure that homework assistance is provided due to needs.[8]

The red-green government kept the promise and abolished the law in 2015. At the same time, the same government introduced a state grant for homework assistance which, via the National Agency for Education, can be applied for by school principals and non-profit organizations. According to the government, the initiative creates better conditions for an equal education, and the government remains critical of subsidizing private homework assistance.

Does this mean that *private* homework assistance has no future? No, the political struggle continues and there are many actors who want to see a reintroduction of this deduction. In addition to the homework assistance companies, the employers' organizations also regret that the homework assistance deduction has disappeared. In this context, it can be mentioned that Almega, by the so-called HOME deduction, wants homework assistance to be included as one of plenty services that should not be defined from a political point of view, but where it is up to "buyers and providers to agree".[9]

Several political parties also want to see a reintroduction of the homework assistance deduction. Both the Liberals and the Center Party want it to be included in the Rut deduction, a deduction which, with the so-called January agreement in 2019, has expanded both in scope and money. In fact, tax deduction for homework assistance is yet again, via the January agreement, allowed for when it comes to babysitting. In a statement, the Tax Agency says that a deduction is allowed for

> Homework assistance and other school work assistance that the babysitter performs for a maximum of 10 percent of the time at each childcare opportunity.[10]

For Europe, shadow education is most widespread in southern European countries, but figures from various studies (e.g. Ireson and Rushforth 2005; Bray 2011) show that 20% of all Austrian parents pay for private extra education, and more than half of all university students in Lithuania, Portugal and Slovakia purchase private tuition. In UK, about 10% of all primary school pupils receive private extra education. Even in countries such as France and Germany, private extra education is quite common. In Spain, about 20% of all pupils between the ages of 6 and 18 receive private extra education in some form

Shadow education is a global phenomenon (Kim and Jung 2019). More than 50% of all Japanese school children received some form of private extra education, so-called Juku, during school hours (Mawer 2015; Entrich 2017). Countries such as Brazil, Hong Kong and Egypt show similar figures. In Canada, it was said to be a "burgeoning industry marked by franchising, marketing, and corporate strategies" (Aurini and Davies 2004).

Private extra education has many inequality-generating effects and in several countries, the private tuition is sponsored by the state through the possibility of tax deductions, deductions which are most utilized by the well-off layers of the population (Welner 2008; Bray 2009; Levin 2018).

Private tuition and homework assistance are something that mainly takes place outside the school area and after school hours. But what about the school itself? Are there explicit tuition fees? Are there hidden tuition fees?

Much of the publicly funded welfare services are nowadays provided via various forms of voucher systems, where each patient/pupil/elderly person comes with a certain amount of tax money to the provider. When it comes to the private welfare companies in healthcare and elderly care, the person who can afford can buy extra healthcare or elderly care in addition to the care level determined by the voucher.

However, the privately run but publicly funded Swedish schools are not yet allowed to sell supplementary services or take out tuition fees.

For the one who launched the idea of a voucher system, Nobel laureate Milton Friedman (Carnoy 1998), there was no doubt that additional fees should be allowed. Actually, it was the possibility of increased private funding that was the main purpose of the voucher system, and Friedman wanted to use it as a battering ram against public funding of healthcare, school and elderly care.

Friedman was mainly focused on the school system. He asked why the parents had the right to spend money on all kinds of things but not on what was perhaps most important to them, the children's schooling. For Friedman, the voucher system was a way to set parents and children free from a state apparatus that kept them prisoners in a system where they could not buy what they requested.

Friedman did not listen to the warnings that such a system would create inequality. He believed that the intellectuals' equalization religion was false, and he argued that even the poorest people can "scrape up a few extra dollars to improve the quality of their children's schooling" and that topping up "would be about as frequent among the poor as among the rest, though perhaps of smaller amounts" (Friedman and Friedman 1980).

Thanks to the voucher system, there would be a gradual move towards a privately funded school system. According to Friedman, the state's role would be to secure a certain minimum standard, "much as it now inspects restaurants to ensure that they maintain minimum sanitary standards" (Friedman 1962). Other scholars modified Friedman's voucher schemes (Jencks 1970).

Because of the inequality-creating effects of the original schemes, they wanted to prohibit the possibilities to charge extra fees and instead give extra resources to schools with larger numbers of disadvantaged children (Barr 2004).

It is the latter, modified version that formally characterizes the Swedish school system. However, according to the original free school reform (1992), schools were allowed to charge some tuition fees. The centre-right-wing parties wanted to keep this opportunity for the private schools, but the motions were rejected and bans on tuition fees were introduced in elementary school. It was not until 2002, however, that the same ban applied also to upper secondary schools (SOU 2013:56).

The prohibition of tuition fees is not as self-evident as it may seem in today's Swedish debate. The 1992 free school reform meant that the Swedish school was organized according to a voucher system, and at first it was thus fully allowed for the schools to charge fees in addition to the income provided by the voucher. The tuition fees should be "reasonable". Exactly what was meant by reasonable fees, and how high these would be, was never specified. The then Minister of Education pointed out in 1993 that many private schools did not charge any fee at all, and that the average fee was only SEK 3000 per year.[11]

Although SEK 3000 per child and year was a small sum in comparison with tuition fees in many other countries, it was large enough to deter many parents from choosing such a school. And some schools charged even higher fees. Several of the right-wing parties still wanted to give the private schools the right to charge reasonable fees. In a motion from 1996, signed by the leaders of the Moderate Party, the Liberals and the Christian Democrats, it is said that there is no motive for further restrictions on tuition fees.[12]

As mentioned above, the centre-right-wing parties lost the battle over tuition fees. Many schools, however, have continued to charge fees even though it is not allowed. I went through reports to the School Inspectorate over a three-year period. In total, 109 different schools were registered under the heading fees, in several cases the same school was also reported several times during different years.[13]

The voucher system in combination with profit-driven school actors entails a natural pressure on different types of extra fees, which can be difficult to prevent even with expensive regulations. In addition, it is difficult for the School Inspectorate to decide what is a fee and what is not. This is because it is still allowed to make voluntary contributions, so the schools design their mailings to parents on the brink between fees and voluntary contribution.

One example is Carlsson's school which received SEK 3.5 million a year in grants/fees the year when the school was reported.[14] In its statement, the School Inspectorate stated that Carlsson's school requests parents to pay SEK 3500 per semester, and sends out a reminder letter to those who choose not to do so.[15]

In addition, the School Inspectorate has been informed that children have been treated separately and received lower grades because their parents did not pay the money, but this is rejected by Carlsson's school.

Carlsson's school maintains that the grant is voluntary, something that the School Inspectorate questions based on the letters that Carlsson's school sent to all parents. The first letter from Carlsson's school states that:

> We therefore hope that all parents will continue to submit to the Board's recommendation to voluntarily contribute SEK 3500 per pupil and semester. Higher amounts are received with gratitude.

The reminder letter states, among other things, that:

> It is easy for a payment note to disappear. In order for us to be able to run the school with the aim of keeping the high goals that we have set for our business (…), great commitment is required of all and also resources in addition to the school voucher.

The School Inspectorate has directed criticism in 24 of the 109 cases mentioned above. In addition to these 109 cases, there may be a lot of hidden statistics. It is a big step for parents to report the school, and it may also happen that they choose not to put their children in that school because they know there is a pressure on high fees. In 2017, the School Inspectorate received 43 notifications under the heading School fees, and in 2018 there were 41 such announcements.[16]

There is a fine line between fees and voluntary contributions. One way to avoid the School Inspectorate is to start parental associations. One month after such a meeting at the school Rudebecks in Gothenburg, it is said that "about SEK 52,000 has come in since April when the parents' association sent out paying-in forms".[17]

Thus, even in school, a pressure is created on income from more sources than just the municipal school voucher. However, compared to healthcare and elderly care, the private school companies' extra income is more regulated and limited. With the entry of private schools and the voucher system, however, with Friedman's words, an opportunity for increased private funding has been opened in the school sector. Soon the time may be ripe, but not yet. As the right-wing think tank Timbro's

CEO expresses it: “And now there is a maturity in public opinion to move forward, not in school, but in healthcare and elderly care”.[18]

Notes

1. Parliamentary publications, protocol 2012/13:37.
2. Parliamentary publications, debate 2013/14:6.
3. Parliamentary publications, bill 2012/13:14.
4. http://www.tcotidningen.se/laxhjalp-en-bransch-i-stark-tillvaxt.
5. http://www.mynewsdesk.com/se/pressreleases/my-academy-rekryterar-vd-fraan-utbildningsbranschen-863141.
6. http://rod.se/skolverket-varnar-f%C3%B6r-or%C3%A4ttvisa-i-l%C3%A4xhj%C3%A4lp.
7. *Aftonbladet*, 3 September 2012. http://www.aftonbladet.se/nyheter/article15348371.ab.
8. *SVT*, 9 October 2014. https://www.svt.se/nyheter/inrikes/stopp-for-laxrutredan-i-januari.
9. Almega, *Ett HEM-avdrag för alla HEM-tjänster*. https://www.almega.se/2016/10/rapport-ett-hem-avdrag-for-alla-hem-tjanster/.
10. https://www.skatteverket.se/foretagochorganisationer/skatter/rotochrutarbete/gerarbetetratttillrutavdrag.4.2ef18e6a125660db8b080001531.html?q=l%C3%A4xhj%C3%A4lp.
11. TT, 18 May 1993.
12. Parliamentary publications, Motion 1995/96:Ub39.
13. https://www.skolverket.se/skolutveckling/statistik/sok-skolinspektionens-anmalningar?typ=A.
14. *Svenska Dagbladet*, 9 November 2010. http://www.svd.se/nyheter/inrikes/bidrag-till-skola-far-allvarlig-kritik_5646885.svd.
15. http://www.skolinspektionen.se/Documents/Nyheter/beslut-avgifter-carlssons.pdf.
16. https://www.skolverket.se/skolutveckling/statistik/sok-skolinspektionens-anmalningar?typ=A.
17. https://www.rudebecks.se/sites/default/files/uploads/130521.pdf.
18. *Dagens industri*, 2 November 2018. https://www.di.se/nyheter/naringslivets-tankesmedja-star-redo-for-nasta-politiska-strid/.

References

Aurini, J., & Davies, S. (2004). The transformation of private tutoring: Education in a franchise form. *Canadian Journal of Sociology/Cahiers canadiens de sociologie, 29*, 419–438.

Baker, D. P., Akiba, M., LeTendre, G. K., & Wiseman, A. W. (2001). Worldwide shadow education: Outside-school learning, institutional quality of schooling, and cross-national mathematics achievement. *Educational Evaluation and Policy Analysis, 23*(1), 1–17.

Barr, N. (2004). *The economics of the welfare state*. Oxford: Oxford University Press.

Bray, T. M. (2009). *Confronting the shadow education system: What government policies for what private tutoring?* United Nations Educational, Scientific and Cultural Organization; International Institute for Educational Planning.

Bray, T. M. (2011). *The challenge of shadow education: Private tutoring and its implications for policy makers in the European Union*. Brussels: European Commission.

Buchmann, C., Condron, D. J., & Roscigno, V. J. (2010). Shadow education, American style: Test preparation, the SAT and college enrollment. *Social Forces, 89*(2), 435–461.

Carnoy, M. (1998). National voucher plans in Chile and Sweden: Did privatization reforms make for better education? *Comparative Education Review, 42*(3), 309–337.

Entrich, S. R. (2017). *Shadow education and social inequalities in Japan: Evolving patterns and conceptual implications*. Amsterdam: Springer.

Friedman, M. (1962). *Capitalism and freedom*. Chicago: University of Chicago Press.

Friedman, M., & Friedman, R. (1980). *Free to choose: A personal statement*. New York: HBJ.

Ireson, J., & Rushforth, K. (2005). *Mapping and evaluating shadow education*. ESRC Research Project RES-000-23-0117. London: Institute of Education, University of London.

Jencks, C. (1970). Giving parents money for schooling: Education vouchers. *The Phi Delta Kappan, 52*(1), 49–52.

Kim, Y. C., & Jung, J. H. (2019). Worldwide shadow education epidemic: From East Asia to Western Hemisphere. In *Shadow education as worldwide curriculum studies* (pp. 25–60). Cham: Palgrave Macmillan.

Levin, H. (2018). *Privatizing education: Can the school marketplace deliver freedom of choice, efficiency, equity, and social cohesion?* New York: Routledge.
Mawer, K. (2015). Casting new light on shadow education: Snapshots of juku variety. *Contemporary Japan, 27*(2), 131–148.
SOU 2013:56. *Friskolorna i samhället: betänkande av Friskolekommittén.* Stockholm: Fritze.
Welner, K. G. (2008). *NeoVouchers: The emergence of tuition tax credits for private schooling.* Lanham: Rowman & Littlefield.

8

Relieve or Hollow Out

What happens to the universal welfare state when 650,000 people buy private health insurance? The advocates of the divided welfare state argue that private insurance *relieves* the public health service, an argument that has been widely spread in the media and social debate. There is an intuitive logic in this statement. If some social groups leave the public welfare, then there will be more resources for those who remain. Or put differently: the more people who leave the public welfare, the better for the public welfare.

The latter obviously sounds a little weird, but as mentioned, there is a logic to it. Oddly enough, it is a logic that is often used by those who in fact want to diminish the public welfare sector and privatize more and more of its functions and funding. One example is the employer organization the Confederation of Swedish Enterprise, which advocates increased private funding and reduced taxes on ownership,[1] on employment[2] and on corporate profits.[3] The organization simply wants a reduced inflow to the public welfare sector. At the same time, it advocates increased tax deduction possibilities for private welfare solutions, i.e. additional tax losses for the state.

J. Lapidus, *The Quest for a Divided Welfare State*,
https://doi.org/10.1007/978-3-030-24784-3_8

Of course, it is strange that those who want to diminish the public welfare sector are those who, with the greatest emphasis, claim that private health insurance relieves the public sector.

A linguistic ambiguity might explain it all. A synonyms search reveals that relieving in Swedish can mean *ease the burden on* or *removing the pressure on* or *loosening*, or *unloading*.

What the Confederation of Swedish Enterprise means by *relieving* is to unload certain elements and tasks, to reduce the public sector's commitment through cutbacks and priorities. But for tactical reasons, it pretends to mean the opposite, namely that the public should be provided with resources.

The employer organization says relieving but mean relieving in a very certain meaning of the word. It promotes the semi-private welfare and has nowhere made itself known as the foremost defender of the public welfare.

In the following chapters, we will discuss some of the factors that mean that the rapid growth of *private* health insurance does not relieve but, on the contrary, erodes the public welfare. On closer inspection, it is quite obvious that this is the case, but the argument that private solutions relieve the public has been made with such frequency and with such an empathy that it has really convinced parts of the population, especially those who have insurance and in different ways want to legitimize this in a country where it can still be seen as something suspicious and odd.

For example, the industry organization Swedish Insurance states that "The insurance relieves and creates space for people who do not have insurance",[4] while the employer organization the Confederation of Swedish Enterprise' responsible for welfare policy issues, in his debate response to me, writes that "The private health insurance in Sweden is an important complement to publicly funded care".[5] The *relief argument* has actually become the favourite argument, and it is found in a multitude of different versions. Another example is the two regional councils from the Moderate Party who, somewhat far-fetched, claim that the "penalty tax" (the benefit taxation) on private health insurance also affects those who have no insurance, since the private insurance relieves the public healthcare.[6]

In what ways do private health insurance gradually erode public healthcare? Let us briefly mention some of these factors and then deepen some of them in the following chapters.

First, it is not true that *more resources remain* for those who stay with the public healthcare. The healthcare budget is updated continuously as is the rest of the state budget, and it reflects the resources that are considered necessary in the public healthcare system. If some citizens choose to leave parts of the public system for the benefit of the private health insurance system, then the public budget will be corrected accordingly. Politicians, constantly pressured by austerity requirements (Blyth 2013), are not late to cut the budget if possible. The healthcare budget is adapted for those who use public health care. The more people who leave the public health service, the less resources politicians have to spend on the public healthcare budget.

Second, there is a decrease in tax willingness among those who buy a private health insurance and thus pay twice for healthcare, partly through the tax and partly through (the certainly subsidized) insurance. The universal welfare model is based on creating welfare services so qualitative that people from different social classes want to use them, something that has been considered extremely important to justify a certain level of taxation. Here, it has been said that "targeted programs and basic security programs stimulate program exit among the middle classes and increase the demand for private insurance" (Korpi and Palme 1998). Hence, the middle class will "perceive social services and benefits programs as policies only for 'the poor'" (Rothstein 2015). And for those who break out of the system, the crucial motive to contribute to the public sector disappears.

Third, it has opinion-related consequences that it is primarily the most vocal social groups that sign private health insurance. These groups now get quick access to healthcare and no longer have to worry about the problems in the public system. On the one hand, the policyholders no longer have a self-interest in that the public health service works as well as possible, this because they solved their needs elsewhere and are very satisfied with this solution. On the other hand, they no longer see the problems in public healthcare, as they no longer use it to the same extent. As a result, a group of citizens who otherwise might have put a lot pressure on politicians to improve public healthcare, disappear. This, in turn, can be quite grateful for the politicians who want to avoid criticism and blame (Weaver 1986) from these groups.

Fourth, on a more general level, private health insurance risks leading to reduced trust in the welfare state legislation and in welfare at large. The Healthcare Act states that "The person who has the greatest need for healthcare shall be given priority", but who can take such a law seriously when the legislators, through direct and indirect subsidies to *private* solutions, encourage citizens to break it? And further: who can believe that the public service delivers the best possible healthcare when there is a parallel system that is obviously faster and better, with guarantees of rapid access to care and with twenty-four-hour access to healthcare coordinators? It is quite obvious that trust is negatively affected by parallel and unequal healthcare systems, a social trust that is actually caused by "two interrelated types of equality, namely, economic equality and equality of opportunity" (Rothstein and Uslaner 2005).

Fifth, private and semi-private healthcare systems tend to be cost-driving (e.g. Gawande 2009; Anderson et al. 2019). Among other things, a demand culture is created where the patients/customers want to get the most out of their insurance, while the private healthcare providers are interested in selling as much healthcare as possible. In addition, we get several other actors who want to make money on the new healthcare market, a market that for various reasons does not work as a normal market should work (Arrow 1978).

Sixth, private health insurance is not as private as the term suggests (e.g. Hacker 2002; Mettler 2011). Usually, benefits received via the employer are taxable, but private health insurance has throughout its growth phase been free from taxation of benefits. Currently, there is a parliamentary majority that once again wants to remove the benefit taxation on private health insurance.

Seventh, insurance policies are cheaper than they should be because insurance companies and private providers are behaving in a rent-seeking (Krueger 1974) and free-riding (Grossman and Hart 1980) way towards the public health sector. We have already mentioned that private insurance is not as private as the concept suggests and that the public sector co-finances them through tax deductions. But in the following, we will instead focus on the fact that taxpayers are building up a healthcare infrastructure in the form of premises, education and much more, something that make insurance companies and their customers come to a set table.

Eighth, there is always a relative scarcity and thus a limited range of healthcare resources in each country: health centres, hospitals, doctors, nurses and more. If a doctor treats an insurance patient, it by definition means not treating a publicly funded patient, something that the doctor could have done at that moment. This means that human resources are withdrawn from the publicly funded healthcare in order to be used instead in the privately funded sector.

Ninth, because of the insurance companies' fear of adverse selection (Cutler and Zeckhauser 2000; Baker 2002), it is both more difficult and more expensive for the unemployed, the sick and the elderly to take out private health insurance, which on the one hand creates a great inequality and which on the other hand makes the publicly funded care handle an increasing proportion of costly patients the more younger and healthier and employed persons who sign private health insurance.

Tenth, the private caregivers get more paid by the insurance companies than by county councils (e.g. Decker 2012; Anderson et al. 2019). In the long run, this may mean that private healthcare providers become less and less interested in the county councils' publicly funded patients, or that they require more payment to conclude contracts with county councils.

Eleventh, for the public, a number of transaction costs (Williamson 1981) are associated with the writing and signing of agreements and, above all, following up agreements with the private providers, in short, install a control mechanism necessary to hinder profit-driven businesses to evade their contractual and costly responsibilities.

High transaction costs are something that characterizes much of the neoliberal development that we have had in Sweden in recent decades. One example is all the companies that, in accordance with the law on public procurement (LOU), put a lot of time and resources into writing tenders but where only one company and one tender ultimately win. There are also several cost-driving effects for the public client. Among these can be mentioned that the client must devote time and resources to writing inquiry documents and then review the various tenders that come in, after which the decision that the client finally makes can be subject to appeal, for example, because of minor shortcomings in the tender documentation, something that leads to legal costs and in some cases imply that the whole process must be taken over from the beginning. Another example of high transaction cost has to do with individual wage setting (Lapidus 2015), for example the doctors' new negotiating position, where they can play off public and private employers against each other.

But above all, speaking about transaction costs, the client must control the provider in different ways and ensure that the provider does not, in order to save money, deviate from what is stated in the contract. All this requires new types of regulation, which have led several researchers (e.g. Majone 1997; Vogel 1996; Levi-Faur 2005) to discuss the following paradox in various ways: the more a market is deregulated, the more regulations and re-regulation these deregulations seem to require, i.e. "privatization leads to the creation of new regulatory bodies and to a considerable widening of the scope of agencies to promote competition" (Majone 1994).

One very concrete example is the City Hospital in Gothenburg, which in a way gives an insight into several of the eroding mechanisms mentioned above, not least when it comes to costs for writing and following up various agreements. The City Hospital caught my attention as they, in a press release on 12 September 2018 announced the happy news that they recruited three dermatologists.

"There is a high demand and needs are increasing", says the hospital's operations manager. "We look forward to offering skin care at the highest level", says the three specialists, one of whom comes directly from the publicly run Sahlgrenska hospital.

The dermatology clinic at the City Hospital is completely private. You may come if you have a private health insurance or pay out of pocket. Price lists are available online. A visit costs SEK 1000 and other thousands if you want to start fast treatment of suspected skin tumour, such as photodynamic therapy (PDT). Please note that costs for materials, blood samples, bacterial cultivation and more may be dependent on the nature of the visit.

If you are broke and have a skin tumour, the City Hospital is closed. But to the otorhinolaryngologist (ear, nose, throat) everyone is welcome, albeit on completely different terms with regard to waiting times and other things. The same applies to several of the City Hospital's departments, while others, like dermatology, are strictly reserved for certain customer groups.

The City Hospital has a number of different agreements with the public. A recently established one applies to Otorhinolaryngology and it contains 40 pages. In the agreement, it is stated that the Supplier (the City Hospital) guarantees the Purchaser (the county council) that healthcare shall be given on equal terms, something which is also stipulated in Swedish law.

Healthcare on equal terms. I ask the public purchasers at the so-called Group office why the agreement stipulates healthcare on equal terms when the City Hospital, seemingly, conducts care on as different terms as possible. There, some departments are completely closed to publicly funded patients, while other departments are a blissful mix of patients with different types of funding. These are sensitive issues also for the public purchasers. One of them says that she absolutely not wants to be quoted, and another makes herself unreachable on the phone.

Instead, I request all documentation about the Ear-Nose-Throat Agreement. Here, it is clear that the City Hospital's operations manager, even before the start-up meeting with the public purchasers, is upset about the fact that the hospital does not get enough referrals from the publicly run hospitals.

"Do you bring the referrals for operations with you then?", she asks the regional developer at the county council before the meeting, in which the Supplier and the Purchaser are supposed to review the agreement. But regional developers do not have access to medical referrals, and they never bring them to any meeting: "No, we do not. You have to contact the respective unit yourself to create routines together how you should go about these matters".

The manager's troubles with the referrals continue during the summer. In mid-June, she takes the matter into her own hands and goes herself, personally, around to the publicly run hospitals. In a mail to the public purchaser, she writes:

> Su / SS ÖNH [Sahlgrenska hospital in Gothenburg] was not ready when I got there and I went into see [XXX] myself. She promised me to bring referrals tomorrow at 11.00 downstairs on level 1 via healthcare unit manager [XXX]. But she said it was difficult to give me referrals on short notice… Some of the surgery was already done. It was the same with patient visits. On the way there, SÄS [Southern Älvsborg's hospital] called and said that they did not want to send referrals anymore due to something that had to do with SU…

Some people feel bad about the operations manager's unconventional and somewhat brusque methods. The coordinator at Alingsås Hospital writes that she had "a rather sad conversation" with the City Hospital's operations manager, who "demands that she can come here and pick up referrals". 50 minutes later, maybe also a phone call later, the coordinator writes again to the regional developer: "I have prepared 12 referrals for her with the help of a nurse".

In another mail, the problem is not the lack of referrals and patients. Instead, the City Hospital's operations manager is upset because some units send "their worst patients" to the City Hospital. The county council's team leader for private healthcare providers responds that "We do not usually refer to our patients as 'worst' and I hope that you, according to our agreement, receive all the patients that are sent to you and need your help".

Does it seem trustworthy? A profit-driven operations manager hunting referrals at every clinic. A public purchaser who tries to appease her in every possible way. I assure: if you had read the entire documentation (hundreds of pages dealing only with the Ear-Nose-Throat agreement), you would have been much more concerned. Here you can find everything from reports from the Patients Board to the operations manager's threatening e-mails copies to the law firm Glimstedt, yet another actor in the increasingly Americanized Swedish healthcare system.

Equally worrying are all question marks about how the agreement should be interpreted. There are a number of uncertainties in the notes from the start-up meeting: What about the supplier's involvement in the Västra Götaland region's infectious disease unit? How about the City Hospital's *option*—a contemporary influence from the stock market—on 200 direct operations?

The county council has several complicated agreements with the City Hospital, and hundreds of other agreements with other private healthcare providers. Effective? Rationally? In addition, the City Hospital, with the same management as today, was involved in a highlighted scandal in 2013 with false invoices to the public purchaser. It is probably the reason why the county council is particularly careful about the financial situation of the City Hospital, and in the memorandums, it is pointed out that the City Hospital "must not treat a patient without a bill of exchange" and furthermore that the supplier should "send invoices often, at least 1 time/month, preferably 1 time/week".

However, most worrying, at least from a legal perspective, is that the City Hospital does not treat their patients equally since some of their nursing departments are closed for publicly funded patients, while others are welcoming different patient groups on very different conditions. The City Hospital is by no means unique. As we have seen, in today's Sweden, hundreds of private providers have a separate entrance for 650,000 people with private health insurance, something which is a violation of the Healthcare Act's writing about care on equal terms.

As mentioned, there are a number of factors by which semi-private welfare solutions erode the public system, but for several reasons, we do not see it happen, for example, *private* health insurance. If 650,000 people overnight had signed such insurance, then there would have been many who had reacted and protested against this development. But that is not how it is been done. The increase in private health insurance has certainly been surprisingly fast, but not so fast that we have been able to see the difference from one day to another. The private health insurance policies have grown from an almost negligible level to a slightly less negligible level to an ever-increasing level where it now comprises one-tenth of the adult population.

The point is that we never noticed the qualitative leap. We were blind to a development that went hand in hand with many other gradual changes, which we were also blind to. Our blindness to gradual change means that there is always a certain lag in our view of the Swedish social development, in our view of the Swedish welfare model, in our own self-image.

Many of us still believe that we have an equal health care for all citizens, this despite the fact that as many as ten per cent of the adult population employ a private insurance company which, through agreements with private providers, fixes faster and better access to healthcare.

How many per cent will buy ahead before we realize that something has happened? Twenty per cent? Fifty per cent? Something that characterizes the hidden welfare is that it develops through seemingly small decisions that rarely are discussed in public. Several political scientists have pointed to these gradual and almost imperceptible changes that together have great effects on the organization and distribution of welfare. The most important concepts for describing such a situation are layering, drift and conversion (Streeck and Thelen 2005; Mahoney and Thelen 2009).

The above concepts and reasoning are some of several possible descriptions of how and in which way we move towards a divided welfare state. It is useful tools for understanding how it all took place, and how it can be that so many of us did not understand what happened.

But in some ways, it is strange that we have such a hard time seeing the overall result of the gradual changes in our own welfare model. Although many figures remain obscure in accordance with the principles of the hidden welfare, we nevertheless have insight into the decisive figures, for example, that "private" health insurance has increased from virtually 0 to 650,000 in twenty years or, on one more general level, that economic inequality has increased steadily since Sweden was world champion inequality in the early 1980s.

Here, parallels can be drawn with climate change. Here is what the psychologist Marta Cullberg Weston says about the psychological causes of our inability to take the climate threat more seriously:

> Many believe that more information to the public is the solution, but it is not so easy that more information leads to action. We must also take into account how the human psyche works. What is complicated with climate change is that it is mainly caused by a transparent and odourless gas – carbon dioxide. It is difficult for people to understand – and easy to distort – the detrimental effect of a threat they neither see nor feel the smell of.[7]

The emergence of an unequal healthcare system can likewise be invisible and odourless, both to the person affected and to the person who benefits from it. How? Well, first, the erosive mechanisms are difficult to measure and quantify, while there is a strong lobby that presents an alternative reality. Second, it is more difficult to notice a deterioration that must not be deterioration in itself, but a deterioration in relation to the development of the surrounding society. It will be quite natural for us that schools and hospitals look a bit worn in comparison with newly built villas and office buildings. We get used to the public being left behind to stagnation. We forget that the public system used to be as modern as anything else in society. We forget Gustav Möller's devise that only the best is good enough for the people. We do not notice that there is a gradual drift where budgets for public purposes are not updated in line with productivity and GDP developments.

We must also realize that there are politicians who want to win votes on our lagging self-image. Politicians who refer to the Swedish welfare model regardless of whether their proposals have anything to do with the model or not, and even though the model has already undergone such major changes that it becomes increasingly difficult to see what is so special about it.

In addition, economic science has made us blind to the fact that improvements for some often mean deterioration for others, that is, if some get more from society's resources, others get less of them. Parts of economic science have erased the question of income distribution and created a desolate economy based on utility maximizing and isolated individuals, households and businesses. Other parts of economic science have approached the question of income distribution by advocating inequality, thus teaching that if some take more of the total resources, it is good for all citizens. Increased gaps are beneficial to everyone. According to the trickle-down economics, the sparrows are also benefited as the horses get a lot to eat.

Trickle-down economics (Anderson 1964; Greenwood and Holt 2010) has many followers. This is what the Swedish entrepreneur Johan Staël von Holstein says on the theme:

> Increased income gaps are only a problem for the jealous and lazy, because as long as everyone gets better it does not matter if a handful gets extremely well, or?[8]

Is it an extreme position? Not really. With reference to the *populist* movement's upswing, liberals can express general concern about the income gaps, but in practice they have no proposals for increased equality and no economic theory saying that income gaps are bad for society.

Notes

1. https://www.svensktnaringsliv.se/fragor/minska-skatt-pa-agande/.
2. https://www.svensktnaringsliv.se/fragor/minska-skatt-pa-arbete/.
3. https://www.svensktnaringsliv.se/fragor/minska-skatt-pa-foretagande/.
4. https://www.svenskforsakring.se/om-forsakring/vad-ar-och-hur-funkar-det/sa-har-fungerar-en-privat-sjukvardsforsakring/.
5. *Svenska Dagbladet*, 20 October 2016. https://www.svd.se/privata-forsakringar-forstarker-sjukvarden.
6. VLT, 23 April 2018. https://www.vlt.se/artikel/debatt/moderaterna-straffskatt-pa-vardforsakring-fel-vag-att-ga.
7. *Svenska Dagbladet*, 29 November 2010.
8. *Metro*, 14 June 2017. https://www.metro.se/artikel/johan-stael-von-holstein-%C3%B6kade-inkomstklyftor-%C3%A4r-bara-ett-problem-f%C3%B6r-den-avundsjuke-och-late.

References

Anderson, W. L. (1964). Trickling down: The relationship between economic growth and the extent of poverty among American families. *The Quarterly Journal of Economics, 78*(4), 511–524.

Anderson, G. F., Hussey, P., & Petrosyan, V. (2019). It's still the prices, stupid: Why the US spends so much on health care, and a tribute to Uwe Reinhardt. *Health Affairs, 38*(1), 87–95.

Arrow, K. J. (1978). Uncertainty and the welfare economics of medical care. In *Uncertainty in economics* (pp. 345–375). New York: Academic Press.

Baker, T. (2002). Containing the promise of insurance: Adverse selection and risk classification. *Connecticut Insurance Law Journal, 9,* 371.

Blyth, M. (2013). *Austerity: The history of a dangerous idea.* Oxford: Oxford University Press.

Cutler, D. M., & Zeckhauser, R. J. (2000). The anatomy of health insurance. In *Handbook of health economics* (Vol. 1, pp. 563–643). Amsterdam: Elsevier.

Decker, S. L. (2012). In 2011 nearly one-third of physicians said they would not accept new Medicaid patients, but rising fees may help. *Health Affairs, 31*(8), 1673–1679.

Gawande, A. (2009). The cost conundrum. *The New Yorker, 1,* 36–44.

Greenwood, D. T., & Holt, R. P. (2010). Growth, inequality and negative trickle down. *Journal of Economic Issues, 44*(2), 403–410.

Grossman, S. J., & Hart, O. D. (1980). Takeover bids, the free-rider problem, and the theory of the corporation. *The Bell Journal of Economics, 11,* 42–64.

Hacker, J. S. (2002). *The divided welfare state: The battle over public and private social benefits in the United States.* Cambridge: Cambridge University Press.

Korpi, W., & Palme, J. (1998). The paradox of redistribution and strategies of equality: Welfare state institutions, inequality, and poverty in the Western countries. *American Sociological Review, 63,* 661–687.

Krueger, A. O. (1974). The political economy of the rent-seeking society. *The American Economic Review, 64*(3), 291–303.

Lapidus, J. (2015). An odd couple: Individual wage setting and the largest Swedish trade union. *Labor History, 56*(1), 1–21.

Levi-Faur, D. (2005). The global diffusion of regulatory capitalism. *The Annals of the American Academy of Political and Social Science, 598*(1), 12–32.

Mahoney, J., & Thelen, K. (Eds.). (2009). *Explaining institutional change: Ambiguity, agency, and power.* Cambridge: Cambridge University Press.

Majone, G. (1994). Paradoxes of privatization and deregulation. *Journal of European Public Policy, 1*(1), 53–69.

Majone, G. (1997). From the positive to the regulatory state: Causes and consequences of changes in the mode of governance. *Journal of Public Policy, 17*(2), 139–167.

Mettler, S. (2011). *The submerged state: How invisible government policies undermine American democracy.* Chicago: University of Chicago Press.

Rothstein, B. (2015). The moral, economic and political logic of the Sedish welfare state. In J. Pierre (Ed.), *The Oxford handbook of Swedish politics.* Oxford University Press.

Rothstein, B., & Uslaner, E. M. (2005). All for all: Equality, corruption, and social trust. *World Politics, 58*(1), 41–72.

Streeck, W., & Thelen, K. A. (Eds.). (2005). *Beyond continuity: Institutional change in advanced political economies*. Oxford: Oxford University Press.

Vogel, S. K. (1996). *Freer markets, more rules: Regulatory reform in advanced industrial countries*. Ithaca: Cornell University Press.

Weaver, R. K. (1986). The politics of blame avoidance. *Journal of Public Policy, 6*(4), 371–398.

Williamson, O. E. (1981). The economics of organization: The transaction cost approach. *American Journal of Sociology, 87*(3), 548–577.

9
A Farewell to Trust and Tax Willingness

The Scandinavian welfare states have previously been characterized by a high degree of trust in the societal institutions and a high degree of trust in each other as citizens (Kumlin and Rothstein 2005; Svallfors 2016). How is trust affected by privatization and half-privatization? How does our view of the universal welfare change when parallel systems develop, for example in the healthcare sector?

The questions are in a way rhetorical. If there is a parallel healthcare system that is faster and more efficient than the (former) universal healthcare system, then by definition the public system is inferior and then the social democrat Gustav Möller's classic devises that "only the best is good enough for the people" (Millares 2015) no longer applies. And if "inequality stands at the beginning of the causal chain" (Rothstein and Uslaner 2005) in explaining low levels of social trust, then it is quite obvious that social trust will be negatively affected when people start to buy ahead the queues in the public health system.

Moreover, if the parallel healthcare system is sponsored directly and indirectly by the state, then it is obvious that the state gives priority to certain citizens in front of others. The state gives those who have certain type of jobs greater opportunity to receive care within the framework

J. Lapidus, *The Quest for a Divided Welfare State*,
https://doi.org/10.1007/978-3-030-24784-3_9

of the parallel healthcare system. The state gives those who are young and healthy and rich more chances to receive care within the framework of the parallel healthcare system. This can explain why more and more Swedes experience that healthcare is not given on equal terms. In the latest survey of Swedish Association of Local Authorities and Regions (SKL), the proportion who perceive that care is given on equal terms is down to 50% among those who responded to this question.[1]

At the same time, also strongly linked to trust: the person who has taken out private health insurance does not notice the problems in the public health service, and no longer has any self-interest in making sure that these problems are solved. The strongest societal groups that politicians would have had the most difficulty dealing with have thus disappeared as opinion-forming force for public healthcare and are instead among those who want to see further semi-privatization of welfare. The politicians feel compelled to meet these groups in their demands for continued semi-privatization, which, through tax loss, further drains public healthcare.

Why should I, if I purchased a private health insurance, also pay taxes for a public healthcare that I no longer use? Through this simple and logical way of reasoning, the creation of parallel welfare systems has a major negative impact on large groups' willingness to pay taxes for publicly funded systems and programmes:

> They will perceive such programs as policies only for "the poor," and the middle class (who are also the swing voters) in particular will turn away from political parties that argue for increasing taxes and social policies. (Rothstein and Uslaner 2005)

As the semi-private system grows and the public welfare programmes are even more directed only to the *poor*, there will be an even greater backlash in terms of tax willingness:

> In effect, the poverty line splits the working class and tends to generate coalitions between better-off workers and the middle class against the lower sections of the working class, something which can result in tax revolts and backlash against the welfare-state. (Korpi and Palme 1998)

Those who manage their healthcare *privately* are, of course, not as keen to contribute to the common, especially if one feels that the public health service is deteriorating and is governed in a corrupt way by incompetent politicians. As we shall see, the advocates of the divided welfare state add a lot of fuel to the beliefs about the general and inherent inability of public health.

Lowering taxes as well as tax willingness require a number of manoeuvres. One of these is, with incorrect calculations, claiming that people pay more taxes (three times!) than they actually do. Another manoeuvre is to continually talk about the inability of public health care, and never ever admit that the functioning of the healthcare system has something to do with resources. "The Left believes that queues are a resource issue, and not a consequence of a socialist economy of shortages", says one journalist. "Our politicians lack competence to lead a complex billion-dollar business", says another. It does not matter whether resources are increasing or decreasing because it is always the *system* that is failing. There is basically no solution. "If the public care had worked properly, then solutions of this nature [private health insurance] would not be needed", it is said, but according to the advocates of a divided welfare state, the public system can never work properly no matter what is done about it.[2]

By focusing so unilaterally on the *system failure* of public healthcare, one reduces people's confidence in the universal welfare model and in their willingness to pay tax. Through the constant and systematic questioning of the *system*, the advocates of a divided welfare state succeed in increasing doubts among the citizens.

Of course, there are, and will always be, different types of deficiencies in public health care. The public health service will never ever *work properly* in the sense completely friction-free and without any waiting time whatsoever. Public welfare will always be a matter of scarcity and of priorities, but this scarcity will, of course, be more acute if resources are withdrawn and given them to those who leave the public system.

And those who leave the public system, why should they trust or even care about a public healthcare characterized by *system failure*? It is more probable that they begin to fight against the public in order to preserve and extend the semi-private benefits that they are now benefiting from.

At first, however, the privileged part of the middle class is uncomfortable with such a struggle against the public healthcare system. The arguments for a semi-private, divided welfare state thus have an element of delusion and moral self-preservation. Deep down, most people understand that the rapid rise of private health insurance is not optimal for a universal welfare state, but it feels good to have an offensive approach: with my private health insurance I relieve the public health sector, yes, by leaving the public sector I actually strengthen it.

The advocates of a divided welfare state nurture the middle class with this kind of arguments and this view of society. It is a way of reducing trust but also to create legitimacy. Initially, it is necessary to persuade the middle class that it does not contribute to destroying the universal welfare model. This is why, for example, the Confederation of Swedish Enterprise attaches so much importance to talking about the insurance as a relief to the public system.

Delusion and moral self-preservation are important factors. It reminds me again of Zimbabwe and Nicaragua, where the staff at the Swedish embassy legitimizes their hiring of plenty maids and gardeners with the argument that it creates jobs. The Zimbabwean and Nicaraguan upper classes, on the other hand, have long since abolished that kind of moral argumentation. And they would never argue that the state-of-the-art private hospital has a positive impact on the dilapidated public hospital for the poor masses.

Things have not come to that pass in Sweden. Here, the middle class still must justify itself. Here, the advocates of a divided welfare state still have to mover very carefully. At the same time, we have already come a long way towards a semi-private welfare, where parts of the middle class have begun to enjoy more and more of their benefits. Moreover, the new privilege system is very difficult to uninstall when it has spread all over. At the same time, there is a natural connection between the new inequality in welfare and increased income gaps. Increased income gaps mean that some groups are starting to demand their own welfare, especially if the state is involved and sponsors that kind of *private* demand. The more they demand their own welfare, the less they will care about what was previously the common one.

On a basic level, it is the increased income and wealth gaps that produce an unequal welfare model. In Sweden, we have had a striking development in terms of income and wealth inequality (Therborn 2018; Almqvist 2016). From being a world champion in economic equality, the income gaps have increased steadily ever since 1980. The gaps have increased for income from work, and the gaps have increased for income from capital partly because politicians, through tax reliefs on different kinds of capital, have made it easier for certain social groups to make a fortune on shares and housing (Lundberg and Waldenström 2018).

In such a situation, it is of utmost importance to keep some societal groups in a good mood. In a situation where the public health service is brought to its knees partly as a result of the tax loss from previous special solutions aimed primarily at some groups, it is important for the politicians to find even more separate solutions for the most critical and vocal groups in society.

In this political manoeuvring, there are elements of blame avoidance and credit claiming (Weaver 1986). By promoting the emergence of *private* health insurance policies, politicians manage to avoid blame in two different ways and from two different social groups. First, since the most vocal groups are offered a way out of the system, politicians avoid blame for the problems in the public sector. Second, as private health insurance in today's debate is said to relieve public healthcare and even have very positive effects on it, politicians avoid being accused of worsening the public healthcare by those who remain a part of it.

Something that characterizes both poor and rich countries with a high degree of inequality is that people have less trust in each other and that no one, neither poor nor rich, trusts the public institutions. The public institutions have major shortcomings, and the only thing that really works is parallel and private or semi-private systems that target some parts of the population.

Trust in other people and in the public institutions tends to be stronger in equal countries with universal welfare models, i.e. models where welfare services are provided on equal terms (Rothstein and Uslaner 2005).

At the same time, trust between the citizens also decreases when these, who previously had access to the same system on equal terms, are now divided into a group that has access to *private* insurance and another group that remains in the public system. Trust will be strengthened between people *within* the group that has private health insurance, that is a strong collective of peaches is created, as the representatives of the insurance industry testify in this book. Meanwhile, trust decreases towards the lemons that are outside this collective.

There are a number of other trust problems built into a profit-driven welfare. The profit interest itself is an incentive to reduce spending and increase income, which creates a natural lack of trust on the part of the authorities. Profit-driven welfare companies must be constantly checked. Profitable welfare companies must be prevented from cutting costs in an improper manner. The emergence of profit-driven welfare companies means that there must be expensive control functions, all in order to handle the lack of trust that is built into the new system.

The Swedish government has noticed parts of the problem. In 2016, the so-called Trust delegation was commissioned to review problems associated with New Public Management (NPM) and its competitive approach to managing welfare. In the directives to the Trust delegation, the government writes

> There is a need to further develop a governance that is based more on trust and increased ability both in municipalities and county councils and with employees to develop the business. Trustful governance is based on mutual trust between stakeholders. This applies to both the state's governance of municipalities and county councils and the latter's own governance of the business.

The chairman of the Trust delegation is Laura Hartman, known as controversial editor of a book (Hartman 2011) whose relatively modest criticism of privatizations gave rise to an outcry from the private welfare industry's debaters and lobbyists. The criticism was so harsh that Hartman had to leave her post as research director at the Centre for Business and Policy Studies (SNS). Hartman, in this highlighted battle, was even opposed by her own SNS board. In retrospect, however, the board was criticized by SNS's scientific council, which urged the organization to unequivocally support the full freedom of the researchers in the future and to prepare and publish a policy so that similar errors should not be repeated.

Why mention the episode about Laura Hartman in this context? Well, because one would think that her chairmanship of the Trust delegation means that it will make certain links between trust and NPM and the ongoing privatization of welfare on the operational and financial side.

As we shall see below, this has not been the case. But first: What is actually NPM and how does it coincide with profits in welfare? NPM has, of course, been described in a number of different ways and given a large number of attributes (Hood 1995; Christensen and Lægreid 2016; Lorenz 2012), but in this context, I consider it most important to understand that it is mainly two things:

NPM is partly a way of making the public sector more similar to markets in a market economy (a kind of steering system in itself) and partly a driving force for profits in welfare and in other public activities (a kind of steering system for itself).

Through NPM, a number of changes were made in the way of organizing the public welfare monopolies. One of the most important changes was dividing public organizations into two parts, one becoming a buyer and the other one a seller. In this way, a *market* was created. And once there was a market, it was natural to argue that the public sellers should compete also with private sellers, and then, later on, it could be argued that public sellers should not compete with the private ones (this chain of event is common, and, for example, it was exactly how large parts of Gothenburg's Traffic Department ended up in private hands).[3]

NPM is thus a system that makes the public more market-like, but it also makes private actors take over what was previously public. At the same time, in its first and more administrative sense, NPM is more important than ever in a welfare model with private actors in publicly funded activities, because without that kind of tight control and administration and regulation, without an "audit society" (Power 1997, 2000) where no one trusts no one, there is nothing to prevent the profit-driven companies from minimizing costs and only focus on what, according to the Swedish Companies Act, is their main purpose: to maximize profits.

Thus, with profit-driven companies in welfare, expensive control functions are required. The so-called deregulations thus required new regulations, ironically more regulations than those needed before the welfare market was *deregulated*. Here, research has talked about the phenomenon of "re-regulation" (e.g. Majone 1997; Vogel 1996; Levi-Faur 2005), and there are many other cost-driving effects and mechanisms built into this public–private collaboration.

A welfare system that is increasingly based on profit-driven companies does not manage without NPM-like regulations and functions. More regulation is, moreover, the centre-right wing parties' response to the Welfare investigation's demand for profit limitation. Here, one can conclude that all parties acknowledge that there are great problems of trust in a privately provided welfare sector.

The trust problems inherent in profit-driven welfare are thus related to NPM, and both NPM and profit-driven welfare are linked to increased private and semi-private funding.

One could thus imagine that a trust delegation would take a holistic approach to the issue, but unfortunately, the government's directives were somewhat superficial. Admittedly, Reepalu's Welfare investigation is mentioned in the directive, but it still seemed to be watertight compartments between issues of trust and profits in welfare. The same goes for the work of the Trust delegation. When I conducted a review of the Trust delegation's current work, it turned out that the delegation has really made an effort to avoid any connection between trust and profits in welfare or between trust and NPM.

In the Trust delegation's main report (Tillitsdelegationen 2018), the palindrome trust (in Swedish: *tillit*) is mentioned 1218 times and it finally means everything and nothing. At the same time, in the real world, as we have seen in this book, a war rages against the trust in Swedish healthcare.

How does the Trust delegation tackle the most burning trust issues? The answer is that they are not considered at all. You get 1218 hits on the word trust but not a single one on profits in welfare. The term private providers is consistently exchanged for *external providers*, and these external performers do not occur at all in the anthology (Bringselius

2018), where about 20 researchers examine a number of different healthcare activities and facilities from a trusted perspective.

Why are there no profit-driven clinics in the research anthology? This is because, in accordance with the disputed NPM, the Trust delegation assumes that there are no specific differences between public and private, profit-driven and "external" providers:

> None of the experimental activities relate to the relationship between a contracting authority and an external supplier of welfare services. In our discussions in the main report, we assume that many of the learning examples, discussions and conclusions that we make can also be used by external providers of welfare services. (Tillitsdelegationen 2018)

It is remarkable. And practical as well, because with such an axiom you do not have to touch the idea that the control apparatus that county councils build up is a consequence of having to monitor profit-making actors. Every deregulation requires new, expensive regulations, which so many scholars have pointed out over the years.

Not even in the sub-report on remuneration models (Tillitsdelegationen 2017), the difference between profit-making and non-profit providers of healthcare is problematized. Well, on page 137 there is one sentence about the fact that crowding out of expensive patients is "often pointed out" as greater if the performer is an "external actor".

From an increasingly fragmented and privatized welfare sector, the Trust delegation paints a peaceful, still life of trust-based governance. The delegation wants a welfare sector characterized by a holistic view, that is a "common structure where all actors have common goals and incentives that go in the same direction".

Common incentives? It is as if the Swedish Companies Act and its explicit paragraphs on profits as the main incentive do not exist. It is as if ten years of debate on profits in welfare has never taken place. It is as if the Trust delegation wants to evoke a "public ethos" (Lundquist 1998; Pierre and Rothstein 2011) from a reality that they do not even dare to describe.

The Trust delegation talks about NPM but still misses what this philosophy ultimately aims at and result in: equating public and private providers to enable privatization of welfare provision and, in extension, privatization and semi-privatization of welfare funding.

How could the Trust delegation neglect the most important parts of trust in relation to welfare? This is mainly due to the fact that the social democratic directives are an unprocessed word mass that reflects the party's *attitude* in the most crucial of welfare issues.

One day the party is in favour of profits in welfare. The next day it is against profits in welfare. One day, it starts an investigation on profits in welfare. The next it allows the investigation to break its own directives and propose a profit limit instead of a ban on profits. One day, the health service will be involved in the investigation. The next day, the healthcare will receive a separate investigation which is not at all about profits in welfare. It is strange that a party that was involved in building the Swedish welfare model cannot take a stand for one or the other, but instead uses this crucial question for a single long-term political tactic.

But the responsibility also lies with the management of the Trust delegation. In view of the babbling directives, the delegation's chairman and research leader could have done what they wanted from this project. And they also have.

Research leader and business economist Louise Bringselius often points out that NPM has gained undeserved bad reputation and that the philosophy is more diverse than most people think (Bringselius 2014; Bringselius 2015). She rarely touches on the purely economic doctrines. But when she does, she regrets that venture capitalists and private performers are denigrated.

The chairman, Laura Hartman, was, as mentioned, renowned in 2011 when she was forced to leave her job after having edited an interesting and mildly critical anthology on profits in welfare. This time, the welfare industrial complex has nothing to complain about.

Notes

1. SKL, Hälso- och sjukvårdsbarometern, 2018. https://webbutik.skl.se/shop?funk=visa_artikel&artnr=7585-769-5.

2. *Göteborgs-Posten*, 5 April 2017; *Svenska Dagbladet*, 5 April 2017; *Östersunds-Posten*, 7 April 2017.
3. The Confederation of Swedish Enterprise, 2006. *Osund konkurrens, kommunalt företagande för miljarder*. https://www.svensktnaringsliv.se/migration_catalog/osund-konkurrens-kommunalt-foretagande-for-miljarder; *Göteborgs-Posten*, 14 February 2005. https://www.gp.se/nyheter/göteborg/95-får-gå-från-gatubolaget-1.1173353.

References

Almqvist, A. (2016). *Den ekonomiska ojämlikheten i Sverige*. Stockholm: Bantorget Grafiska AB.

Bringselius, L. (2014). New public management–ett enkelt penseldrag som förklarar det mesta. *Organisation & samhälle, 2*, 34–39. http://org-sam.se/wp-content/uploads/2016/05/OS_nr_2_2014.pdf.

Bringselius, L. (2015). Sverige behöver en mer nyanserad debatt om NPM. *Dagens nyheter*.

Bringselius, L. (2018). Styra och leda med tillit: forskning och praktik. *Statens offentliga utredningar* (2018: 38).

Christensen, T., & Lægreid, P. (2016). *The Ashgate research companion to new public management*. Abingdon: Routledge.

Hartman, L. (2011). Konkurrensens konsekvenser. *Vad händer med svensk välfärd, 2*.

Hood, C. (1995). The "new public management" in the 1980s: Variations on a theme. *Accounting, Organizations and Society, 20*(2–3), 93–109.

Korpi, W., & Palme, J. (1998). The paradox of redistribution and strategies of equality: Welfare state institutions, inequality, and poverty in the Western countries. *American Sociological Review, 63*, 661–687.

Kumlin, S., & Rothstein, B. (2005). Making and breaking social capital: The impact of welfare-state institutions. *Comparative Political Studies, 38*(4), 339–365.

Levi-Faur, D. (2005). The global diffusion of regulatory capitalism. *The Annals of the American Academy of Political and Social Science, 598*(1), 12–32.

Lorenz, C. (2012). If you're so smart, why are you under surveillance? Universities, neoliberalism, and new public management. *Critical Inquiry, 38*(3), 599–629.

Lundberg, J., & Waldenström, D. (2018). Wealth inequality in Sweden: What can we learn from capitalized income tax data? *Review of Income and Wealth, 64*(3), 517–541.
Lundquist, L. (1998). *Demokratins väktare: ämbetsmännen och vårt offentliga etos*. Lund: Studentlitteratur AB.
Majone, G. (1997). From the positive to the regulatory state: Causes and consequences of changes in the mode of governance. *Journal of Public Policy, 17*(2), 139–167.
Millares, M. (2015). *Att välja välfärd: politiska berättelser om valfrihet*. Doctoral dissertation, Statsvetenskapliga institutionen, Stockholms universitet.
Pierre, J., & Rothstein, B. (2011). Reinventing Weber: The role of institutions in creating social trust. In P. Lagreid & T. Christensen (Eds.), *The Ashgate research companion to new public management* (pp. 407–419). Burlington: Ashgate.
Power, M. (1997). *The audit society: Rituals of verification*. Oxford: Oxford University Press.
Power, M. (2000). The audit society—Second thoughts. *International Journal of Auditing, 4*(1), 111–119.
Rothstein, B., & Uslaner, E. M. (2005). All for all: Equality, corruption, and social trust. *World Politics, 58*(1), 41–72.
Svallfors, S. (2016). Who loves the Swedish welfare state? Attitude trends 1980–2010. In *The Oxford handbook of Swedish politics* (p. 22). Oxford: Oxford University Press.
Therborn, G. (2018). *Kapitalet, överheten och alla vi andra: klassamhället i Sverige – det rådande och det kommande*. Lund: Arkiv förlag.
Tillitsdelegationen. (2017). *Jakten på den perfekta ersättningsmodellen: vad händer med medarbetarnas handlingsutrymme?/delbetänkande av Tillitsdelegationen*. Stockholm: Wolters Kluwer.
Tillitsdelegationen. (2018). *Med tillit växer handlingsutrymmet: tillitsbaserad styrning och ledning av välfärdssektorn/huvudbetänkande av Tillitsdelegationen*. Stockholm: Norstedts juridik.
Vogel, S. K. (1996). *Freer markets, more rules: Regulatory reform in advanced industrial countries*. Ithaca: Cornell University Press.
Weaver, R. K. (1986). The politics of blame avoidance. *Journal of Public Policy, 6*(4), 371–398.

10
A Spiral of Rising Costs

And the winner is… If a competition were to be announced between all the contradictions of the semi-private healthcare, it would not be difficult to find the winner. The greatest contradiction is that semi-private healthcare systems spend more of society's resources despite the fact that many people hardly get access to healthcare. The classic example is the United States, which spends 17% of its GDP in health care, even though millions of people do not even have legal rights to basic care.

There are many reasons why semi-private healthcare systems tend to devour more of society's resources. Above all, healthcare providers and healthcare consumers have a greater self-interest in the fact that a lot of resources are spent on care. Consumers want as much care as possible for the money they have spent on their insurance, something that, among other things, leads to a demand culture where one requires care efforts that are not always necessary. Profit-driven healthcare providers and other actors (insurance companies, loan institutions, etc.) have to earn as much as possible in healthcare. The healthcare company that does not make as much profit as other care companies will soon be outcompeted.

J. Lapidus, *The Quest for a Divided Welfare State*,
https://doi.org/10.1007/978-3-030-24784-3_10

The above is some of the reasons that make the US healthcare system so expensive compared to other countries. Other things that have been pointed out are, for example, a highly complex and fragmented payment system (Reinhardt et al. 2004), an unregulated distribution and utilization of expensive new technologies (Bodenheimer 2005), high administrative costs (Woolhandler et al. 2003), high advertising costs (Applequist and Ball 2018), high salaries and remuneration levels to doctors (Schroeder and Frist 2013), high drug costs and high drug use (Kantor et al. 2015) defensive medicine (Panella et al. 2015), that is doctors who order a number of unnecessary and costly samples and treatments because of fear of being sued by the beneficiaries for malpractice.

By making healthcare a market, and by mixing private and public provision, funding and regulation into an ever-increasing mess, Sweden has also increased the risks and conditions for a cost-driven healthcare system that will become increasingly costly for the economy.

One example is the online doctors. There is an enormous potential in digitalization of healthcare, not least in terms of cost-saving, but without judgment and government regulations, it may be the other way around, namely very expensive. The Swedish online doctors' private companies have grown explosively, and this means an equally explosive increase in the tax revenue that was pumped into these privately run but publicly funded companies. Take the company Kry, for example, which went from a turnover of SEK 14 million to 100 million between 2016 and 2017. In order to further increase its turnover, in 2018 there was a costly and highlighted advertising campaign, where KRY filled the capital Stockholm with the following message:

> Hello pre-school infections, day-care diseases, hay fever and cold seasons. Meet a doctor within 30 minutes – without leaving home.

The advertising campaign received a lot of criticism. One should not burden the public budget by seeking care for cough, many argued. One of them was Elin Karlsson, who is a member of the Medical Association's board and is chair of the Council for Medicines, IT and medical technology. She said:

> I think their marketing is inappropriate. It seems to be aimed at creating medical contacts and a need for care where there is not one. It is unfortunate from a socio-economic and ethical perspective. /... / We have a limited bag of money that will suffice for all healthcare. If we publicly fund medical visits when it is not justified, we risk not having the resources to treat those who really need it.[1]

The online doctors' companies have grown in an unregulated manner, and they are very cost-driving. The same go for GP locums (freelance general practitioners), that is the doctors who are hired for shorter assignments and cost the public large sums because of the salaries that these doctors are able to demand (e.g. Skinner et al. 2006) Privatizations have made it the doctors' market. Privatizations have allowed doctors to play out different care providers against each other, but now the Swedish Association of Local Authorities and Regions (SKL) and also the government want to put an end to this. In January 2017, a document was published saying that the healthcare system must "achieve an independence from hired personnel by 2019-01-01".[2]

However, a reading of the document shows that the sharp measures are few if any, but instead, it is about "knowledge transfer between county councils and regions", "produce proposals on how to follow-up different measures", "scheduled communication for supporting the project's goal". Neither the government nor SKL have taken any tough measures, and in September 2018, it was revealed that the costs actually increased in 12 of 21 county councils.[3] The same goes for England. There, the "average hourly pay rates for locums employed by NHS trusts in England rose in 2016 despite the introduction of a locum pay cap" (Rimmer 2017).

Let me exemplify some of the cost-driving mechanisms with previously mentioned private provider GävleDalakirurgin in the Swedish town Gävle.[4] On September 18, 2017, the provider publishes a press release that catches my attention. Under the heading *GävleDalakirurgin faces an exciting autumn*, the company's founder and CEO says that:

> I knew that there was a need for extended healthcare facilities in Gävle and it feels incredibly fun that the demand is even greater than I had expected.

How does the clinic earn its money? GävleDalakirurgin is a fully private clinic that opened in 2015. According to the press release, the clinic has signed agreements with all major insurance companies, and the number of insurance patients during the second quarter of 2017 doubled compared to the same period the year before.

There is also the possibility to pay out of pocket for the person who visits GävleDalakirurgin. On its website, under the heading *General Surgery*, surgery of umbilical hernia is offered for SEK 18,000 and groin hernia for SEK 32,000. Under the heading *Orthopedic Surgery*, you De Quervain's syndrome is treated for SEK 8000, while Carpal Tunnel Syndrome and Dupuytren's contracture costs SEK 11,000.

Note, however, that there is an extra cost associated with anaesthesia. According to GävleDalakirurgin, most operations can be done under local anaesthesia. But, it is said on the website, "if the patient wants to sleep during the procedure, the cost is between SEK 3,000 (sedation) and SEK 5,000 (anaesthesia)".

We have previously seen how GävleDalakirurgin is aimed at employers and employees with information on favourable gross salary deductions. Another idea is to take a bank loan to pay for the operation. According to GävleDalakirurgin, it is a common procedure, and it is said on the website that:

> One common approach to financing an operation is to expand your existing mortgage.

But maybe you have trouble getting more money from your bank? GävleDalakirurgin has the solution:

> If you want support with the payment for your operation, we cooperate with the company Medical Finance, which is a credit company that specializes in healthcare financing.

Then follows contact information for Medical Finance, which according to its own website,[5] has been operating since 2003 and has more than 10 years of experience in financing with industry-adapted solutions for private healthcare providers. Medical Finance writes that "we are of course available for financing all types of healthcare" and further that "we offer simple and secure financing with flexible loan products from SEK 1,000 to SEK 200,000".

The collaboration between a private healthcare provider such as GävleDalakirurgin and a credit company such as Medical Finance is another example of how new actors are drawn to the new healthcare market. Anyone who can make money from healthcare wants to be there. However, at first glance, Medical Finance which according to the website is "a subsidiary of Promentor Finans" seems to be driven by purely altruistic instincts. Some loans are completely interest-free. There are different types of loans to choose from, but "Healthcare 0% is our preferential interest-free loan" where you can borrow up to SEK 50,000 "completely interest-free".

Here, however, I recommend you to check out the small print, where you can read more about various arrangement fees and monthly fees for your *interest-free* loans.

Back to GävleDalakirurgin. The clinic's website states that visits that take place more than one year after surgery are counted as a new consultation and thus imply a new cost for the client. Furthermore, the cost of the operation must be paid no later than 14 days before the operation day. It is also argued that if you cancel your operation later than 10 working days before the operation, you will owe 10% of the operation cost.

In the above, there are elements of a further cost-driving mechanism in a semi-private healthcare system, namely the aforementioned transaction costs. That is, the cost of arriving at an agreement, i.e. the time and money spent for a producer and a consumer to approach each other and finally reach an agreement.

In a semi-private healthcare system, the customer must gather information about the companies' prices, and at the same time ask whether it is more beneficial to take a private insurance or try to get the operation through the public system or, in some countries, choose whether to go to public hospitals as insurance clients or as public patients (Colombo and Tapay 2003; Keleher 2016). But it is not just about prices for surgery and the like, but also about the small print about anaesthesia and return visits and many other things that have to do with general conditions. At the same time, the company has to spend time and money preparing prices that provide reasonable returns and profits and also make a set of rules that sometimes have to be adapted for the individual customer, as a purchase of an operation is not like buying fruit at the grocery store.

Buying healthcare is not like buying fruit. There are many crucial differences, and the most important one is that you never know when you get sick and how much it will cost. Further, it is a question of information. The healthcare market does not work at all in accordance with neoclassical theories and principles of perfect information, that is that both the buyer and the seller are fully informed about the nature of the goods or the service. When you buy fruit, you can look at it and compare with other fruits that you bought there and elsewhere. The grocery store has no major information advantage against you as a customer when it comes to your fruit purchases. It is a completely different situation with the ignorant patient and all the doctor's experience and education. These and other kinds of critical remarks were made in a classical article (Arrow 1963) which is referred to by Reinhardt (2001):

> First, the minimal conditions for the functioning of the competitive markets assumed for the theorem are (1) that both sellers and buyers fully understand and can assess the relevant dimensions of the particular goods and services traded in the market, (2) that both of them are price takers in the sense that as individual participants in the market they are too insignificant to have any influence at all over prices, and (3) that all relevant prices are known to all participants before transactions are consummated. It is left to the reader to assess how well even now, four decades after Arrow's article was published and almost two decades into the information revolution, the typical transaction in health care meets even these minimal requirements of a competitive market.

Because of the information asymmetry between doctors and patients, private caregivers can give excessive treatment that the patient actually does not need. At the same time, the patient wants to have as much healthcare as possible for the money spent on private health insurance, so the patient is normally happy to receive what the doctor offers.

Here, of course, the insurance company can put its foot down and say that the policyholder is not entitled to this or that care, something that Michael Moore's film *Sicko* highlights in a quite striking way. This can lead to lawsuits in every direction, which further drives costs for the healthcare system.

Here, a few more words can be said about the previously mentioned clinic GävleDalakirurgin. One way to earn money for the business is via the customers' own payments for operations and other treatments, but "Most of our customers have health insurance and come through an insurance company". It is thus the insurance patients who are a dominant element of the clinic's activities, something which is confirmed by the company's CEO when I interviewed him.

In this respect, GävleDalakirurgin is different from many other private healthcare providers in today's Sweden. How? Well, it is not because insurance patients dominate over those who pay out of pocket, since that is the case with most private healthcare providers. No, what I am thinking of is of course that GävleDalakirurgin lacks an agreement with the county council and thus also lacks the right to, parallelly, receive publicly funded patients.

Why cannot GävleDalakirurgin build up the parallel system that so many Swedish healthcare providers have built up? For the CEO, it would be a "dream to offer public health care", but it is the politicians in the north of Sweden who throw a spanner in the works:

> We are north of Dalälven, here it is a politically red as it can be. Thus... It characterizes everything, and this with private clinics and private doctors and hi-ho... In primary care it is accepted throughout Sweden and also in the northern parts, but inpatient care is severely limited, there is no tradition and it is very difficult to get procurements, yes, you know to be involved as a local private actor it is very difficult. In the city Uppsala, which is quite close, hundred kilometers from us, it is another thing, there it is more like the big cities, lots of private gynecologists and criss-cross with private doctors, here there is almost nothing, except primary care. It is a completely different tradition, so I am a little pioneer here.[6]

As we have seen, there are a lot of private healthcare providers who today have built up this type of parallel healthcare system at one and the same clinic. The publicly funded patients take the usual route through the public health care guarantee, while the insurance patients take the fast track through the insurance companies' fast access guarantees and healthcare coordinators.

There are a number of cost-driving mechanisms that are built in to the parallel healthcare system. First, the administration costs increase when creating two parallel systems at one and the same clinic. Someone must keep track of who is supposed to be in one queue and who should be in the other and set aside the right amount of staff for the erratic number of patients who come with private health insurance. Increased costs are also created outside the clinic, among other things through the healthcare coordinator services that insurance companies set up. Many nurses are employed in this kind of services, and the insurance company Euro Accident announces in a press release that they will employ another 11 nurses to their medical customer's centres.[7]

Second, the higher prices that insurance companies are willing to pay may mean that private healthcare providers also demand more of the county councils, especially if the insurance system grows stronger and becomes an increasing source of income for the private providers.

Third, another type of transaction costs, where private healthcare providers must enter into agreements with more actors as new insurance companies and banks enter the market. Is there a template for these agreements? Exactly what do the banks and insurance companies pay for the services they purchase from the private healthcare providers? There are a number of question marks that remain because of the inherent invisibility of the hidden welfare state.

More generally, in terms of cost-driving mechanisms, there is often a particular healthcare culture in countries where healthcare is not a human right but a commodity almost like any other. In short, privatization creates a sort of hysteria around healthcare that traditionally has not existed in countries like Sweden, where no one has had to calculate and compete for healthcare.

It is all about a new kind of concern about economics and health, a concern that not only affects the poor but one that cuts across the whole society. Some people may not have noticed it yet. But it will soon become obvious in the same way that other neoliberal solutions have become obvious and created similar anxiety in many more areas than healthcare.

Of course, the poor are the most affected. In an unequal healthcare culture like the US-American, many people worry about how they will afford healthcare for themselves and for their family at all. But even those who have a lot of money are worried that they will not get healthcare in absolute top class.

In the United States, healthcare is available everywhere—on radio, on television, in newspapers and on large advertising pillars along each highway—and there is always some insurance policy or treatment method or doctor who is better than the one you have. You do not want to be falling behind your neighbour who has just signed a gold or even platinum insurance. And as an employer, you do not want to be worse than other employers, because it is a major competitive disadvantage not to offer insurance policies to your employees.

These kinds of mechanisms are well described in Frank (2013). He shows how an unequal society creates a constant arms race with the people in the same residential area, a constant and nervous comparison of material status in all possible areas.

So far, healthcare is present in people's lives in a completely different way in the United States than in Sweden. It became clear when I did a study trip in five US southern states and interviewed everyone who came in my way. How difficult is it to get US-Americans to talk about healthcare? Like pressing a button. Ask anyone—motel cleaners, gun dealers and petrol stewards—and they can talk for hours about their relation to healthcare; what insurance policy they have and what they would like to have, how high or low their deductible is, how they dare or dare not go to the doctor because of costs associated with such a visit.

One of the many people I interviewed was James, a gun salesman and retired electrician in Dothan, Alabama. Previously, he had private health insurance through the job but now he goes on Medicare, the state insurance for people over 65. Medicare covers 80%, and James worries about the remaining 20, because it can be terribly expensive if he is hospitalized. Another person I interviewed was Meg, the holder of a souvenir shop in New Orleans. She herself has acquired insurance, but her colleague has not. Meg introduces me to the young woman who shyly tells me she can't afford Obamacare.

Another example is Kelly, a cleaning lady at a motel in Thomasville, Georgia. Despite all her ailments, she has not been seeing a doctor for 21 years. She dares not. One of her colleagues was there last year, but it became so expensive that the credit rating was run at the bottom. Kelly gets angry when I ask why she didn't buy a cheaper health insurance through Obamacare. She still cannot afford, she says, and then the state forces her to pay a penalty tax because she does not buy insurance. She hates big government and the big fishes in Washington.

Kelly is not rich enough to afford a *private* health insurance within the framework of the hidden welfare state, but also not poor enough to gain access to Medicaid within the framework of the visible welfare. She falls headfirst between these two welfare systems. The abyss between the hidden and the visible welfare is something that characterizes a divided welfare state like the US-American. It is in that crack that millions of Americans fall down. They are not rich enough to buy private insurance, but not poor enough to be entitled to publicly funded healthcare.

With Obamacare, there was an intention to make healthcare insurance cheaper through government subsidies. As a result, between September 2013 and February 2015, "22.8 million people gained coverage and that 5.9 million people lost coverage, for a net increase of 16.9 million people with insurance" (Carman et al. 2015). The downside is that the US-American healthcare system is still a market system and that there are still several million people who do not, or do not believe they can, afford to buy even a cheaper insurance. Those who do not take out insurance may have to pay a penalty fee. There has been a lot of confusion regarding the penalty tax, and some people "believe that paying the tax penalty was actually more affordable for them than paying for health insurance annually" (Patel et al. 2018). Obamacare thus becomes even worse than the old system for persons like Kelly.

So far, there is a big difference between the healthcare culture in a country like the United States and a country like Sweden and thus also a big difference between the social costs associated with healthcare in these two countries. Healthcare is sold everywhere in the United States. It was the feeling we got when we drove through five southern states; in the car radio, every other advertising item was healthcare related and, in the window, we saw pharmacies large as the largest Swedish supermarkets.

Our observations proved to be consistent with actual conditions (e.g. Angell 2005). Americans buy twice as much prescription drugs compared to Europeans. US companies spend huge sums on drug advertising, up to $7 billion a year, and the United States is one of the few countries in the world that allows direct mail for prescription drugs. Advertising is most evident on TV. A survey showed that 72% of all advertising breaks in the evening news in CBS contained at least one notice about drugs.[8]

In 2015, the American Medical Association (AMA) attempted to ban direct mail for prescription drugs (Applequist and Ball 2018). AMA believed that advertising created increased demand for new and expensive medicines, whether or not these drugs were appropriate. However, a ban on direct mail seems far away. Earlier attempts to ban direct mail have lost against the powerful drug lobby, which among other things referred to freedom of expression and that advertising provides valuable information for the patients.

The American healthcare culture is very cost-driving, and it is characterized by people's general concerns about their health and how they should make ends meet economically. A concern that is further whipped up by insurance companies wanting to sell insurance, by lenders advertising for cheap healthcare loans, by clinics that do radio advertising for new treatment methods, by pharmacies that advertise on cheap drugs, and by lawyers who want you to hire them to run your case against the healthcare provider or insurance company.

In addition, ill health is more common in unequal countries with unequal healthcare systems. A well-known and readable book on this theme (Wilkinson and Pickett 2010) shows that inequality and ill health have a close relationship, that is unequal countries have relatively large health problems and thus relatively large healthcare costs. From several perspectives, it is obvious that Sweden is becoming increasingly unequal. As a consequence, we will probably see more ill health and higher healthcare costs.

Notes

1. *Breakit*, 11 October 2018. https://www.breakit.se/artikel/15994/kry-spenderar-miljoner-pa-att-locka-forkylda-till-lakaren-sagas.
2. SKL, 20 January 2017. https://skl.se/download/18.18d9e79f159d8e-a51823eaa/1485438457636/06-2017-WEBB-Oberoende%20av%20inhyrd%20personal.pdf.
3. *Dagens Medicin*, 21 September 2018. https://www.dagensmedicin.se/artiklar/2018/09/21/kostnaden-for-hyrlakare-okar/.
4. https://gavledalakirurgin.se.
5. https://medicalfinance.se/.
6. Interview, 14 November 2017.
7. Euroaccident, 28 March 2019. https://www.euroaccident.se/Om-oss/Aktuellt/Aktuellt-detalj/Forsta+forstarkningen+har+anlant.
8. *USA Today*, 16 March 2017. https://eu.usatoday.com/story/money/2017/03/16/prescription-drug-costs-up-tv-ads/99203878/.

References

Angell, M. (2005). *The truth about the drug companies: How they deceive us and what to do about it*. New York: Random House.

Applequist, J., & Ball, J. G. (2018). An updated analysis of direct-to-consumer television advertisements for prescription drugs. *The Annals of Family Medicine, 16*(3), 211–216.

Arrow, K. (1963). Uncertainty and the welfare economics of medical care. *American Economic Review, 53*(5), 941–973.

Bodenheimer, T. (2005). High and rising health care costs. Part 2: technologic innovation. *Annals of Internal Medicine, 142*(11), 932–937.

Carman, K. G., Eibner, C., & Paddock, S. M. (2015). Trends in health insurance enrollment, 2013–15. *Health Affairs, 34*(6), 1044–1048.

Colombo, F., & Tapay, N. (2003). *Private health insurance in Australia: A case study* (OECD Health Working Papers 8). Paris: OECD Publishing.

Frank, R. (2013). *Falling behind: How rising inequality harms the middle class* (Vol. 4). Berkeley: University of California Press.

Kantor, E. D., Rehm, C. D., Haas, J. S., Chan, A. T., & Giovannucci, E. L. (2015). Trends in prescription drug use among adults in the United States from 1999–2012. *JAMA, 314*(17), 1818–1830.

Keleher, H. (2016). The private health sector and private health insurance. In *Understanding the Australian health care system* (p. 35). Chatswood: Elsevier.
Panella, M., Leigheb, F., Rinaldi, C., Donnarumma, C., Tozzi, Q., & Di, F. S. (2015). Defensive medicine: Defensive medicine: Overview of the literature. *Igiene e sanita pubblica, 71*(3), 335–351.
Patel, M. R., Jensen, A., Ramirez, E., Tariq, M., Lang, I., Kowalski-Dobson, T., et al. (2018). Health insurance challenges in the post-Affordable Care Act (ACA) era: A qualitative study of the perspective of low-income people of color in metropolitan Detroit. *Journal of Racial and Ethnic Health Disparities, 5*(1), 78–85.
Reinhardt, U. E. (2001). Can efficiency in health care be left to the market? *Journal of Health Politics, Policy and Law, 26*(5), 967–992.
Reinhardt, U. E., Hussey, P. S., & Anderson, G. F. (2004). US health care spending in an international context. *Health Affairs, 23*(3), 10–25.
Rimmer, A. (2017). Locum pay rates have risen despite hourly rate cap. *BMJ, 356*, j135.
Schroeder, S. A., & Frist, W. (2013). Phasing out fee-for-service payment. *The New England Journal of Medicine, 368*(21), 2029–2032.
Skinner, C. A., Riordan, R. L., Fraser, K. L., Buchanan, J. D., & Goulston, K. J. (2006). The challenge of locum working arrangements in New South Wales public hospitals. *Medical Journal of Australia, 185*(5), 276–278.
Wilkinson, R., & Pickett, K. (2010). *The spirit level: Why equality is better for Everyone*. London: Penguin Books.
Woolhandler, S., Campbell, T., & Himmelstein, D. U. (2003). Costs of health care administration in the United States and Canada. *New England Journal of Medicine, 349*(8), 768–775.

11
A Burden for the Common

How can *private* health insurance be as cheap as it actually is? If you are young and healthy, you can get away with a few hundred SEK a month, but shouldn't the insurance be more expensive considering everything it promises? In this chapter, we will see how *private* health insurance policies in different ways is a rent-seeking (Tollison 1982) free-rider (Grossman and Hart 1980) on public health care, and how prices therefore can be kept lower than would otherwise have been the case.

However, it should also be said that the insurance companies have raised the prices of many premiums and deductibles in recent times. The prices will probably continue to rise the more services and privileges that are baked into the insurances, but the point here is that they would have been even higher if the private was not able to freeride on the public sector.

There is an *indirect* sponsorship that is extra under-researched within the framework of the under-researched hidden welfare state. It is certainly the case that the *direct* sponsorship in the form of statutory tax deductions—or "tax incentives, tax subsidies, tax breaks, tax returns or, in a more derogatory vein, tax loopholes" (Levi-Faur 2014)—that has been called *Fiscal welfare* (Titmuss 1958), *Social tax expenditures*

J. Lapidus, *The Quest for a Divided Welfare State*,
https://doi.org/10.1007/978-3-030-24784-3_11

(Morel et al. 2018), *Tax breaks for social purposes* (Adema 1997), *Private social benefits* (Hacker 2002) can be regarded as the engine of the hidden welfare state, but this machine or this system also consists of a number of indirect sponsorship methods, and they are an even more invisible part of it.

We have already seen how tax breaks for semi-private supplementary services, such as private health insurance, constitute a burden for the state in the form of lost tax revenue. But purely cost-wise, it is not the insurance companies, but the policyholders who earn from the tax breaks, this because the policyholders only have to pay half the insurance premium. Since the tax breaks do not directly benefit the insurance companies (indirectly there is of course a positive effect, since the insurance companies can sell more insurance the more favourable the deductions their customers may make), then it should not be tax breaks that affect the price and make the insurance cheaper than what they *should* be.

So, what kind of freeriding are we talking about? In what ways can the insurance companies go sponge on the public to make their insurance policies cheaper and more attractive to customers?

The answer is that insurance companies and their customers come to hospitals and health centres where most things have already been set up and paid for. The insurance companies can keep low prices on their insurance, as their customers come to private healthcare providers who have their healthcare infrastructure built up of tax funds. There are many private providers who receive the bulk of their income from the county councils and who see the insurance patients as a *bonus*. Further, there are many private providers who make use of publicly paid staff as well as of premises and other materials financed by the public.

Here is a concrete example: in 2011, the private provider Capio Lundby Hospital and the county council Västra Götaland region signed a six-year agreement, from 1 January 2012 to 21 December 2017, with the possibility of extension. At a meeting on 17 October 2017, the Gothenburg Health Care Board decided to extend the agreement with Capio Lundby Hospital until 31 December 2020 with unchanged conditions.

The agreement consists of 34 pages and contains, in addition, a dozen appendices. In the agreement, the client (the public) specifies as detailed as possible what the supplier (the private hospital) is supposed to do for the money and what should be offered at the hospital.

Here are some of the hundreds of requirements that the client needs the supplier to fulfil in order to sign the contract:

> The patient environment must be designed to contribute to the patients' well-being, e.g. possibility to wear own clothes during dialysis. /…/ Physical activity e.g. exercise equipment must be designed to contribute to patient well-being. Newspapers, image and data entertainment should be designed to meet the patients' needs and wishes. Patient / relative co-operation should be designed to contribute to the patients' well-being.
>
> All equipment used in the business must comply with established standards, values and requirements for reliability, performance and quality in order to ensure an effective function. The supplier is responsible for uninterrupted power supply where required.

The supplier has, through its signature, agreed that the above shall be fixed within the framework of the contract with the client. All of the above is thus included in the price between client and supplier. The *private* insurance customer therefore comes to a hospital with electricity, newspaper subscriptions and everything between heaven and earth that has already been settled in the contract between the private hospital and the public client.

And how about the rent? Must not the insurance companies and their customers, who use the premises in the same way as the publicly funded patients, at least pay their share of the rent?

No, the rent is already paid by the public. It is clear from the contract that the business will be conducted at the Wieselgrensplatsen in Gothenburg and that the rent amounts to SEK 10,500,000 per year. According to the contract, the public client shall pay rent to the private supplier from the time the contract period commences.

The insurance patients thus come to premises where the rent is already paid by the public, i.e. by the taxpayers. But do insurance companies really have the right to let their customers go to the hospital?

In the above contract, under the heading *Localization and premises*, there is an addition that could mean that the private healthcare provider must not lend their premises to those patients whose insurance companies have not paid a penny in rent.

> Activities that are not included and financed in the agreement and which are not financed by VGR [the county council] or other healthcare practitioner may only be conducted in the premises after approval by the client.

From the above, it appears that the supplier, the private healthcare provider, needs an approval from the client in order to receive insurance patients in their premises. Has the supplier requested such approval? Has the client given such approval?

I have interviewed several representatives of the supplier as well as the client, and it seems that everything is completely in order. Private Lundby Hospital is fully entitled to conduct other activities in the premises for which the public pays the entire rent. After a few calls to different people at Capio Lundby Hospital, I got a longer conversation with the company's CEO and operations manager, who believes that everything is very transparent and that Capio regularly reports to the client what types of activities that are conducted in their premises.[1]

The CEO is of course correct in the fact that it is not a secret for anyone that the hospital conducts other and more *private* activities on its premises, for example, on the website it says:

> Through the Private Team, we have developed a concept that is a good complement to public health care. We offer good quality and high service levels at all levels. We have agreements with most insurance companies regarding private health insurance. Do you want to seek care from us and use your health insurance? Contact your insurance company directly and they can book an appointment with you at Capio Lundby Hospital.

Then I get a clear message also from the client or at least as clear as one can expect to get within the framework of the hidden welfare. First, I speak with the chairman of the Gothenburg Health and Medical Care Board. He refers me to the so-called Group office at the county council, where there are several people who work on contract issues and the like. Having spoken to some of these contractual persons, I am referred to one who has special knowledge about the agreement between the county council and Lundby Hospital. She confirms that Lundby Hospital has an approval to conduct other activities on its premises and that the county council receives regularly reports on the nature and scope of this activity.

However, for me as a researcher, it is impossible to get to see these reports, as they are confidential. The county council's representative says:

> The knowledge we have about the insurance companies, it is confidential. /... / You have to settle with the fact that the county council has the knowledge, so to speak.[2]

The public thus gets some information from and about the private sector, but the information is not public enough to be passed on to someone else. It is another example of the invisibility of the hidden welfare state, where journalists and researchers can get some information, but where the exact data remains hidden behind the wall of business secrecy that is now a natural feature of the welfare model. It is a culture of secrecy that is spread from the private sector. The public also has to relate to the rules in the *private* market, and even the public is nowadays secretive with things that have to do with the private.

Capio Lundby Hospital, although the public pays the rent, has the right to conduct other activities on its premises. It is one of many examples of how the insurance companies and their customers freeride on the public sector.

An example that touches upon the above is found in Australia, where insurance companies make money paying less to public hospitals than they pay to private hospitals (Seah et al. 2013):

> In addition, when private patients are treated in public hospitals, the public hospital can only charge the fixed rate that is set by the federal government. This fixed rate is less than what private hospitals charge for the same services, and thus the government further subsidises the care of

> privately insured patients. Such funding discrepancies are possible because all private hospitals are involved in contractual relationships with PHI companies. It has been estimated that the insurers of private patients are charged only a third of the $1000 a day they would pay in private hospitals.

Let us now look at another example, namely the remuneration of the staff receiving patients within the framework of the semi-private welfare. A first observation, as we have already noted, is that the country's overall welfare resources are not endless. There is a limited range, for example, of the staff group that we are going to focus on here, namely the doctors.

As we have seen in previous chapters, private providers may allow their doctors to alternate between publicly and privately funded patients, but a physician cannot at the same time treat patients from both of these categories. At any given moment, a doctor is either employed with a patient in the public health queue or employed with a patient who has bought ahead with private health insurance. This means that some of the personnel resources that could have gone to public healthcare, in this case the limited number of active doctors, instead go to the semi-private healthcare.

But the private doctors are private, right? No not at all. First, as mentioned, they are included in an activity that is state-sponsored on both the supply side and the demand side: their patients can do tax breaks, and their employer, the private healthcare companies, can mix privately and publicly funded patients in the most profitable possible doses.

However, it does not stay there. As we shall see, it is not just that the doctors are part of an environment that is more public than private in nature, but it is also the case that their medical career is public to a very high degree.

First, the doctors' education is publicly funded. The medical education in Sweden is financed by state resources, so it is the public that, at the most basic level, enables there to be doctors who receive patients who have bought themselves ahead the public health queue.

But for a doctor, it is not just the publicly funded and five and a half year long basic education we talk about. Moreover, a doctor should also do almost two years of general medical training programme, and most doctors then do another five years to reach specialist expertise in their area.

Who pays for the doctors' almost seven years of supplementary training? In most cases: the public sector. I have to say that I was surprised when I began to inform myself of who pays the doctors' salaries during the five years of specialization, because it turns out that county councils often pay these salaries even though the doctors are employed at privately run clinics.

The private providers receive a free workforce that produces at least an 80% level of a specialist doctor, and the private providers then charge the county councils for the healthcare produced by these county council-paid doctors. The private healthcare providers can also charge the insurance companies for the doctors' services, because there is nothing to prevent these doctors paid by the county councils from taking care of patients who bought themselves ahead the county councils' own care queues.

It is very remarkable that the county councils pay doctors who perform healthcare for which the county councils have to pay again, even when the doctor's receive insurance customers.

In some county councils, this model has actually been questioned. In the region of Uppsala, in 2016 it was decided to let the private providers pay for their doctors' supplementary training. Bertil Kinnunen, social democratic county commissioner for the Uppsala region, argued that the previous model was a pure profit business for the private healthcare providers. He told Swedish public television:

> It is clear that the private health centers have previously had a great advantage of not having to pay for any salary costs. Now they have to be involved in financing some of the services.[3]

In a survey conducted by the Swedish Medical Association,[4] it was found that all Swedish county councils paid the majority of the doctor's salary while doing there supplementary training, regardless of whether the doctor was employed by public or private healthcare providers. In the region Blekinge, the county council accounted for 100% of the salary cost. The allowance covered the entire salary, including social security contributions, holidays and more.

The same was true of the regions Dalarna, Kronoberg, Västmanland, Örebro and Östergötland. Other county councils—such as Norrbotten, Skåne, Sörmland and Västernorrland—paid between 75 and 90% of the salaries.

This is a little debated but highly costly affair for the public sector. Not only does the public pay for the healthcare provided by the private caregivers, but the public must also pay their salary during the first seven years. This type of freeriding has also been highlighted in England, where the British Medical Association (BMA) has argued that "the private sector is free-riding on English education of doctors and medical research" (Olesen 2010).

Nevertheless, representatives of the private providers have expressed dissatisfaction with the state of affairs. For example, Håkan Tenelius and his colleague Karin Liljeblad at the Association of Private Care Providers argue that county councils should compensate the private providers "not only for healthcare efforts, but also for educational assignments that they undertake".[5] Here, Tenelius/Liljeblad refers to the qualified specialist doctors who supervise doctors during the training, and it is believed that this tutoring means less time for patient work and thus an income loss for the private healthcare provider.

In a laconic reply to Tenelius/Liljeblad's article, four doctors on supplementary training state that they are, after all, free labour for the private providers:

> The health care providers point out the need for compensation in order to get the educational assignment to work. In this context, we want to clarify that we come without pay requirements. We are free labor for the healthcare provider. Our salary is paid by SLL [Stockholm county council] and the respective health center. After introduction and during supervision, we contribute to the health care production that the healthcare provider is compensated for.[6]

The public sector thus bears the costs for the doctors' education and salary during the early years of their careers. Still, doctors are free to work for a private healthcare provider and receive private and *private* patients, even during the training period. In the 1970s and 1980s, attempts were made to limit these possibilities (Heidenheimer and Elvander 1980; Immergut 1990). When the public health monopoly was expanded, the doctors' opportunities to work in privately run healthcare with *private* funded patients were also circumscribed.

Today it is completely different. The public monopolies have long been disrupted and privately employed doctors can mix their patient groups haphazardly, that is receiving publicly funded patients and insurance patients and patients who pay out of pocket in any way they like.

But what about the publicly employed doctors, that is the doctors who work in publicly provided—they actually still exist—health centres and hospitals such as Sahlgrenska in Gothenburg or Karolinska in Stockholm? Another purpose of the 1970s and 1980s circumscription of private providers was to prevent publicly employed doctors having their private clinic alongside the public, something that meant less time and commitment for the public duty.

In what way? Well, there are many countries whose medical laws stipulate, just like the Swedish one, that all citizens have the right to healthcare on equal terms and due to needs. There are many countries that have publicly run hospitals where all citizens are welcome and where many doctors are employed. The problem is that it can be difficult for the patient to find the doctor. The problem is that the doctor has his/her own private reception which is prioritized before the employment at the publicly run hospital. There can thus be a very inclusive legislation, while the public is eroded into an empty shell.

Multiple public–private jobholding or "moonlighting" (Biglaiser and Albert Ma 2007) is a very common phenomenon in developing countries (Berman and Cuizon 2004) but also in rich countries (Eggleston and Bir 2006; Socha and Bech 2011). In Sweden, too, we have opened up for secondary activities and jobs of various kinds (Erlingsson and Öhrvall 2013), something that also applies to publicly employed doctors. For these, there are rules that are intended to ensure that the doctors are available at their workplace. Thus, the publicly employed physician may not have a secondary occupation that affects the work tasks or is competing or damaging to the work. According to the Swedish Medical Association, however, it is easier for public employees than for privately employed doctors to work with other tasks, since the competition aspects are more prevalent in the private sector.[7]

In the public sector, it is thus easier to get a secondary occupation approved. This definitely seems to be the case in the region Skåne, where an inventory showed that Skåne's university hospital approved 450 out of 480 applications for secondary occupation, while western Skåne approved 103 out of 104 of these applications. The only doctor, who did not get approved in western Skåne, was he who planned to start his own online company for prescription of aphrodisiac.[8]

The Moderate Party's Caroline Wessel, who is a member of the Staff Committee in Region Skåne, highlights the easy-going approval of secondary jobs. She worries that it may take too much power and energy from the regular work. She wants to see an investigation into possible connections between secondary jobs and sick leave at the regular workplace, and she says:

> It is problematic if doctors use the holiday after on-call duty for other types of work. Region Skåne is the main employer and it is we who have rehabilitation responsibility if someone gets burned out.[9]

Furthermore, Caroline Wessel believes that doctors who work at 100% for a public employer should work 100% for the same. She says:

> The goal must be for our employees to work one hundred percent for Region Skåne. If you want variation, it should be possible to arrange within the business.

In January 2019, the specialist magazine Dagens Medicin revealed that three orthopedic surgeons at publicly run Karolinska Hospital in Stockholm received secondary jobs approved for the same work by a privately run healthcare provider.[10] The most noteworthy in this case is that Karolinska has a close referral collaboration with private orthopedists in outpatient care, which means that doctors can steer simple cases to the private healthcare provider. Dagens Medicin writes:

> It is thus possible for the orthopedists who decide on referrals to choose to keep costly investigations and operations within Karolinska, and vice versa: forward financially favourable patients to themselves or colleagues on the secondary job. In a document that Dagens Medicin has taken note of, one of the doctors claims that he is paid per patient in the private clinic, something that can encourage treating as many patients as possible.

The above is another example of private and semi-private activities becoming a burden for the public, in this case by the fact that well-paid doctors supplement their already high incomes by using their public employment in a questionable way. There are many examples of how the medical profession strengthens its position in the semi-privatized welfare, where they can exploit the fact that the public becomes an increasingly weaker party in relation to the private and semi-private.

Doctors tend to receive a completely different and much better negotiating position. The public goes cap in hand and ask for a doctor who has been trained with public funds within the framework of a legislation where healthcare should be given on equal terms for everyone. The ultimate example is the medical locums. In Australia, "Locums earn up to three times the award rate, with agencies charging 10%–15% commission per shift" (Skinner et al. 2006). The same goes for Sweden. The locums earn a lot of money from their strong position towards the public sector, and I myself have seen county council politicians tear their hair over the extravagant salaries they are forced to pay for these doctors.

Notes

1. Interview, 7 December 2017.
2. Interview, 8 December 2017.
3. SR, 1 February 2016. https://sverigesradio.se/sida/artikel.aspx?programid=114&artikel=6357794.
4. Sveriges läkarförbund, *System och strategier för att öka antalet ST-läkare.*
5. *Dagens Samhälle*, 7 June 2016.
6. *Dagens Samhälle*, 15 June 2016.
7. https://slf.se/rad-och-stod/flera-arbetsgivare-bisysslor/anstallningsvillkor-vid-fler-an-en-arbegtsgivare/.

8. *Sydsvenskan*, 26 September 2016.
9. *Sydsvenskan*, 26 September 2016.
10. *Dagens Medicin*, 7 May 2019. https://www.dagensmedicin.se/artiklar/2019/01/17/karolinska-godkande-tvivelaktiga-bisysslor/.

References

Adema, W. (1997). What do countries really spend on social policies? A comparative note. *OECD Economic Studies, 28*(1), 153–167.

Berman, P., & Cuizon, D. (2004). *Multiple public-private jobholding of health care providers in developing countries: An exploration of theory and evidence*. Issue paper-private sector. London: Department for International Development Health Systems Resource Centre Publication.

Biglaiser, G., & Albert Ma, C. T. (2007). Moonlighting: Public service and private practice. *The RAND Journal of Economics, 38*(4), 1113–1133.

Eggleston, K., & Bir, A. (2006). Physician dual practice. *Health Policy, 78*(2–3), 157–166.

Erlingsson, G. Ó., & Öhrvall, R. (2013). Kommunerna brister i hanteringen av anställdas bisysslor. *under utgivning i Ekonomisk Debatt*.

Grossman, S. J., & Hart, O. D. (1980). Takeover bids, the free-rider problem, and the theory of the corporation. *The Bell Journal of Economics, 11*, 42–64.

Hacker, J. S. (2002). *The divided welfare state: The battle over public and private social benefits in the United States*. Cambridge: Cambridge University Press.

Heidenheimer, A. J., & Elvander, N. (Eds.) (1980). *The shaping of the Swedish health system*. London: Croom Helm.

Immergut, E. M. (1990). Institutions, veto points, and policy results: A comparative analysis of health care. *Journal of Public Policy, 10*(4), 391–416.

Levi-Faur, D. (2014). The welfare state: A regulatory perspective. *Public Administration, 92*(3), 599–614.

Morel, N., Touzet, C., & Zemmour, M. (2018). Fiscal welfare in Europe: Why should we care and what do we know so far? *Journal of European Social Policy, 28*(5), 549–560.

Olesen, J. D. (2010). *Adapting the welfare state: Privatisation in health care in Denmark, England and Sweden*. Doctoral dissertation.

Seah, D. S., Cheong, T. Z., & Anstey, M. H. (2013). The hidden cost of private health insurance in Australia. *Australian Health Review, 37*(1), 1–3.

Skinner, C. A., Riordan, R. L., Fraser, K. L., Buchanan, J. D., & Goulston, K. J. (2006). The challenge of locum working arrangements in New South Wales public hospitals. *Medical Journal of Australia, 185*(5), 276–278.
Socha, K. Z., & Bech, M. (2011). Physician dual practice: A review of literature. *Health Policy, 102*(1), 1–7.
Titmuss, R. (1958). *Essays on the welfare state.* London: George Allen and Unwin.
Tollison, R. D. (1982). Rent seeking: A survey. *Kyklos, 35*(4), 575–602.

12

Rhetoric and Practice

All political parties, from right to left, claim that they safeguard the Swedish welfare model. All parties endorse the Swedish healthcare's public funding via taxes. But rhetoric is one thing and reality another. Just as the advocates of a divided welfare state, the politicians and their parties, from right to left, are aware of the popularity of the Swedish welfare model in broad layers of the population. This means that politicians, regardless of the actual content of their proposals, often claim that these proposals are fully in line with the Swedish welfare model.

Political scientist Robert Cox (2004) has named the phenomenon *the path dependency of an idea*. He argues that a welfare model can be so popular that politicians feel compelled to refer to it even if their proposals go in a completely different direction. Meanwhile, as an effect of these contradictory proposals, the welfare model gradually—often through mechanisms such as layering, drift and conversion (Béland 2007)—loses its fundamental characteristics. Finally, the Swedish welfare model simply means the model practised in Sweden.

However, some changes can be quite difficult to obtain by this type of gradual and almost invisible means. A large majority of the population associates the Swedish welfare model with healthcare on equal

J. Lapidus, *The Quest for a Divided Welfare State*,
https://doi.org/10.1007/978-3-030-24784-3_12

terms for everyone, a healthcare that is not determined by the thickness of the wallet. The emergence of private health insurance challenges that notion, and, among the public, it creates questions and concerns that the politicians feel obliged to react on.

In this chapter, we take a closer look at the so-called Stop Law in 2006. The law was presented by the Social Democrats as a way to stop the possibility to buy ahead the public queue to healthcare, but at the same time, there was an abundance of loopholes and exemptions in the government bill, which even included a calming message to those private providers who continued to welcome policyholders and publicly funded patients on totally different conditions.

What is the basis for these contradictions? Why did the Social Democrats say they were establishing a law that would stop the VIP lanes in healthcare, while they established a law that did not stop the VIP lanes in healthcare? Why this divergence between rhetoric and reality?

Before discussing the why-question, the actual divergence between rhetoric and reality must be investigated. Here, a combination of discourse analysis (Brown et al. 1983) and immanent ideology critique (Burbules 1992; Liedman and Nilsson 1989; Boréus and Bergström 2012) is quite suitable. The immanent ideology critique "challenges a belief system not by comparing it against a set of external standards, but by showing that it does not measure up to its own (perhaps unstated) standards" (Burbules 1992). This is done by comparing the difference between what is said and what is actually done or even more refined: by comparing the difference between what is said in different circumstances or even differences between what is said in one and the same circumstance.

One method that combines the above is critical discourse analysis (Van Dijk 2008; Fairclough 2013). It is a strand within critical theory (Calhoun 1995), and it is one of the several types of discourse analysis (Jørgensen and Phillips 2002). Critical discourse analysis seeks "more insight into the crucial role of discourse in the reproduction of dominance and equality" (Van Dijk 1993), and it is fundamentally concerned with "analysing opaque as well as transparent structural relationships of dominance, discrimination, power and control as manifested in language" (Wodak 2001).

In his critical discourse analysis of New Labour, Fairclough (2002) gives many examples of "the reality-rhetoric dichotomy" within that party. The most obvious dichotomy is the differences between what is said and what is done, but Fairclough also finds differences between what is done and what is done, i.e. different types of actions regarding one and the same political issue. This was the case with increased child benefit, which was regulated in the law but which still did not reach all groups that it was supposed to reach.

Another example of "the reality-rhetorical dichotomy" is when New Labour talks about their proposals in one way in certain circumstances and in another way in other circumstances. This was the case with the Freedom of Information Bill, where Tony Blair was very clear on the supposedly broad scope of the new bill which should put an end to the "obsessive and unnecessary secrecy which surrounds government activity", and even "signal a new relationship between government and people". Blair linked the new type of openness to the politics of the Third Way, but when the bill was finally published, it was met with a lot of criticism and regarded as going against what was said from the beginning, for example in a White Paper published two years earlier. The White Paper differed a lot from the published bill, which contains many more exemptions and lacks some of the requirements included in the White Paper. Fairclough summarizes:

> The gap between rhetoric and reality in this case is the gap between the language of the Bill and the language of New Labour's political discourse about the Bill. /…/ So the gap between rhetoric and reality in this case is not between language and something else—it is between language used in one place and language used in another: language used in political discourse and language used in government action.

As we shall see below, our example (the Stop Law) is even more conspicuous. It is not just about the sayings and doings in one circumstance compared to another, but it is also about two different languages to two different groups *within* one and the same government bill.

There is much to be said about the reasons for this behaviour from a political point of view, not least with regard to the Social Democratic Party that is the historical bearer of the Swedish welfare model. Somehow, it is the ultimate example of politics without principles, politics that rhetorically is trying to please all groups at the same time while, in reality, do not by any means hinder the rise of a divided welfare state.

The Stop Law, introduced by a social democratic government in January 2006 and repealed by a centre-right wing government one and a half years later, was widely considered a way of slowing down the rapid growth of private health insurance. According to the law, private providers had to make a choice between policyholders and publicly funded patients. According to the law, the private provider who had an agreement with the county council, and thereby welcomed publicly funded patients, could not agree with the insurance companies on welcoming their patients.

Private and public funding would not be mixed. The private providers would have to decide which kind of patients they wanted. A privately run healthcare facility could not have a slow queue for publicly funded patients and a faster one for policyholders.

Or? Well, that was how it was presented in the media by the social democratic minister with that portfolio and that was also how it was presented in the government bill.[1] However, there are a lot of other things presented in the same bill, things that contradict the above and make the law mean something else than it was supposed to. First, it is stated that:

> The county council, if it delegates to someone else to carry out healthcare provided at a *hospital* [my emphasis], the agreement shall contain conditions that the care shall be conducted exclusively with public funding and publicly decided healthcare fees.

Upon closer reading, it turns out that the law only involves hospitals. As already mentioned, private health insurance is available and applicable at all levels of care. Restricting the law to hospitals therefore entailed a limitation of the reach of the law. It was pointed out by several referral bodies, including the National Public Health Institute, the Swedish

Confederation of Professional Employees and the Swedish Association of Local Authorities. The Swedish Association of Health Professionals also criticized the fact that the law would only involve hospitals, and it was stated that "the possibility of receiving patients with private funding may be a threat to the vision of healthcare on equal terms".

The social democratic government insisted on the decision not to involve primary care. The government bill has a section with a heading that explicitly says it will account for the reasons for excluding primary care, but, strangely enough, the section does not contain any explanation whatsoever.

Moreover, and very important in this context, the distinction between hospitals and primary care is misleading. There are evermore specialist clinics that are neither hospitals nor traditional primary care units, and all of them would also be exempt from the Stop Law since they are obviously not hospitals. One of hundreds of examples is the HandCenter[2] which is present in four different Swedish cities and which, at least in Gothenburg, has an agreement with the county council while also welcoming policyholders and patients who pay out of pocket.

Here, at the HandCenter in Gothenburg, the patient can choose to pay SEK 2809 out of pocket for a visit, which does not include "X-ray, sampling, treatment and surgery". Policyholders are of course another group entitled to quick access to all services. Among the HandCenters' partners, there are insurance companies like Skandia and Euro Accident and banks like SEB.

In the slowest queue to HandCenter, we find the publicly funded patients. Observe that HandCenter has a "limited access by phone"[3] for this group of patients, an information that was removed soon after my debate with one of HandCenters' surgeons in one of the largest Swedish newspapers.[4]

So, the Stop Law would only involve hospitals. Or? No, the law only involved former public hospitals and not those that were privately run from the beginning. Not surprisingly, the former public hospitals that were supposed to be hit by the law argued that this implied a sort of arbitrariness that clashed with the *competition neutrality* mentioned both in Swedish and in EU legislation.

So, the law would involve only some hospitals. Or? Well, first, it is difficult to specify what a hospital really is, and the official report that formed the basis of the bill puts a lot of effort into answering that question (Vårdens ägarformer 2002). Second, the private hospitals could simply stop calling themselves hospitals and instead, in order to bypass the Stop Law, use titles like *local healthcare units*. Third, it was allowed to withdraw parts of the operation from the reach of the Stop Law. The government bill expresses itself generously at this point, and it mentions several activities that can be separated from the hospital's organization.

Thus, it was highly doubtful whether the law even applied to some hospitals. But if it did, and if county council politicians broke the law by reaching agreements with hospitals that received policyholders, then nothing would happen. The social democratic government could not find "sufficient reasons for imposing sanctions on county councils that violate the regulations". The lack of means to sanction law-breaking actions was criticized by several referral bodies, and the Swedish Municipal Workers' Union gave mention to county council politicians who would, deliberately, go against the law for ideological reasons.

In conclusion, the Social Democrats had thus created a law that was explicitly intended to curb the growth of health insurance policies ("We want to put an end to VIP lanes", as the responsible minister Ylva Johansson put it in parliamentary debates and in newspaper interviews), but which in fact was so packed with loopholes and exemptions that it had no effect.

In fact, the entire 40-page bill, signed by Prime Minister Göran Persson and Ylva Johansson, is very contradictory. The bill states that private healthcare providers should not be able to have agreements with both county councils and insurance companies. Then, exemption after exemption, loophole after loophole, and at the end, there is even a calming message to all private providers:

> The absolute majority of private healthcare providers [will] continue to receive patients whose care is financed with private health insurance or with their own funds.

So, once again: Why do the Social Democrats say that they are establishing a law that will stop the VIP lanes in healthcare, while they establish a law that does not stop the VIP lanes in healthcare even though it is said to do so? Why this dichotomy between rhetoric and reality?

One of several answers is that the radical rhetoric has had an important function. The rhetoric of the party leadership has often been directed to an external opinion and to an internal opposition which still advocates the traditional Swedish welfare model and which surprisingly often have been satisfied with the empty words. In practice, the party has played a key role in privatizing the welfare and laying the foundation for a divided welfare state.

It is thus an internal opposition and an external opinion that makes a law like the Stop Law come about, but other mechanisms that make it as watered down as possible. It is about a general ideological shift (Kitschelt 1994) backed up by a liberal or even neoliberal third way (Callinicos 2001; Cammack 2018), and it is obviously about a leadership that wants to give the impression of defending traditional principles but who, in practice, are breaking them. Leading party figures who still have a certain measure of radicality but keep it for themselves for a number of reasons: they do not want to confront the vocal voters who benefit from the hidden welfare state, they do not want to confront the private welfare-industrial complex that they themselves have helped to build, they do not want to be in conflict with centre-right wing media that is always on the welfare industry's side, they have developed into an economic elite who has a self-interest in inequality, and they do not want to be too radical during their term of office and thus lose out on well-paid jobs, often within the welfare-industrial complex, that wait for them after the political career.

At the same time, the party is becoming less of a people's movement and more of an election machine, where it is difficult to make a career without coming into line. It is particularly evident at the congresses. The delegates come there with tough motions about such things as profits in welfare, but the party board gathers the delegates in thematic groups where they all agree in advance on writings that can be interpreted in any way by the party leadership.

In this context, it must also be pointed out that within Social Democracy there is an internal disagreement—and thus an opening for future change—which does not exist in the centre-right wing parties. To re-exemplify with the Stop Law, we can conclude that the centre-right wing parties tore it up and replaced it, in January 2007, with the so-called Start law.

This meant that the centre-right wing parties prevented even the vaguest attempts to slow down the development towards a divided welfare state in the healthcare area. Nevertheless, representatives of these parties, including the responsible minister Göran Hägglund from the Christian Democrats, meant that they were opposed to the possibility of buying ahead the public queue.

How can the centre-right wing parties be opposed to two queues in public healthcare and, at the same time, implement a Start law manifesting exactly the parallel system with two separate queues? How can these two positions be reconciled? They cannot, of course, but as previously mentioned, the centre-right wing parties insist that proposals that promote the divided welfare state are fully in line with the Swedish welfare model. It gives rise to a kind of newspeak where two queues are not two queues and where private solutions are the best that can happen to the public sector. It is a rhetoric they are forced to use because of the public opinion's positive attitude towards the Swedish welfare model.

But is it really true that the centre-right wing parties, in practice, have pursued such a clear policy on these issues? Yes absolutely. The centre-right wing government 1991–1994 was very keen on privatization (e.g. Blomqvist 2004), and, thus, "a number of new legislative enactments promoted private alternatives to state-provided services" (Clayton and Pontusson 1998), while the centre-right wing government 2006–2014 created several of the semi-private tools are used to build the divided welfare state (e.g. Carlén et al. 2013; Etzler 2013). The first thing that the government 2006–2014 did was, as mentioned, to abolish the Stop Law and replace it with the Start law. The second thing the government did was to launch different types of tax breaks, the so-called Rut deductions, within schooling and elderly care.

Indeed, the centre-right wing parties are not the only ones advocating a divided welfare state, using a rhetorical strategy that reminds a lot of Orwellian newspeak. In fact, what we see is a hegemonic paradigm (Cerny 2008) or a hegemonic bloc (Jessop 1997) comprised by a number of different actors and shaped by a process that is evident not only in Sweden but in all countries that have moved towards neoliberalism, i.e. most of the countries that we can possibly think of. It is an ongoing process that changes our countries and our ways to think or as Harvey (2007) puts it:

> Neoliberalism has, in short, become hegemonic as a mode of discourse. It has pervasive effects on ways of thought to the point where it has become incorporated into the common-sense way many of us interpret, live in, and understand the world.

Thus, the above is a general trend with many similar expressions and actors in many different countries, but of course, each country has some characteristics of its own. Something that characterizes Sweden is that it, in a relatively short period of time, has moved from one extreme to another at least in some aspects, for example by destroying the public welfare monopolies and creating possibilities for welfare companies to make unregulated profits in all welfare sectors.

Such a transition would not have been possible without the determination of many different actors who, knowingly or unknowingly, form a bloc that becomes even more powerful due to the evermore actors comprising it and due to the surprising weakness or even total absence of counter-hegemonies (Carroll 2009).

What does the hegemonic bloc look like? In terms of advocating continued privatization and half-privatization of welfare services, it is a mixed bag of actors such as (1) the centre-right wing parties and their increasingly clear but still veiled criticism of the universal welfare model, (2) Parts of Social Democracy and especially former leading representatives who have close links to, or even work for, the private welfare industry, (3) the far-right political party the Sweden Democrats, which was ambivalent for a few years but then, due to unsurpassed pressure from a variety of lobby organizations,[5] took a clear stand for the private welfare industry, (4) the most central employer organization (the Confederation of Swedish Enterprise) as well as the more industry-specific ones (e.g. the employers' organization for the Swedish Service Sector, the Association of Private Care Providers) which, as representatives and propagandists for the private welfare industry, have an interest in continued privatization, (5) the branch organizations for private providers, for example the Swedish Association of Independent Schools, which promotes privatization while neutralizing the non-profit organizations by gathering them under the same umbrella, (6) the branch organization for insurance companies, Swedish Insurance, which has been the most insistent promotor of the rapid rise of private health insurance and which, in June 2019, managed to convince the Swedish Tax Agency to more or less half the benefit taxation of private health insurance,[6] (7) the right-wing think-tanks such as Timbro, which have had a growing influence over the past decades and now, more openly than ever before, promote a divided welfare state, (8) the centre-right wing Swedish media, which is characterized by its dominant position especially when it comes to newspapers, something which is partly due to owner concentration, (9) the business magazines like Dagens Industri,[7] which has advocated closer ties between the centre-right wing and the far-right wing political parties in order to create an even stronger bloc for, among other things, privatization of welfare, (10) the increasingly larger group of people from the middle class who benefits from half-private welfare services while alienating itself from the ideals of the universal welfare model, (11) the welfare companies and their leading representatives, for example the CEO of Academedia, Marcus Strömberg, who is frequently debating and highlighting the interests of the private welfare industry, (12) the risk capitalists who made major investments in the private welfare industry, for example Rune Andersson who, in 2017, doubled his ownership of Academedia from 10 to 20%,[8] (13) the multitude of minor stockholders who fear the risk of falling share prices in the event of any type of regulation of profits in welfare, (14) the professionals and/or small entrepreneurs within the private welfare industry, for example doctors who get a better negotiating position when they are allowed to play off different clients against each other and set up lucrative businesses where they can, arbitrary, mix different patient groups on different conditions, and (15) the white-collar unions (e.g. the Swedish Confederation of Professional Employees and the Swedish Confederation of Professional Associations), which are suddenly happy to offer their members half-private welfare solutions within the framework of the divided welfare state.

In the light of today's craze for semi-private welfare solutions, it is interesting to see how actors have changed their positions over time. One such example is the centre-right wing parties and their contribution to the original Healthcare Act, which speaks of "a healthcare on equal terms for the whole population" and a healthcare where "the one who have the greatest need for healthcare must be given priority".

In the bill for the 1983 law, signed by the Center Party's Thorbjörn Fälldin and the Liberals' Karin Ahrland, there are a number of paragraphs that emphasize the importance of healthcare on equal terms.[9] In one of them, it is said that waiting times may not be affected by such things as ability to pay:

> The possibilities of receiving healthcare must not be affected by age, gender, ability to take initiative, education, ability to pay, nationality, cultural differences, the nature of the disease and the duration of the disease. Not even waiting times may be affected by such conditions.

The bill further states that society must eliminate all factors that prevent healthcare due to needs:

> Only health needs must determine the extent and nature of the intervention. Society must eliminate economic, social, linguistic, religious, cultural and geographical barriers for the individual to benefit from the healthcare.

Something that is striking in this early 1980s bill is the paragraphs on total societal planning and an overall and public responsibility for healthcare, terms that are hardly viable after several decades of neoliberal social development. But now is now and then was then. The image of an inclusive and universal welfare model under construction and expansion was very strong at that time in Swedish history, and it obviously spread to some of the centre-right wing parties.

These spots have long been washed away from the centre-right wing political parties. Today, they promote the development towards a divided welfare state while at the same time, for tactical reasons, claim to safeguard the traditional Swedish welfare model. In some respects, the same goes for Social Democracy. We have previously seen how the Social Democrats, via the Stop Law in 2006, criticized the possibility to buy ahead the public queue while at the same time allowing it. How did the Social Democrats look upon the parallel healthcare system the following years?

At first glance, it is the same appearance as before, i.e. a unilateral social democratic resistance to the so-called VIP lanes in healthcare. The Health Care Policy Program from 2009 states that the bourgeois parties have paved the way for private-paying patients, and it is also said that the Social Democrats are strongly against the possibility to buy ahead the public queue within the public health system.

Similarly, the matter is expressed in 2019 on the Social Democrats' national website, under the tab *Our Policy A to Z*,[10] where it is said that the party wants to put an end to VIP lanes in healthcare. The same sentence was present already in 2013, but also then with the same slide away from VIP lanes in general to VIP lanes in some hospitals, which, as we have seen, is something significantly different. If one reads the party's statements from the congress in 2013, it becomes even clearer that it is all about hospital care and not healthcare in general. In their statements, the party board is careful to point out that it is the hospital care that matters and nothing else. For example, it is said that (my emphasis) "The Social Democrats want to prohibit the possibility of buying ahead in publicly funded *hospitals*" and "The one who has been able to take out a private health insurance or can pay extra should not be able to receive faster care than others in a publicly funded *hospital*".

The Future Contract, which was adopted by the same congress, also states that it is the hospital care that is intended, even here with a clear slide away from care in general to the hospital care:

> Provide care due to needs. It should only be the health status that determines when and how to get part of publicly funded healthcare – never private funding or various private insurance policies. The possibility of buying ahead on publicly financed hospitals should be stopped.

Thus, the Social Democrats still wanted to stop VIP lanes only in some hospitals, if even that. In 2016, there was a new proposal in the same area.[11] Supposedly, it should ensure that "no one can buy ahead the queue in publicly funded healthcare regardless of who is performing it".[12]

The proposal, however, was even more toothless than the Stop Law, and the proposed legal text was not at all in par with the critical writing in the media. In short, the proposal was to add one paragraph to the Healthcare Act's already existing writing on everyone's right to care on equal terms, i.e. one single phrase claiming that private health insurance can only be accepted if the principles of the Healthcare Act is not disregarded.

What effect will such a supplement have? Probably no effect at all. In fact, each county council will be permitted to make its own reading, and those readings will differ a lot depending on political colour and conviction. Here, it can also be mentioned that there is a tendency to decentralize major principles and decisions on Swedish welfare to municipalities and county councils, something which cannot be considered typical of the traditional welfare model. According to the proposal above, it is important to reduce the regional differences that have arisen in healthcare. However, it is difficult to create equality across the country by letting county councils individually interpret a fuzzy legal text or, as in another highlighted suggestion for decentralization, allowing individual municipalities to veto against profits in welfare.[13]

To summarize a bit drastically, one can say that the left-wing parties do half-hearted and alleged attempts to slow down the development towards a divided welfare state, while the centre-right wing parties openly promote the development while insisting that they protect the Swedish welfare model.

On the whole, the divergence between rhetoric and practice remains significant in terms of welfare state politics. It is a democratic problem that political parties say one thing and do another.

Notes

1. Parliamentary publications, bill 2004/05:145, *Driftsformer för offentligt finansierade sjukhus*.

2. https://www.handcenter.se/.
3. https://www.handcenter.se/soka-till-handcenter-goteborg/ (23 September 2018).
4. https://www.expressen.se/debatt/ni-gor-ett-mini-usa-av-svensk-sjukvard/.
5. *Dagens Industri*, 25 September 2015. http://www.di.se/artiklar/2015/9/25/allt-om-den-tata-kontakten-mellan-sd-och-naringslivet/.
6. Swedish Tax Agency, 10 June 2019. https://www4.skatteverket.se/rattsligvagledning/377241.html?date=2019-06-10.
7. https://www.di.se/.
8. *Dagens Industri*, 13 February 2017. https://www.di.se/nyheter/rune-andersson-dubblar-agandet-i-academedia/.
9. Parliamentary publications, bill 1981/82:97, *Om hälso- och sjukvårdslag*.
10. http://www.socialdemokraterna.se/Var-politik/Var-politik-A-till-O/Sjukvard/ (8 May 2013).
11. Parliamentary publications, Departementsserien 2016:29, *Privata sjukvårdsförsäkringar inom offentligt finansierad hälso- och sjukvård*.
12. *Dagens Nyheter*, 22 August 2016. https://www.dn.se/debatt/universitetssjukhusen-ska-vara-kvar-i-gemensam-ago/.
13. *Aftonbladet*, 18 February 2012. https://www.aftonbladet.se/ledare/a/a24K45/veto-behovs-for-valfarden.

References

Béland, D. (2007). Ideas and institutional change in social security: Conversion, layering, and policy drift. *Social Science Quarterly, 88*(1), 20–38.

Blomqvist, P. (2004). The choice revolution: Privatization of Swedish welfare services in the 1990s. *Social Policy & Administration, 38*(2), 139–155.

Boréus, K., & Bergström, G. (2012). *Textens mening och makt: metodbok i samhällsvetenskaplig text-och diskursanalys*. Lund: Studentlitteratur.

Brown, G., Gillian, B., & Yule, G. (1983). *Discourse analysis*. Cambridge: Cambridge University Press.

Burbules, N. C. (1992). Forms of ideology-critique: A pedagogical perspective. *Qualitative Studies in Education, 5*(1), 7–17.

Calhoun, C. (1995). *Critical social theory: Culture, history, and the challenge of difference*. Oxford: Wiley-Blackwell.

Callinicos, A. (2001). *Against the third way: An anti-capitalist critique*. Cambridge: Polity.

Cammack, P. (2018). Giddens's way with words. In *The third way and beyond*. Manchester: Manchester University Press.

Carlén, S., Persson, C., & Suhonen, D. (2013). *Reinfeldtkoden: den ädla konsten att rasera den svenska modellen*. Föreningen Ordfront och Ordfront magasin.

Carroll, W. K. (2009). Hegemony, counter-hegemony, anti-hegemony. *Socialist Studies/Études Socialistes, 2*(2), 9–43.

Cerny, P. G. (2008). Embedding neoliberalism: The evolution of a hegemonic paradigm. *The Journal of International Trade and Diplomacy, 2*(1), 1–46.

Clayton, R., & Pontusson, J. (1998). Welfare-state retrenchment revisited: Entitlement cuts, public sector restructuring, and inegalitarian trends in advanced capitalist societies. *World Politics, 51*(1), 67–98.

Cox, R. (2004). The path-dependency of an idea: Why Scandinavian welfare states remain distinct. *Social Policy & Administration, 38*(2), 204–219.

Etzler, A. (2013). *Reinfeldteffekten: hur nya moderaterna tog över makten i Sverige och skakade socialdemokraterna i grunden*. Stockholm: Karneval Förlag.

Fairclough, N. (2002). *New labour, new language?* London: Routledge.

Fairclough, N. (2013). *Critical discourse analysis: The critical study of language*. London: Routledge.

Harvey, D. (2007). *A brief history of neoliberalism*. New York, USA: Oxford University Press.

Jessop, B. (1997). A neo-Gramscian approach to the regulation of urban regimes: Accumulation strategies, hegemonic projects, and governance. *Reconstructing Urban Regime Theory: Regulating Urban Politics in a Global Economy, 5*, 1–74.

Jørgensen, M. W., & Phillips, L. J. (2002). *Discourse analysis as theory and method*. London: Sage.

Kitschelt, H. (1994). *The transformation of European social democracy*. Cambridge: Cambridge University Press.

Liedman, S. E., & Nilsson, I. (Eds.) (1989). *Om ideologi och ideologianalys: uppsatser och texter*. Göteborg: Institutionen för idé- och lärdomshistoria.

Van Dijk, T. A. (1993). Principles of critical discourse analysis. *Discourse & Society, 4*(2), 249–283.

Van Dijk, T. A. (2008). *Discourse and power*. London: Macmillan International Higher Education.

Vårdens ägarformer. (2002). *Vinst för vården: idébetänkande från utredningen Vårdens ägarformer - vinst och demokrati*. Stockholm: Edita Norstedt.
Wodak, R. (2001). What CDA is about—A summary of its history, important concepts and its developments. *Methods of Critical Discourse Analysis, 1*, 1–13.

13
The Ambivalent Actors

The ongoing semi-privatization of Swedish welfare creates new actors, such as insurance companies and private healthcare providers, who are pushing for continued semi-privatization. At the same time, there are other community actors who have a more split attitude. Among these ambivalent actors are trade unions, non-profit organizations and some political parties.

This kind of privatization processes normally change reality in a way that strengthens the actors with a clear interest in continuing privatization, while other and more ambivalent societal actors are beginning to abandon approaches and positions that were previously obvious to them (e.g. Pierson 1996; Hacker 2002). Important changes also occur at the individual level (e.g. Soss and Schram 2007; Finlayson 2009), where the welfare that was previously seen as a civil right might finally be seen as a commodity in a market for some and a means-tested assistance for others.

It is not difficult to establish that the industry organization Swedish Insurance is positive to the rapid growth of private healthcare insurance. And it is just as obvious that profit-making welfare companies such as Attendo, Capio and Academedia are positive about the profits in welfare that, according to the Swedish Companies Act, are the main purpose of their business.

J. Lapidus, *The Quest for a Divided Welfare State*,
https://doi.org/10.1007/978-3-030-24784-3_13

But what about welfare companies that are not profit-driven? How do they look upon privatization and semi-privatization of the Swedish welfare sector? To begin with, it may seem contradictory that a non-profit organization would be a member of an organization that takes a strong position for profit-driven companies. But it is a fact that non-profit organizations and profit-making companies often join the same industry organizations.

One example is the Swedish Association of Independent Schools, a trade association with 600 members run by associations, cooperatives, foundations and limited liability companies. The association takes a strong position for profits in welfare and believes that one

> should not favour some forms of business over others / … / and should not discriminate between existing and potential actors, business forms, business models or technologies.

In accordance with this profit-permitting attitude, the association opposed, among other things, the 2014 government proposal on a municipal veto against profit-making private schools, a proposal that no longer has a parliamentary majority since the political party the Sweden Democrats have changed their opinion on this issue. In a report on the theme, the association believes that the principles from the 1992 free school reform would be suspended if the municipalities got a veto against profit-driven private schools.

One reason why businesses with completely different forms of provision (i.e. profit-driven and not profit-driven) can be joined in the same industry organizations is that they have a lot in common. Almost all private schools—whether they are profit-driven or not profit-driven—have the 1992 free school reform to thank for their existence. And above all, they have since been governed by the same regulations in large and small matters, both when it comes to the rules for school fees and when it comes to applying to the School Inspectorate and decisions from the same. In this situation, an organization such as the association of independent schools can help with support and advice for private schools with completely different types of operating mode.

As long as companies with completely different forms of operations are united within the Swedish Association of Independent Schools, it will be important for this organization to highlight what unites the large corporate groups with the small non-profit organizations. That is, highlight the similar rules and not least highlight the common history, where the pursuit of freedom of choice and diversity is keywords and where the fight against the public education monopoly unites all private actors regardless of the mode of operation.

The profit-making companies obviously welcome an organization that takes a strong position for their interests and at the same time, neutralizes any criticism from the non-profit organizations by gathering them under the same umbrella. The large groups have several members on the board of the Swedish Association of Independent Schools, and at the same time the large corporate groups are those who contribute most to the association's finances.

The Swedish Association of Independent Schools has a membership fee which is 0.07% of the member's annual turnover up to SEK 150 million and 0.01% on additional turnover. The minimum fee is SEK 2500. The maximum fee is SEK 400,000.

A large corporate group like Academedia, with a turnover of several billion, will have to pay the maximum amount to be a member of the association. In the board of directors elected by the association on 19 April 2018, Academedia is represented by Lisa Oldmark, HR director and head of Academedia Academy.

The association, under the leadership of former leader of the Liberal Party, Lars Leijonborg (chairman), and the Moderate Party's Ulla Hamilton (CEO), thus takes a clear position for profits in welfare.

At the same time, there are smaller industry organizations that are critical of profits in welfare. One example is the Association for Idea-based Schools with about 50 members. The association says that it works for a non-profit school system, an opinion presented for example in a referral to the so-called Ownership Review in 2015.

The critical opinions held by the Association for Idea-based Schools cause Academedia's CEO Marcus Strömberg to react. He believes that the association creates counterproductive antagonism between different schools. "We who believe in freedom of choice must stand united", writes Strömberg in a debate article, and he further believes that the polarization that the Association for Idea-based Schools creates is both "unfortunate and difficult to understand".[1]

At the same time, Strömberg makes an interesting tactical manoeuvre when he claims that a profit-driven company like Academedia is also idea-based. Strömberg exemplifies the idea-based character of Academedia with the company's policy:

> Everyone who has chosen us should have the conditions they need to reach their full potential and we provide guarantees regarding education, quality, openness and security.

The profit-driven welfare companies have a lot to gain from approaching the non-profit organizations and even appropriating their good reputation. Another example of this is a highlighted debate article, where four welfare entrepreneurs write emotionally under the heading *Our entrepreneurship in welfare is idea-based*.[2]

Here, however, the welfare entrepreneurs are criticized by representatives of two non-profit organizations (Famna and Forum), who oppose the profit-driven companies' attempts to appropriate the concept of *idea-based*.

> What the entrepreneurs do is try to benefit from the positive connotation that the word "idea-based" has come to receive, and how it is now used in political decisions and public debate. We turn against these attempts to parasite on the good reputation.[3]

The non-profit organizations are a mixed bag of small and large companies and cooperatives with different backgrounds, modes of operation and conditions for working on the welfare market. Here, for example, are small village schools run as cooperatives and here are large hospitals run as foundations.

An example of the latter is Ersta Hospital in Stockholm. Ersta is a non-profit hospital that itself emphasizes that all surplus is reinvested in the business. Does it mean that Ersta Hospital is in any way opposed to the profit-driven welfare industry? No, hardly. The hospital's CEO

Stefan Nilsson believes that the *idea-based* sector should strive for French and German levels, i.e. moving from 3 to 25% of welfare production in Sweden.[4] But Ersta's hospital management has no fundamental objections to profits in welfare. In an interview,[5] Nilsson claims that profit restrictions hardly lead to better healthcare, while hospital manager Jan-Åke Zetterström believes that one should focus on other things than profits in welfare.

Similar opinions have often been expressed. Just like the advocates of profits in welfare, Ersta wants to steer the debate away from the issue, and Stefan Nilsson thus believes that "It is regrettable that the debate is about profit levels rather than about what quality we want in welfare services".[6]

At the same time, Ersta Hospital is part of the private welfare industry in the sense that it has agreements with the insurance companies on private health insurance, where some patients get faster care than others. Ersta writes on his website that

> If you want to come as an insurance patient, you indicate to your health care coordinator that you want to come to Ersta Hospital. At Ersta Hospital, insurance patients have their own administrator who will help your health care coordinator and yourself to fast access to healthcare.

Ersta was early out with its collaboration with the insurance companies. Ersta Hospital was included in the insurance company Länsförsäkringar's network of private healthcare providers even before the big boom for this type of insurance.[7]

Something else that could be investigated is the level of remuneration and other benefits that some non-profit organizations have to employees and to board members. Foundations are non-profit, but tax resources can sometimes be wasted on high salaries and board fees, conference trips and more. In the United States, non-profit hospital foundations can pay millions of dollars to their managers and the chairman of the board. One example is the head of the non-profit North Shore hospital chain, Michael Dowling, who earned $10 million in 2014.[8]

The non-profit organizations are rarely being antagonists to the profit-driven welfare industry. One of several reasons for joining the industry is the natural fear of the non-profit organizations to be hit by welfare restrictions, especially if the restrictions aims at recreating public monopolies on welfare services. This kind of fear is expressed by Ersta Hospital when it criticizes one of the trade union's investigations on profits in welfare[9] and writes that "The risk is that LO, in its eagerness to attack what is perceived as a problem, strikes blindly against everyone".[10]

In order to reduce this type of concern among the non-profit organizations, the Left Party's Ali Esbati claims in a reservation to the party's programme commission that it should, in order to "avoid political own goals", erase the sentence saying that welfare "should be publicly owned and run":

> Who are and can be our allies? It is both reasonable and very important to involve people who work in, let's say, church organizations or in cooperative child care. Incidentally, this particular type of non-commercial private business is outperformed by commercial giants. There are potential problems to discuss in all this, as well as with municipal organization for that matter. But it is crucial for political success to draw the conflict lines right. And it's right to draw it against commercial logic.[11]

For the critics of profits in welfare, it can certainly be wise to focus on the profit-making welfare companies. At the same time, there is a political naivety in the exaggerated praises of the non-profit sector. The government now "wants to see more idea-based organizations in the welfare sector",[12] and it has started an investigation[13] that will look into the non-profit sector in order to "promote increased idea-based participation in welfare". Hopefully, the investigation will skip the "romanticism about [the] inherent purity" (Salaman 1995) of non-profits and develop a more "complete picture of the extent and character of the private, nonprofit delivery system and its interaction with the public sector" (Salamon 1987). Hopefully, with the help of interesting and critical articles (e.g. Evans et al. 2005; Bode 2006; Valentinov 2012), the investigation will not only praise but also problematize the non-profit sector.

For example, there are many non-profit organizations that can never become allies in any fight against the emergence of a divided welfare state. As mentioned above, it will be difficult to turn Ersta Hospital against the profit-driven welfare industry and in particular against the rapid rise of private healthcare insurance that the hospital receives some of its income from.

Just like the non-profit organizations, the trade union movement is divided in its view of the profit-making welfare industry and the emergence of a divided welfare state. In some cases, the union movement "seek to protect and narrowly promote the policy interests of their remaining core membership" (Clegg et al. 2010). Such an attitude can be crucial for the outcome, and the union's acceptance of semi-private welfare solutions was actually one of the factors behind the rapid rise of private health insurance in the United States (Dobbin 1992; Hacker 2002; Starr 2008).

In Sweden, so far, blue-collar and white-collar unions have had somewhat different motives for their ambivalent attitude. For the white-collar unions, it is above all about the fact that their members demand the semi-private welfare services provided by the private welfare industry, such as health insurance and household services. For the blue-collar unions, the ambivalent attitude has more to do with the fact that their members are employed in and by the private welfare industry.

The increased interest in semi-private welfare solutions has given the white-collar unions incentives to meet the members' wishes. A survey[14] showed that seven out of ten member unions within Swedish Confederation of Professional Associations (Saco) and the Swedish Confederation of Professional Employees (TCO) offered *private* health insurance for their members. It was most common within Saco, where 20 out of 23 member unions offered insurance. At TCO, the corresponding figure was six of fourteen unions.

The white-collar unions, in particular the high-salary-unions in this category, want to meet the members' wishes in consuming semi-private welfare services, which are mostly used by the higher income layers in the population. Crouch (2000) has expressed it in the following way:

> Finally, unions may come to represent secure labour market insiders whose position is envied and resented by outsiders drifting between temporary work and unemployment, against whose interests unions then start to work.

In this context, it can be said that the white-collar unions used to discuss this in moral terms. They choose between a defence of the Swedish welfare model's principles and an adoption of a new welfare model, based on semi-private funding of healthcare. TCO's then social policy manager reasoned about the union's decision to offer private health insurance to its members:

> There is a moral problem in that the legislation assumes that one should have healthcare due to needs while we establish a parallel system where one can buy healthcare.[15]

Another example is the Teachers Unions included in the TCO, which through one of the insurance intermediaries Teacher Insurance has taken one of the most

> controversial but at the same time most humanitarian and thoughtful decisions – to offer you as a teacher a private health insurance.[16]

In recent years, TCO has taken a more unambiguous position for profits in welfare, sometimes expressed in debate articles written by leading representatives of the union. For example, TCO's team manager Thomas af Bjur, in a reply to the chairman of the Welfare investigation Ilmar Reepalu, means that welfare companies should have the right to make a profit and that this is an important prerequisite for developing the business.[17]

The blue-collar unions have also been split in their view of the profit-driven welfare industry. On an overall level, however, the Swedish Trade Union Confederation (LO) has been criticizing privatization of provision since the very beginning. One example is a response[18] to the government inquiry that followed up the Competition Act in 1993 (Konkurrenslagsutredningen 1997). There, LO speaks about the competition as a dogma and attacks the Swedish Competition Authority which is considered to apply the legislation in a counterproductive and "one-eyed, doctrinal way, without regard to what negative effects the Agency's promotion of competition get in other respects".

According to LO, it has been shown that the Swedish Competition Authority has a particular aversion to activities in the public sector. The Swedish Competition Authority's objective has been that everything must be exposed to competition, an objective that is superior to all other goals in society. According to LO, privatization, corporation and deregulation of public activities have become "an ideal, an end in itself".

LO's criticism of competition policy has continued. In 2012, LO's Congress made a decision to promote a ban on profits in healthcare, school and elderly care, and that the Act on Freedom of Choice (LOV) should be overturned.

In terms of the rapid rise of private health insurance, LO has had a very clear stance. In a debate article in April 2019, leading representatives state that "private health insurance is an ingredient in the poisonous cocktail that threatens the welfare system".[19]

However, it has not always been as easy to interpret LO's opinion on the issue, and this applies even more to some of its member unions. One example is the Swedish Municipal Workers' Union (Kommunal), which has had a lot of problems deciding what to think about profits in welfare. But the congress in 2010 was quite clear on the subject. It established that the union should

> take up an active struggle against continued privatization and for a re-democratization and expansion of the public sector.

The Congress decided to instruct the National Board of Directors to prepare a plan for this active struggle, something that resulted in a report that was published two years later.[20] The congressional decisions had been interpreted by many as a clear no to profits in welfare, but on the contrary, the report authors adopted a relatively permissive attitude to the same. An attitude that was further emphasized by the then president Annelie Nordström in a series of interviews on the theme, where she also questioned the positions of the other LO member unions.[21]

The president's actions were criticized by a number of representatives of the LO and the Kommunal itself, who said that she must follow democratically made decisions and not choose a separate position in terms of profits in welfare.[22] At the same time, there was a continued criticism of profits in welfare of a majority of the union's members, which meant that the federal leadership's permissive stance was voted down at the 2013 congress.[23]

Yet, the union, or at least the federal leadership, continues to have an ambivalent attitude on this issue. A small but striking example can be found on the Kommunal's website where, even under the heading *Opinions on welfare issues*, not a single word is said about profits in welfare.

What determines the ambivalent position on profits in welfare? On a general level, it can be said that Kommunal, just like the Social Democratic Party, has long been characterized by antagonism between so-called renewers and traditionalists. The renewers have acknowledged the ideological reversal that the traditionalists opposed. For the union Kommunal, the starting point for this turnaround can be said to be the introduction of individual wage setting in 1993, which has also given rise to recurring congress debates in recent decades (Lapidus 2015).

More specifically, there are a number of points of contact between a trade union such as Kommunal and the private welfare industry, where the most important is that an increasing proportion of Kommunal's members are employed within the welfare industrial complex. As long as the Swedish welfare model rested on the public monopolies with its public provision of welfare services, the welfare workers of Kommunal were almost exclusively employed by the public.

Of course, this has changed with the emergence of the private welfare industry. In the early 1990s, 12% of the union's members were private employees. In 2011, this figure had increased to 23%, corresponding to 115,000 private employees and 355,000 employees in municipalities and county councils. The proportion of private employees has increased further in recent years.

The fact that the private welfare industry employs an increasing share of Kommunal's members means that these actors must approach each other in different ways. A clear example is that the large welfare companies are now represented with staff and stands at Kommunal's congresses. In this context, a contradictory picture was given to me at the 2013 Congress. When I got there, I noticed that the congress hall's foyer was wallpapered with the radical artist Robert Nyberg's work and paintings, criticizing the increasing individualization (e.g. individual wages and the increased presence of profit-making healthcare companies) of social life. Upstairs, and quite contradictory, the visitors were met by the profit-driven healthcare companies' stands and Kommunal's own stand, where members could learn more about individual wage setting.

Of much greater importance is the fact that the private welfare companies have become an important negotiating partner to Kommunal. In the wage negotiations in 2016, Kommunal negotiated about 50 collective agreements, of which a number concerning the private welfare companies. Under the heading *Actual situation for the wage negotiations for your professional area*, six occupational areas were listed, two of which are directly linked to the private welfare companies, namely *Private schools and private preschools* as well as *Private healthcare and Personal assistance companies.*

The fact that the private welfare companies have become a major employer may be one of the reasons why Kommunal avoids the open battle that a clear no to profits in welfare would entail.

One can also imagine that a no to profits in welfare would be rejected by the members who work in the private welfare industry. However, this does not seem to be the case. A survey conducted by Kommunal shows that 84% of the privately employed members think that surpluses in tax-financed activities should mainly go back to operations and not to shareholders.[24]

There are also some political parties who have had an ambivalent attitude towards the emergence of the private welfare industry and the semi-privatized welfare. Let us focus on the two parties that have really distinguished themselves in this area: the Social Democrats who have gradually adapted to the growth of a welfare market since the mid-1980s, and the Sweden Democrats who adapted almost overnight.

In 2014, the Sweden Democrats had a critical attitude towards profits in welfare. This was especially true of the school sector where the Sweden Democrats had adopted a programme according to which private schools would not be allowed to make profits at all.[25] Leading representatives referred to the party programme, for example in 2013 when it was questioned why the National Union of Teachers avoided mentioning that the Sweden Democrats wanted a ban on profits in welfare.

So, for example, the then and current party secretary, Richard Jomshof, meant that "The Sweden Democrats have pointed out that any profits should be reinvested in school activities". In a post on his blog in March 2013, he is thus upset that the chairman of the National Union of Teachers, Metta Fjelkner, only mentions the Left Party when she talks about parliamentary parties that are critically inclined to profits in welfare.[26]

To prove the profit-critical attitude of the Sweden Democrats, Jomshof cites from the programme adopted on the party's national days in autumn 2011:

> The Swedish school is about to become a billion industry where companies invest money and do profits as in any other company, for example through lower teacher density and higher proportion of unauthorized teachers, profits that can also be moved abroad. But is the school really like any other company? We don't like it. [...] It is unacceptable that tax money intended for education be transferred to dividends. Instead, we mean that Sweden should follow other Nordic countries, where private schools must not take any profits out of the business.

After the 2014 elections, the new government decided on an investigation into profits in welfare. The centre-right-wing opposition was critical. The opposition proposed another type of investigation, something that the Sweden Democrats suddenly agreed on. The party had suddenly swung on the issue of profits in welfare, and the private welfare industry had now received the parliamentary majority that it wanted for a permissive attitude to profits in welfare.

In a series of articles from 2015, the magazine Dagens Industri has shown how the Sweden Democrats almost overnight changed their perception of profits in welfare, from having a restrictive attitude to advocating a permissive ditto shortly after the election.[27] It is the story of a rarely watched number of visits and courtships from a wide range of stakeholders—employer organizations, branch organizations, private providers and others—with the stated purpose of getting the Sweden Democrats to change sides, something that eventually succeeded.

The Sweden Democrats' rapid reversal can be explained in different ways. One explanation is that the far-right party is grateful for friendly relationships with anyone who may offer them, including the private welfare industry and their lobbying organizations. A more ideological explanation is that the party is basically right-wing, and that it is not particularly surprising that the Sweden Democrats now have the same opinion as the other right-wing parties on this issue.

How, then, should the Social Democrats' ambivalence and more gradual reversal be explained? And where does the party stand today? These are issues that are difficult but important to answer. Difficult because they have many bottoms. Important because the Social Democrats are still Sweden's largest party and, moreover, for historical reasons, the party has a particular weight on issues relating to the provision and funding of the welfare sector.

At one level, it can be said that the Social Democrats have been ambivalent ever since employers chose the neoliberal way and ceased to compromise on continued expansion of the public welfare sector. During the model's glory days, the Social Democrats had created an ideology that demanded eternal consensus with employers, which under certain economic conditions could accept the reformist policies. When the employers suddenly attacked this spirit of consensus, it became a shock to the labour movement.

Gradually, the Social Democrats have also moved away from issues related to economic equality. The Swedish Social Democrats were inspired by the Third Way, a movement that was strongly associated with British sociologist Anthony Giddens (1998) and with Tony Blair's leadership of the Labor Party, one of the parties transformed in accordance with the Third Way (e.g. Powell 2000).

There are liberal or even neoliberal elements in the Third Way policy. One of the most important is the emphasis on equal chances of life and the simultaneous avoidance of traditional social-democratic slogans of an active policy of equalizing income and wealth gaps. Furthermore, the Third Way sanctioned the extensive privatizations within the welfare sector, i.e. public–private partnership in sectors that had previously been closed to private actors.

Some go even further and claims Gidden's Third Way to be purely neoliberal, for example Cammack (2018) who states that:

> Anthony Gidden's The Third Way (published in 1998, and followed two years later by The Third Way and its Critics) was advertised and widely understood as presenting a new politics of the 'Centre-Left', adapted to the circumstances of globalisation – a 'Renewal of social democracy', as its sub-title proclaimed. Close examination of the text reveals something different – a process in which the vocabulary and values of social democracy are systematically redefined in order to bring them into alignment with an unabashedly pro-capitalist agenda.

No matter how to interpret the exact meaning of the Third Way, it is a fact that Swedish social democracy gradually changed its view of the organization of welfare. It actually started long before Giddens wrote his book. For example, there were early proposals for New Public Management and subsequent privatization of provision. In a bill from 1991, signed by Prime Minister Ingvar Carlsson and Minister of Industry Rune Molin, it is said that:

> The public sector must therefore be exposed to more market-like conditions. This means that producer and purchaser relations should be developed and that contracts and procurement should be systematically examined in the public sector.[28]

During the 1990s, the Social Democrats became even more competitive. In a bill from the year 2000,[29] signed by Prime Minister Göran Persson and Labor Minister Mona Sahlin, it was clear that competition would permeate every part of society. It has been said that the competition policy was given a "firmer ideological foundation" (Edwardsson 2003) than in the centre-right-wing bill of 1992, and it has also been emphasized that the Social Democratic bill was the prime example of a "clear stance in favour of an active state competition policy and competition as a guiding principle" (Bernitz 2011).

Since then, the criticism of the increasingly privatized welfare sector has increased within the party, but apart from party leader

Håkan Juholt's short term of office, the party leadership has tried to limit this criticism as much as possible. A couple of months before the congress in 2017, it became known that the party board wanted to exempt healthcare and elderly care from profit restrictions. Here, they got tough criticism from the Left Party who threatened to quit all budget cooperation. Many Social Democrats were also critical. The media reported about an "internal uprising" and a high-ranked Social Democrat such as the municipal commissioner in Malmö, Anders Schönström, said that "Profit restrictions shall apply to the entire welfare sector".[30]

At the congress, the party board was defeated by the delegates in this matter. Or? Most analysts interpreted that the party leadership suffered defeat, among them Swedish public television, who wrote that "The party leadership only wanted to stop profits in the school sector, but was run over by the congress".[31]

On closer inspection, however, the congress's letter was so fuzzy (*A regulatory framework is needed that puts an end to the profit hunt in school, healthcare and elderly care*) that the party leadership still felt free to exempt healthcare from profit restrictions.

Notes

1. *Dagens Samhälle*, 23 June 2015.
2. *Dagens Nyheter*, 14 November 2016.
3. *Dagens Nyheter*, 16 November 2016.
4. *Svenska Dagbladet*, 25 December 2017.
5. *Dagens Nyheter*, 6 March 2015.
6. Ersta Hospital, January 2013.
7. *Dagens Medicin*, 26 September 2007.
8. *New York Post*, 29 November 2015.
9. Rautio et al. 2013, *Åtgärder för att begränsa vinst i välfärden*. https://www.lo.se/home/lo/res.nsf/vRes/lo_underlagsrapport_valfard_webb_pdf/$File/Underlagsrapport_valfard_webb.pdf.
10. Ersta Hospital, January 2013.
11. https://www.vansterpartiet.se/debatt/tank-strategiskt-om-vinster-i-valfarden/.

12. https://www.regeringen.se/pressmeddelanden/2018/06/regeringen-vill-se-fler-ideburna-aktorer-i-valfarden/.
13. https://www.regeringen.se/49c71f/contentassets/f57e6665339742c69616be0d72bba21e/en-tydlig-definition-av-ideburna-aktorer-i-valfarden-dir.-201846.pdf.
14. *Dagens Arena*, 5 September 2016.
15. *Tidningen Vision*, 12 October 2011.
16. https://www.lararforsakringarbloggen.se/tag/valfard/.
17. *Dagens Nyheter*, 21 March 2016.
18. Referral answer to Konkurrenslagsutredningen 1997.
19. *Aftonbladet*, 28 April 2019. https://www.aftonbladet.se/debatt/a/707y69/privata-forsakringar-hotar-svensk-valfard.
20. Kommunal, *Vägval välfärd*. https://www.kommunal.se/sites/default/files/rapport_vagval_valfard_121217.pdf.
21. *Dagens Opinion*, 17 October 2012. http://www.dagensopinion.se/kommunal-varf%C3%B6r-lo-mot-vinster-enbart-v%C3%A4lf%C3%A4rden; Kommunalarbetaren, 15 January 2013. http://www.ka.se/kommunal-non-profit-blir-frivilligt.
22. *Arbetet*, 10 May 2012. http://arbetet.se/2012/10/05/tror-nordstrom-pa-demokrati/.
23. *Arbetet*, 30 May 2013. http://arbetet.se/2013/05/30/kommunal-ska-kampa-mot-vinster-i-valfarden/.
24. https://www.kommunal.se/sites/kommunal.se/files/privatanstallda_i_valfarden_om_vinster_.pdf.
25. https://sd.se/wp-content/uploads/2013/08/Sverigedemokraterna-Inriktningsprogram-2011-Skola.pdf.
26. https://richardjomshof.wordpress.com/2013/03/28/lararnas-riksforbund-fortsatter-med-att-utelamna-sverigedemokraterna/.
27. *Dagens Industri*, 25 September 2015. http://www.di.se/artiklar/2015/9/25/allt-om-den-tata-kontakten-mellan-sd-och-naringslivet/.
28. Parliamentary publications, bill 1990/91:184.
29. Parliamentary publications, bill 1999/2000:140.
30. *Aftonbladet*, 24 February 2017.
31. *SVT*, 10 April 2017.

References

Bernitz, U. (2011). *Svensk och europeisk marknadsrätt 1, tredje upplagan*. Stockholm: Norstedts Juridik AB.

Bode, I. (2006). Disorganized welfare mixes: Voluntary agencies and new governance regimes in Western Europe. *Journal of European Social Policy, 16*(4), 346–359.

Cammack, P. (2018). Giddens's way with words. In *The third way and beyond*. Manchester: Manchester University Press.

Clegg, D., Graziano, P., & van Wijnbergen, C. (2010). *Between sectionalism and revitalisation: Trade unions and activation policies in Europe*.

Crouch, C. (2000). The snakes and ladders of 21st-century trade unionism. *Oxford Review of Economic Policy, 16*(1), 70–83.

Dobbin, F. R. (1992). The origins of private social insurance: Public policy and fringe benefits in America, 1920–1950. *American Journal of Sociology, 97*(5), 1416–1450.

Edwardsson, E. (2003). *Konkurrenslagen och konkurrensbegränsande offentliga regleringar* (Doctoral dissertation).

Evans, B., Richmond, T., & Shields, J. (2005). Structuring neoliberal governance: The nonprofit sector, emerging new modes of control and the marketisation of service delivery. *Policy and Society, 24*(1), 73–97.

Finlayson, A. (2009). Financialisation, financial literacy and asset-based welfare. *The British Journal of Politics and International Relations, 11*(3), 400–421.

Giddens, A. (1998). *The third way: The renewal of social democracy*. Cambridge: Polity Press.

Hacker, J. S. (2002). *The divided welfare state: The battle over public and private social benefits in the United States*. Cambridge: Cambridge University Press.

Konkurrenslagsutredningen. (1997). *Konkurrenslagen 1993–1996: betänkande av Konkurrenslagsutredningen*. Stockholm: Fritze.

Lapidus, J. (2015). An odd couple: Individual wage setting and the largest Swedish trade union. *Labor History, 56*(1), 1–21.

Pierson, P. (1996). The new politics of the welfare state. *World Politics, 48*(2), 143–179.

Powell, M. (2000). New Labour and the third way in the British welfare state: A new and distinctive approach? *Critical Social Policy, 20*(1), 39–60.

Salamon, L. M. (1987). Of market failure, voluntary failure, and third-party government: Toward a theory of government-nonprofit relations in the modern welfare state. *Journal of Voluntary Action Research, 16*(1–2), 29–49.
Salamon, L. M. (1995). *Partners in public service: Government-nonprofit relations in the modern welfare state*. Baltimore: Johns Hopkins University Press.
Soss, J., & Schram, S. F. (2007). A public transformed? Welfare reform as policy feedback. *American Political Science Review, 101*(1), 111–127.
Starr, P. (2008). *The social transformation of American medicine: The rise of a sovereign profession and the making of a vast industry*. New York: Basic Books.
Valentinov, V. (2012). Toward a critical systems perspective on the nonprofit sector. *Systemic Practice and Action Research, 25*(4), 355–364.

14

Right or Commodity

Civil rights, human rights and social rights are broad and elastic concepts and political ones. In a 1960 election manifesto, the Democrats in the United States make a list of civil rights, such as the right to healthcare and education. The list is criticized by the philosopher Ayn Rand. She believes that the only rights are ownership and freedom of action, and similar thinking is found in various forms and packaging. In his book *The Sleeping People*, former Prime Minister (Moderate Party) Fredrik Reinfeldt writes that "We do not want to see a society where people are starving, but no standard requirements more than that should be tax-financed" (Reinfeldt 1993). The Swedish author Lena Andersson also focuses on lazy individuals when she attacks the state, which is actually stealing money from the hard-working parts of the population.[1]

And why not? Why not turn healthcare, school and elderly care into commodities like all the rest? Why should these services be financed jointly and more or less distributed to all citizens?

These are appropriate issues for a straightforward and honest debate. Issues that, given that we already have a parallel healthcare system where people buy ahead, are burning ones.

J. Lapidus, *The Quest for a Divided Welfare State*,
https://doi.org/10.1007/978-3-030-24784-3_14

However, the questions are not asked in that way. This is partly because the advocates of the divided welfare state want to avoid a debate that up to now is political suicide (Cox 2004), which in turn is due to the fact that the Swedish welfare model is still popular among large parts of the population (Svallfors 2011). Sweden is not the United States. Swedes in general still think that healthcare should be provided on equal terms, even if the values gradually are changing as a result of such things as the rapid growth of *private* health insurance and clinics that are locked for publicly funded patients and clinics that turn to employers rather than to county councils.

There is also another reason for the questions not being asked: the advocates of the divided welfare state are simply allowed to avoid a straightforward and honest debate, which in turn depends on the opponent's ignorance of what semi-privatization actually means and how far we have actually gone in that direction. The advocates of the divided welfare state are allowed to say that it is best for the universal welfare state that more and more people leave the same. Or stand unchallenged in arguments like "employers must quickly have their employees back to work", when the other side of the coin is that we shall have a healthcare for people with good and safe employment and another healthcare for everyone else.

The advocates of a divided welfare state are allowed to take small and unnoticed steps, while warning that we will have more of private solutions in the future (Jordahl 2004; Borg 2009; Lyttkens 2010; Sanandaji and Sahlgren 2019). It is much easier to speak out loud about the future, but here and now great changes are taking place. Here and now we have received a parallel healthcare system that is growing every year, so there is nothing to wait for when it comes to a straightforward debate about welfare as a right or commodity.

Soon enough, however, the advocates of a divided welfare state will be more willing to take the debate. As the rhythm of half-privatization continues, and as the values continue to change among the population, the advocates of a divided welfare state will become increasingly clear on the subject. In an interview in Svenska Dagbladet, the Christian Democrats' party leader Ebba Busch Thor is said to open "a controversial door in a country where the vast majority of healthcare is paid through public funds".[2] This door will finally be wide open if things continue to develop in a certain direction, but up until now it has been closed for tactical reasons.

The first thing that has to be said in this debate is that welfare could always be bought for money, even when the Swedish welfare model was at the most *Swedish* in the early 1980s. You have always been able to go to Sophiahemmet in Stockholm and pay the full price for your health-care. What is now advocated is not pure merchandise and pure markets, however, but instead state-sponsored services in all the imaginative ways that are described in this book. The privatizationists have never been fundamentalists in that sense.

Let us forget the state sponsorship for a moment and pretend that *private* health insurance is merchandise in the true sense of the word. What are the arguments for making health care into a commercial service like anyone else?

To a large extent, it is about philosophy and ideology, or in short about the view of human beings. Some believe that welfare services are part of civil, social or human rights, while others argue that this type of rights is in conflict with property rights and individual freedom. Of course, there are also a number of intermediate positions, and the issue of the welfare services' status has been problematized and nuanced in many different ways (e.g. Nussbaum 1997; Sen 2005; West 2017). The question relates to even broader theories of justice (Nozick 1974; Rawls 1971; Sen 2009) and these theories have, in turn, been interpreted with regard to welfare services in general and health care in specific.

One example is Moskop (1983), who discusses whether Rawls' theory of justice may be used to justify a human right to health care. Moskop is cited in Rumbold (2017), whose overview article covers a lot of philosophical opinions and aspects of the right to health care, a right that is "increasingly enshrined in national constitutions around the world – present today in a slight majority of written constitutions" (Kavanagh 2016). It is even the case that

> Following endorsement by WHO, the World Bank, and the UN's Sustainable Development Goals, the drive towards universal health

> coverage (UHC) is now one of the most prominent global health policies. (Rumbold et al. 2017)

The same type of aspirations is found in the *Second Bill of Rights*[3] proposed by US President Franklin D. Roosevelt in 1944. For example, according to the bill, all people have "The right to useful and remunerative job", "The right to adequate medical care and the opportunity to achieve and enjoy good health", "The right to a good education", and "The right of every family to a decent home".

The philosopher Ayn Rand makes fun of the bill. At whose expense is all this service provided, she asks, and she explains that "Jobs, food, clothing, recreation (!), homes, medical care, education, etc., do not grow in nature" (Rand 1964).

It is part of Rand's philosophy—the so-called objectivism (Peikoff 1993a)—to reject this type of civil rights. No one can force anyone to contribute anything to the common. Tax, for example, is a form of theft. This means that every social right—the right to healthcare, the right to eat—results in a restriction of individual freedom.

Ayn Rand believes that public welfare services are plain theft of those who "pay for" it all. It's even worse than theft! In fact, it is about slave labour:

> If some men are entitled by right to the products of the work of others, it means that those others are deprived of rights and condemned to slave labor. (Rand 1964)

Whoever pays tax has thus been forced to perform a slave labour. This applies even if the money goes to the disabled and the sick, because even in such cases you do not have the right to enslave people.

In Rand's world, there are two kinds of people. There are, on the one hand, strong, healthy, enterprising people and on the other hand weak, almost retarded people. The latter should almost be considered as animals. It is an Übermensch ideal that appears everywhere in Ayn Rand's writings:

> If some men do not choose to think, but survive by imitating and repeating, like trained animals, the routine of sounds and motions they learned

> from others, never making an effort to understand their own work, it still remains true that their survival is made possible only by those who did choose to think and to discover the motions they are repeating. The survival of such mental parasites depends on blind chance. (Rand 1964)

The sub-humans are often ordinary workers. The Übermensch is often successful entrepreneurs, for example, in the book *Atlas Shrugged* (Rand 1957) about which the Centre Party leader Annie Lööf once wrote that:

> This summer I read Ayn Rand's Atlas Shrugged and was totally captivated. The book is by far the best book I've ever read. It carried me away, it touched me and it made my mind grow.[4]

Others have written more critically about the book. Here is how it is summarized by the writer Aron Lund:

> It is a pubertal Übermensch tall tale about heroic big businessmen with blue steel look and perfect chin, who in protest against the parasitic public breaks out of the welfare state and flees to a secret valley to build a new beautiful world without socialists and weakness.[5]

In the midst of all brutality, Ayn Rand can appear to be consistent and logical in her thinking. Really? Here is the journalist Eva-Lotta Hultén's exposé of the logical shortcomings in the same book:

> Despite Ayn Rand's tribute to the logic, much in the book is rather illogical. When subhumans fail, it's their own fault, when superhumans fail it is the fault of the subhuman. When egoists cooperate it is noble, when altruists or poor cooperate it is dangerous. When workers resort to violence, it is abominable. When capitalists do so, it is exemplary. When superhumans intentionally destroy property (to punish the subhuman), it is good, when subhumans (out of clumsiness) do the same thing, it is despicable. When a company manager determines the wages, they automatically become fair, if the union interferes, they automatically become unfair.[6]

Aren't these extreme thoughts and ideas? Are there really people who sympathize with this? Yes, to a great extent. Philosophers like Rand

(2013), Friedman and Friedman (1962) and Hayek (1944) have great global influence, and if we look at the United States, we find millions of people—including leading politicians—who openly question the right of the poor to healthcare and who would argue that "To call it a Right when the recipient did not earn it is merely to compound the evil" (Peikoff 1993b). The poor are seen as parasites. Ayn Rand would have been proud of all the bumper stickers with crude texts such as *Work harder—millions on welfare depend on you* and *I gotta go to work today cause millions on welfare depends on me.*[7]

But what about Sweden and Ayn Rand? The neoliberal philosophers are often published in Swedish by Timbro, a think tank financed by the employer organization the Confederation of Swedish Enterprise. Timbro's task is "forming a long-term opinion for market economy, free enterprise, individual freedom and an open society".[8]

One of the Timbro's favourite authors is Ayn Rand. On the website, it is advertised for an "exclusive and unique collection box" with all her classics (Rand 2013). Ayn Rand is appreciated by many Swedes. One who has read everything is the author Lena Andersson, who has presented Rand's ideas in many articles.

One of these articles was published in the newspaper Dagens Nyheter and is about the state being a criminal pimp.[9] Lena Andersson puts, in the spirit of Rand, two talented entrepreneurs against a slouch who "only thinks about himself and not on all the needs that he fails to cover where he is sitting and resting". In a follow-up article, Andersson clarifies the conclusions of the previous article:

> It was about tax as coercion and the fundamental unreasonability, which most people so far advocate and find reasonable, that one can vote on what to buy for other people's money.

According to Lena Andersson, it is unreasonable for people to vote for politicians who decide that a certain amount of tax money is needed for healthcare, school and elderly care. The state is criminal when it receives funds in this way. Like Ayn Rand, Lena Andersson believes that charity is the only legal way:

> Most sympathetic would be if these funds were not enforced but received through persuasion. It must be a rest from the days of the autarchy that we so easily accept that it is a crime not to abandon parts of one's property, and that it is not crime to steal it.

There is much to be said about this view of the welfare state and the view of human beings. There is obviously a neoliberalism that not only leads to the greatest possible inequality, but also—consciously or unknowingly—advocates an Übermensch ideal in which people are divided into two groups: capable and inept.

The good people can afford to buy welfare on the open market. The inept are allowed to beg not to go under. Ayn Rand says it plainly. So does the Swedish author Lena Andersson, but in her case, it might be due to political naivism and ignorance, because it is not certain that she really grasps what kind of a *society* her ideas would lead to.

Maybe I underestimate Andersson. It is easy to believe that the Übermensch ideal is the result of a temporary blackout, but the view of different groups of people is progressing strongly in Sweden. It is noticeable, among other things, in the debate on meritocracy and simple jobs. Meritocracy is basically a sensible concept (it aims, among other things, that merit and skill must be crucial when people are employed, not friendship and nepotism), but the neoliberals are turning it into a battering ram for ever-increasing income differences. The same goes for the concept of *simple jobs*. No matter how low the wage for these jobs, it can always be much lower. What is even a simple job? Does she who now comes in and cleans my office have a simpler job than me, where I sit at my computer and produce text? In terms of number of years of education, yes, of course my job seems to be more complex or even more difficult. But in many ways, I think she seems to have a tougher and more tiring job, while my job seems to me to be more stimulating. In addition, I have received an interesting education funded by the state.

Meritocracy and simple jobs have become concepts that legitimize extremely low wages for some and ever higher salaries for others, the capable ones. At the same time, these *simple jobs* are supposed to increase in number by the state sponsoring the middle and upper classes' household requirements of cheap labour, which will further strengthen the higher classes in their view of their own excellence and high qualifications.

In a sense, Ayn Rand's sincerity is preferable to the Swedish centre-right wing politicians and their argument that semi-privatization is the best thing that can happen to the universal welfare. The debate should therefore be directed to the question of whether welfare such as healthcare, in a modern society and in one of the richest countries in the world, should be part of the civil rights or buyable and saleable just like any service or product.

At the same time, we must not forget what we would forget for a moment, that is, that the state is always involved in *free* markets for welfare. Ayn Rand's and Lena Andersson's societies do not exist. Instead, in their real-world type of liberal welfare models, it is normally the case that the state subsidizes the welfare of the rich in a multitude of ways, while the universal welfare state is eroded to means-tested services of varying quality.

Notes

1. *Dagens Nyheter*, 15 April 2016. http://www.dn.se/ledare/kolumner/lena-andersson-skatt-ar-den-sanna-girigheten/.
2. *Svenska Dagbladet*, 21 January 2018.
3. http://www.ushistory.org/documents/economic_bill_of_rights.htm.
4. *Svenska Dagbladet*, 26 July 2014. https://www.svd.se/jag-budskapet-ligger-loof-nara.
5. *Uppsala Nya Tidning*, 13 April 2011. https://www.unt.se/ledare/vem-ar-ayn-rand-1312388.aspx.
6. https://evalottahulten.com/2014/07/01/ayn-rand-och-den-banala-objektivismen/.
7. https://www.amazon.com/working-millions-welfare-depend-Sticker/dp/B006L998TI.
8. https://timbro.se/.
9. *Dagens Nyheter*, 16 April 2016.

References

Borg, P. (2009). *Den långsiktiga finansieringen: välfärdspolitikens klimatfråga?* Finansdepartementet, Regeringskansliet.

Cox, R. (2004). The path-dependency of an idea: Why Scandinavian welfare states remain distinct. *Social Policy & Administration, 38*(2), 204–219.

Friedman, M., & Friedman, R. (1962). *Capitalism and freedom.* Chicago: University of Chicago press.

Hayek, F. A. (1944). *The road to serfdom.* London: G. Routledge.

Jordahl, H. (2004). Vårdkonsument eller soffpotatis. *Nya balanspunkter för hälsa och sjukvård. Timbro Hälsa.*

Kavanagh, M. M. (2016). The right to health: Institutional effects of constitutional provisions on health outcomes. *Studies in Comparative International Development, 51*(3), 328–364.

Lyttkens, C. H. (2010). Sjukvårdens långsiktiga finansiering. In A. Anell & U. G. Gerdtham (Eds.), *Vårdens utmaningar* (pp. 114–147). Stockholm: SNS Förlag.

Moskop, J. C. (1983). Rawlsian justice and a human right to health care. *The Journal of Medicine and Philosophy, 8*(4), 329–338.

Nozick, R. (1974). *Anarchy, state, and utopia* (Vol. 5038). New York: Basic Books.

Nussbaum, M. C. (1997). Capabilities and human rights. *Fordham Law Review, 66,* 273.

Peikoff, L. (1993a). *Objectivism: The philosophy of Ayn Rand.* London: Penguin.

Peikoff, L. (1993b, December). Health care is not a right. In *Speech delivered at the Town Hall Meeting on the Clinton Health Plan on Dec* (Vol. 11).

Rand, A. (1957). *Atlas shrugged.* New York: Random House.

Rand, A. (1964). *The virtue of selfishness.* London: Penguin.

Rand, A. (2013). *Förnuft, egoism, kapitalism och en romantisk livskänsla: texter i urval.* Stockholm: Timbro.

Rawls, J. (1971). *A theory of justice.* Cambridge, MA: Harvard University Press.

Reinfeldt, F. (1993). *Det sovande folket.* Stockholm: Moderata ungdomsförb.

Rumbold, B. E. (2017). The moral right to health: A survey of available conceptions. *Critical Review of International Social and Political Philosophy, 20*(4), 508–528.

Rumbold, B., Baker, R., Ferraz, O., Hawkes, S., Krubiner, C., Littlejohns, P., et al. (2017). Universal health coverage, priority setting, and the human right to health. *The Lancet, 390*(10095), 712–714.

Sanandaji, N., & Sahlgren, G. H. (2019). *Ålderskris: Vad kan Sverige lära av sjukvården i Japan?*
Sen, A. (2005). Human rights and capabilities. *Journal of Human Development, 6*(2), 151–166.
Sen, A. K. (2009). *The idea of justice*. Cambridge, MA: Harvard University Press.
Svallfors, S. (2011). A bedrock of support? Trends in welfare state attitudes in Sweden, 1981–2010. *Social Policy & Administration, 45*(7), 806–825.
West, R. (2017). Rights, capabilities, and the good society. In *Justice and the capabilities approach* (pp. 189–220). Abingdon: Routledge.

15

The Twisted Debate

Have you met the System Man? He is a stubborn opponent of profits in welfare, a numbskull who is supposed to embody the ignorant criticism of the private welfare industry. The Association of Private Care Providers ordered him for the simple reason that it was impossible to win the debate against real opponents. In his interesting and revealing book (Tenelius and Selling 2016), the association's commercial chief Håkan Tenelius, tell us how it happened:

> The PR agency MSL, one of those who invited themselves to the procurement, stated frankly that we would never win the fight against our current opponents. We did not even have the prerequisite to get a draw against Jonas Sjöstedt [the leader of the Left Party], this sympathetic and kind-hearted man from Västerbotten. Therefore, we must create a new opponent.

It all started when the Association of Private Care Providers wanted to make an advertising campaign for profits in welfare, and while Tenelius and his colleagues prepared the procurement of suitable advertising agency, they confirmed that the member companies' willingness to campaign was very strong. Tenelius writes: "In a few months,

J. Lapidus, *The Quest for a Divided Welfare State*,
https://doi.org/10.1007/978-3-030-24784-3_15

600 companies had undertaken to invest an average of SEK 10,000 on our advertising project".

The healthcare companies invested 6 million of taxpayers' money in the System Man, created by the advertising agency MSL (another agency that had interesting proposals was Honesty, but it was MSL that got the contract). Tenelius offers fascinating reading when he describes how he gets various celebrities to participate in advertising movies with the freedom-hating System Man.

In one of these films, the broadcaster Carl Schulman manages script and direction. The protagonist is the retired television reporter Elisabet Höglund, also famous for her hairstyle, who sits at the hairdresser and explains how she wants her hair cut. Tenelius remembers the film with some delight: "Then the System Man appeared and declared outright that this was now over with Mrs Höglund's extravagant hairstyles". In another movie, the System Man discovers the two football players Anton Hysén and John Alvbåge in the same bed. Håkan Tenelius remembers the film: "Of course, the System Man had no objections on two men, as he said, conducting lovemaking. However, he had clear instructions on how to do it".

For some reason, Håkan Tenelius invited me as a panel participant on the release for his and Niels Selling's book *The Welfare Lobbyist*. It is an astonishingly frank story of how private stakeholders act in the welfare sector, and I can imagine that many people in the audience wished it had never been written.

The event took place on Uggleviksgatan in Stockholm. During the champagne mingle, I came to talk to some employees at the Association of Private Care Providers. They told me how the crisis of the elderly care company Carema in 2011 affected them on a personal level. They were almost weeping when they talked about it. They remembered how the media and the whole society had turned against them. They talked about how the crisis brought them together to fight the resistance, and the slander of, profits in welfare.

Large parts of the Stockholm private provider's elite took part in the release party on Uggleviksgatan. And the same elite was there when I participated in the annual and exclusive (entrance fee: SEK 4995 excluding VAT for five hours) Private Healthcare Day arranged by the magazine Dagens Medicin.

The Social Democrat Ilmar Reepalu was also there. He had the hardly enviable task of presenting his Welfare investigation about profits in welfare to these leaders of Swedish private healthcare providers.

The operations managers of the private healthcare providers were angry. The economists were even more angry. But angriest of all were the directors and entrepreneurs, a rare mix of well-dressed brands (Johan Fredriksson, CEO of Praktikertjänst and Sveneric Svensson, medical director of Capio) and rude venture capitalists.

There were also representatives of the public health system in the audience. Their silence was a clear example that the private welfare industry lacks a natural counterpart. The private healthcare providers have their battle organizations fighting for continued privatization at all levels of healthcare, but the Swedish Association of Local Authorities and Regions (SKL) is hardly involved in any corresponding struggle for publicly provided healthcare.

The silence of the public health representatives was in stark contrast to the anger of the private welfare industry's representatives. It was an anger directed against the Social Democrat Ilmar Reepalu. It was also possible to discern a fear of Reepalu and his investigation, but at the same time a determination to spell out some truths to this gray man. However, it did not ramble on. Apart from a couple of entrepreneurs who got so upset that I could not what they were saying, it was in a quite polite way that the private welfare industry's representatives formulated their negative attitude towards Reepalu and his investigation.

It is not surprising that the private welfare industry's representatives felt threatened. It is private interests that are challenged and huge revenues at stake. And here came a Social Democrat who wanted to regulate or even close a market on which they made their profits in welfare. In this new welfare market, there are many actors with different types of self-interest in the fact that it remains and develops. We have got 650,000 citizens who are happy to buy themselves ahead the public queue at a subsidized price. We have got private providers who make profits by selling their services to county councils and to insurance companies. We have a number of insurance companies and banks that have found a new business with great potential. We have got credit institutions that make money from lending money to operations and other treatments. We have got shareholders who want the healthcare companies to make as big profits as possible. We have employers who, at the expense of the state, can offer the services of the private welfare industry to their employees. We have a large number of lobbyists who make their living from fighting for the survival and further development of the private welfare industry. We have got unions who want to be able to offer the services of the private welfare industry to their members. We have got politicians who have strong ties to the private welfare industry, politicians who get well-paid jobs and board assignments within the same as soon as the political career is completed.

In short, there are many actors who have reason to be angry with Reepalu and his investigation even though it became much vaguer than it could and should have been, had it just followed its own directives that surpluses must be returned to the activities where they occurred.

Despite the fact that the advocates of a divided welfare state are very determined, they find it very difficult to convince people of the blessings of it. The traditional welfare model continues to be popular. A popularity that means that the welfare industry's representatives cannot speak plainly about which model they themselves want.

The result is a twisted debate. A debate that avoid factual matters. A debate that uses the ABC's of lobbying, among other things, by combating fictitious opponents and ignoring the most obvious facts.

We have already mentioned some of these questionable and newspeak-like debate tricks: two queues for healthcare are not two queues for healthcare and the policyholders' subsidized double payment to the health service is rather a triple or quadruple payment. Another of these misconceptions is about the fatal consequences of a possible ban on profits or profit restriction for the privately provided healthcare facilities.

This is how the often-repeated myth reads: if we forbid profits in welfare, much of the welfare will disappear. It will affect people in every county council, at all levels of care. Hundreds of thousands of people will simply stand without access to healthcare.

This myth is spread through media, not least editorials of centre-right-wing newspapers who have repeatedly argued that people will be left without healthcare if private welfare companies are forced to shut down because of profit restrictions. It is a myth with a dramatic effect and the purpose is exactly that, to make people scared of restrictions of profits in welfare.

Why is this a myth? Why is it just ridiculous? The answer is very simple: almost all of the healthcare is funded through taxes, and all of this money continues to flow into the healthcare system with or without profit-making providers. There is, therefore, no healthcare that *disappears* if the profit-making healthcare companies close down their business. There would a continuous flow of exactly the same amount of money to hospitals and health centres which, in the case of a profit ban, get the name *County Council* instead of the name healthcare company. The difference is instead that more money would go to the healthcare of publicly funded patients, and less money would go to subsidizing insurance patients or simply disappearing out of the system as dividends to shareholders.

Nevertheless, this myth has been widely distributed and it has been packaged in more or less interesting ways. An example of more intricate packaging is the employer organization Almega who, under the heading *Private companies crucial for future welfare*, put the above myth in connection with a demographic development which will take place regardless of whether the healthcare is privately or publicly provided. Almega writes:

> While the need for new capacity in the welfare sector is very high, a large part of today's independent schools, health centers and care services are threatened with the Government's forthcoming bill on profit restrictions for companies in the welfare sectors. /... / Without the private actors, public-run primary care must find room for another 26 million patient visits by 2020 – this represents a 60% increase in the public's own care production. But the municipalities would also be hard hit by the government's proposal for profit restriction. Without the support of private actors, today's need for 150,000 new students by 2020 will instead be a need of 450,000, while the number of elderly people in need of municipal elderly care in 2020 will increase from 25,000 to 80,000.[1]

According to Almega, the municipalities would thus be "hard hit" by the government's proposal for profit restriction. However, these municipalities would have at least the same amount of tax resources to dispose of regardless of whether the businesses were run by private or public providers. Almega does not say a word about this. Instead, Almega insinuates or even explicitly states that the welfare is threatened and that the municipalities are hard hit if they choose another mode of operation for their businesses.

The above is an example of how to frame a message and to "select some aspects of a perceived reality and make them more salient in a communicating text" (Entman 1993). It is also a way to make the message more frightening, just as when ordinary benefit taxation suddenly became *triple taxation* or *health tax*. A similar example is the US-American beer association NBWA's attempts to go against the estate tax, something that at first did not create much fuss. Neither did the expression "inheritance tax". Then, the NBWA got the idea to call the estate tax a "death tax" (McGrath 2007).

Framing and "venue shopping" (e.g. Pralle 2003; Baumgartner and Jones 2010; Klüver et al. 2015) are important tools when it comes to lobbying. Here, to the welfare industrial complex, it is of utmost importance to avoid the debate to be about distribution or greed or profits or cost-driving or resource-consuming effects of a semi-privatized welfare. Selling (Tenelius and Selling 2016) argues that "While the opponents want to discuss tax fraud and greed, the companies want a discussion about quality and freedom of choice".

Questions about freedom of choice and quality can indeed be quite tricky for the welfare companies (when it comes to freedom of choice there is a concentration to a few groups such as Capio, Academedia and Attendo, and in terms of quality, there are disputable mechanisms built into the profit interest). However, these questions are always less problematic than questions of profit, equality and erosion of the universal welfare state. Moreover, a comprehensive measure of quality is difficult to determine in the welfare sector, and the concept of freedom of choice is so diffuse that it can mean virtually anything.

Ideally, the companies and their associations would like to completely depoliticize this type of welfare debate, that is, remove it from the political agenda and thus avoid having to defend their profits in welfare. From the point of view of the private welfare industry, the best thing would be if profits in welfare could be an issue that, like the monarchy or democracy, could have its enemies, but which, on the whole, are things that people take for granted. Or as Håkan Tenelius (Tenelius and Selling 2016) notes:

> I would like us to get to where the dental care is today, where people in general shrug their shoulders over the fact that there are both private and public actors. Where people have stopped caring about the mode of operation. You go to the dentist you think is good, end of story. If we end up there, then we will not continue with our opinion formation.

Maybe the lobbyists eventually will get what they want. In the January agreement (2019) between the Social Democrats, the Environmental Party, the Liberal Party and the Center Party, there are several paragraphs indicating that restrictions on profits in welfare will no longer be on the agenda. Further, the more actors with self-interest in profits in welfare, the greater the possibility of eventually depoliticizing the issue and erasing it from the political agenda. The lobbyists want people to get tired of discussing the issue, and one who is very tired is the journalist Lena Mellin. In an article titled *Profits in welfare make me exhausted*,[2] she seems to mean that we have talked enough about it and that we simply have to accept profits in welfare.

Mellin is correct when she argues that the issue has been very long drawn out and discussed for decades. Here, one can draw some parallels to the so-called Socialization Investigation which the Social Democrats appointed in 1920 and the same party put to an end fifteen years later. Then there were many Social Democrats who did not want any socialization but in order to appease the internal opposition and public opinion, they continued to investigate infinitely, until people were so exhausted that they had forgotten what it was all about.

The same can actually be said about Ilmar Reepalu and his Welfare investigation. Instead of following the directives and making it easy—profits or not profits in welfare—the investigation complicated things as much as possible with a multitude of calculations around profit levels and percentages. When not even experts can figure out what the proposals mean, then people in general, even those who were recently engaged in the issue, get tired of it all.

However, the private welfare industry and its lobbyists have not yet come all the way to a total depoliticization of the issue. Therefore, they still have to avoid the most sensitive issues and instead focusing on the more elusive concepts of quality and freedom of choice. Or use other debate tricks, for example arguing emotionally and at the same time accusing the opponents of doing just that. Håkan Tenelius writes in a reply to one of my debate articles that:

> John Lapidus is right in saying that the System Man was born when we saw how difficult it is to win the debate against the real opponents of profits in welfare. The reason is that these are happy to argue based on emotions instead of facts.[3]

Another who answered my debate article was Anders Morin, responsible for welfare policies at the Confederation of Swedish Enterprise. He writes that private health insurance "contributes to relieving public health",[4] which is the ever-recurring argument for private health insurance. As I said, it is remarkable that this argument is put forward by those who want to relieve the public sector in a completely different way, namely to take away from public health some of its commitments and to privatize or semi-privatize it as much as possible.

One of the advocates of privatization is Anders Morin himself. In the case of private health insurance, he wants to further promote its growth by making them free from tax both for employees and for employers, something that he has stated in several reports and referral responses.

The demands for privatization of large parts of the healthcare funding have a long history. However, in contrast to this fact, there has been, among politicians as well as researchers, a Swedish self-image and lingering belief in a consensus that health care should be publicly funded.

One example of this is a book (Blomqvist and Rothstein 2000) where two political scientists who have made many important contributions to welfare research, argue that there is hardly anyone who believes that a central welfare service such as healthcare should not be publicly funded. In the next sentence, they take Assar Lindbeck as an example that even market-liberal economics professors consider that joint and solidaristic funding of healthcare is necessary.

Does Lindbeck really think so? In an article in the newspaper Dagens Nyheter, on the contrary, he argues that taxes provide "justice at a low level" and that a number of other, private funding forms are required that enable "people to express their willingness to pay for further consumption of human services".[5] According to Lindbeck, there is a reason to initiate a debate on alternative future forms of funding of school, healthcare and elderly care, a debate that can "tear down some ideological and political barriers that today prevent a reform of organization and funding in these important areas".

The public funding of healthcare has been questioned from different angles and directions. Here, it is not surprising that the insurance industry, with its own interest in private and semi-private solutions, was early on. Thus, for example, Kent Andersson, then Nordic manager of health insurance at the insurance company Trygg-Hansa, meant in an article from 2009 that the trend towards increased private funding has already come a little way, so far that this can be "a period that we will look back on and see that significant changes began to take place".

Similar ideas are found, for example, at the much broader Health Care Forum, an organization consisting of a number of actors from private and public welfare activities. In one of its reports, written in 2004 (Bröms 2004), it is regretted that healthcare is a "planned economy in the middle of a market economy".

According to the report, healthcare must to a much greater extent be privately funded, and it is proposed that today's healthcare organization "be broken into two systems that are governed and developed on the basis of very different political value-systems". One system should include the "heavy healthcare" and remain publicly funded. In the other system—primarily primary care—it is the "market conditions that should apply" and the forms of private funding can be, for example, patient fees, collective agreement-regulated insurance and private family insurance.

A "critical factor" that will be the subject of debate in this two-tier healthcare system is, according to the report, the safeguarding of "everyone's access to urgent care". According to the report, there are reasons to worry, partly because some individuals' need for care can be so large that no healthcare provider wants them, and partly because the individuals have such a weak economy that they do not consider themselves able to afford the healthcare. In both cases, there is reason to consider to what extent the municipalities have the capacity to act as a "reasonably comprehensive last safety net".

However, it will never be as it has been before, according to the report, and "today's dogma" of equal treatment in healthcare is no longer as obvious. In a report from the right-wing think tank Timbro, Henrik Jordahl agrees:

> Just like in other markets, the economically well-off together with the smart and active consumers will have more and better healthcare. This can of course be regretted, but on the other hand, Sweden's traditional and egalitarian health policy is not able to attract the resources needed to meet the growing health needs.

The aforementioned reports are inspired by the Ministry of Finance's Long-Term Survey 2003/04 (Statens offentliga utredningar 2004), which is frequently cited. In the Long-term Survey, it is stated that the welfare state's dilemma is "ultimately a consequence of the fact that it is mainly financed by taxes".

In the next chapter, we will talk about the strange myth that tax-financed welfare would be more difficult to maintain the richer a society becomes, but here we content ourselves with finding that the Long-term study spreads the myth further. It is thus established that "continuous increases in the tax levy cannot be considered a long-term path to finance a development of the welfare systems". This may, for example, mean that the tax-financed services must be "restricted to a limited basic supply" which is supplemented by citizens with their own, voluntary payments. By restricting the public commitment "vertically" while giving private funding increased room for manoeuvre, "a valve" is created that let individuals express increased demand.

However, increased private financing of healthcare was the subject of debate well before the Long-Term Survey 2003/04. So, in 1991, economist Lars Söderström predicted that the financing of healthcare would become the central healthcare policy issue of the 1990s. He himself wished for a model in which 50% of healthcare consumption is privately financed, hence 20% via private health insurance and 30% via individual fees. The public commitment would thus be reduced from today's slightly more than 80–50%, a level comparable to US-American conditions.

In a book from 2010, Carl Hampus Lyttkens is inspired of Söderström's ideas for increased individual fee financing. Lyttkens proposes a gradual increase of the high-cost ceiling by some per cent per year, until it reaches "the desired level", and he also wants to transfer certain forms of healthcare entirely to private financing.

Lyttkens refers to the 2009 ESO report *The long-term funding—the climate issue of welfare policy* (Borg 2009) (a title that indicates that something must be done now, not in the future when it can already be too late), where the report author Per Borg believes that the political system has not acknowledged that there is a problem that requires system changes.

According to the ESO report, it is rather that there is a reverse consensus compared to what was stated by Rothstein and Blomqvist, at least in the scientific world where "a more or less united circle of experts and researchers points to necessary future changes". The problem is, among other things, populist politicians who "compete to emphasize that healthcare should be tax-financed and not dare to discuss such a sensitive issue as alternative financing".

It is true that the political parties in their rhetoric tend to agree that healthcare should be publicly funded, something that may have contributed to false notions of common opinions in this area. In practice, there has never been any consensus in either way. Instead, the perceptions have ranged from the opinion that all healthcare must be publicly funded to the opinion that the public sector only has to pay for a basic and shrinking supply of hospital care.

Many politicians still hesitate to say what they think about welfare, but there are others who are more outspoken. An example is the think tank Timbro's CEO Karin Svanborg-Sjövall, who says:

> It is time for us to step up our efforts and seriously challenge the sacred cow that no one dares to ride: namely the purely private funding of welfare. We have outsourced the welfare services, but there have been no real privatizations. It is about looking more at insurance solutions of various kinds. Not least if we go into a recession, we will be forced to very tough

> priorities, and then the discussion on how the welfare will be financed will come to work seriously. And now there is a maturity in public opinion to move forward, not in the school sector, but in healthcare and elderly care.[6]

The think tank Timbro is really on the offensive these days. Under the heading *Welfare funding beyond taxes—Like swearing in church*, together with the think tank ECEPR,[7] they claim that:

> To emphasize a new form of financing for welfare in Swedish policy context, which means that funding via tax funds is greatly reduced, is a bit like swearing in the church. But the political leadership in Sweden must wake up to the real financing problems of welfare. Now, investigations must be started around the transition to a new financing model. The current model is not sustainable, and the effect of this will be quite noticeable when the next economic crisis strikes. The political parties, those in government as well as the opposition, must begin to tackle the difficult work of shifting towards a more sustainable form of funding. The alternative, not to reform, will lead to a deep economic crisis for the welfare sector.[8]

Timbro is apparently explicit with its willingness to fundamentally reshape the Swedish welfare model, and like other advocates of a divided welfare state they are more and more successful in spreading their ideas due to, among other things, a situation where lobbyism grows stronger (Hermansson et al. 1999; Garsten et al. 2015) and where the welfare industrial complex is more powerful (Svensson 2014; Unsgaard and Werne 2014). Partly, it is also due to the non-existent Swedish quarantine rules for politicians to engage in the private welfare industry. Here, the private sector has been very successful not least with retired social democratic politicians (Mona Sahlin, Thomas Bodström, Göran Persson, Björn Rosengren, Thomas Östros, Per Nuder and many more). The welfare industry has also made inroads into the active labour movement, something that has been little noticed even though it has sometimes been quite extravagant. One example is the Prime scandal (e.g. Suhonen 2014), where a number of Social Democrats, including Niklas Nordström, via the PR agency Prime, was bought by the

Confederation of Swedish Enterprise to guide the Social Democratic Party towards right-wing politics.

Notes

1. https://www.almega.se/en-ny-naringspolitik/privata-foretag-avgorande-for-framtidens-valfard/.
2. *Aftonbladet*, 10 September 2017.
3. *Svenska Dagbladet*, 21 October 2016.
4. *Svenska Dagbladet*, 19 October 2016.
5. *Dagens Nyheter*, 27 February 2005.
6. *Dagens Industri*, 2 November 2018. https://www.di.se/nyheter/naringslivets-tankesmedja-star-redo-for-nasta-politiska-strid/.
7. https://www.ecepr.org/.
8. *Dagens Samhälle*, 26 April 2019. https://www.dagenssamhalle.se/nyhet/valfardsfinansiering-bortom-skatten-lite-som-att-svara-i-kyrkan-27330.

References

Baumgartner, F. R., & Jones, B. D. (2010). *Agendas and instability in American politics*. Chicago: University of Chicago Press.

Blomqvist, P., & Rothstein, B. (2000). *Välfärdsstatens nya ansikte: demokrati och marknadsreformer inom den offentliga sektorn*. Stockholm: Agora.

Borg, P. (2009). *Den långsiktiga finansieringen: välfärdspolitikens klimatfråga?* Finansdepartementet, Regeringskansliet.

Bröms, J. (2004, December). *Makten över behoven-Kan sjukvårdens två kulturer förenas*. Rapport till Vårdforum. Stockholm.

Entman, R. M. (1993). Framing: Toward clarification of a fractured paradigm. *Journal of Communication, 43*(4), 51–58.

Garsten, C., Rothstein, B., & Svallfors, S. (2015). *Makt utan mandat: de policyprofessionella i svensk politik*. Stockholm: Dialogos förlag.

Hermansson, J., Lund, A., Svensson, T., & Öberg, P. O. (1999). *Avkorporativisering och lobbyism*. Stockholm, Sweden: SOU.

Jordahl, H. (2004). Vårdkonsument eller soffpotatis. *Nya balanspunkter för hälsa och sjukvård. Timbro Hälsa*.

Klüver, H., Mahoney, C., & Opper, M. (2015). Framing in context: How interest groups employ framing to lobby the European Commission. *Journal of European Public Policy, 22*(4), 481–498.

Lyttkens, C. H. (2010). Sjukvårdens långsiktiga finansiering. In A. Anell & U. G. Gerdtham (Eds.), *Vårdens utmaningar* (pp. 114–147). Stockholm: SNS Förlag.

McGrath, C. (2007). Framing lobbying messages: Defining and communicating political issues persuasively. *Journal of Public Affairs: An International Journal, 7*(3), 269–280.

Pralle, S. B. (2003). Venue shopping, political strategy, and policy change: The internationalization of Canadian forest advocacy. *Journal of Public Policy, 23*(3), 233–260.

Söderström, L. (1991). *Hur skall sjukvården betalas?-Om alternativa betalningsmodeller* (Vol. 1). Stockholm: SNS Förlag.

Statens offentliga utredningar. (2004). *Långtidsutredningen 2003/04, SOU 2004:19*. Stockholm: Fritzes offentliga publikationer.

Suhonen, D. (2014). *Partiledaren som klev in i kylan*. Stockholm: Leopard Förlag.

Svensson, S. (2014). *Oligarkerna: vinnarna i slaget om välfärden*. Stockholm: Tankesmedjan Tiden.

Tenelius, H., & Selling, N. (2016). *Välfärdslobbyisten: om caremadrevet, vårdvinster och demokratins nya utmaninger*. Stockholm: Ekerlids förlag.

Unsgaard, O. F., & Werne, K. (2014). *Den stora omvandlingen. En granskning av välfärdsmarknaden*. Stockholm: Leopard förlag.

16
Future Funding of Welfare

Do we have to move towards a divided welfare state? Is it a kind of economic necessity that forces us to create more private and semi-private welfare solutions? The advocates of the divided welfare state want to portray it that way. The public welfare services become more expensive and expensive every year, they reason, and therefore we will not be able to afford them in the future.

The advocates of a divided welfare state are inspired by William Baumol and his so-called cost disease, according to which services become relatively more expensive over time as it is more difficult to increase productivity in the service sector compared to the goods sector (Baumol and Bowen 1966; Nordhaus 2008; Baumol 2012).

Unfortunately, they have completely misunderstood Baumol's theories. This is despite the fact that Baumol himself has done everything to avoid these misunderstandings. Time and again, William Baumol emphasizes that the cost disease is a completely natural part of every society's development. Time and again, he points out that a society that becomes richer and richer will have an increasing opportunity to pay for an ever-better welfare for all its citizens.

How can one think that a society that is getting richer will have more difficulties to fund a good welfare system for all citizens? What

J. Lapidus, *The Quest for a Divided Welfare State*,
https://doi.org/10.1007/978-3-030-24784-3_16

is the basis for these misunderstandings of Baumol's theories, misunderstandings that he himself points out as dangerous to society? How can Baumol be so misunderstood when his theories are so logically consistent and intuitively obvious?

As we shall see, it is easy to misunderstand Baumol's theories, especially for those who want to misunderstand them. The misunderstanding is based on the exclusive and excluding focus on Baumol's first thesis, namely that services become relatively more expensive over time.

That is undoubtedly the case: services are becoming relatively more expensive over time, but if something becomes relatively more expensive then something has to be relatively cheaper. According to Baumol's second thesis, if something gets cheaper, then you will be able to afford what is more expensive, especially as this price shift is based on the whole society becoming richer and richer.

The misunderstanding is thus based on disregarding Baumol's second thesis, namely that productivity growth in the goods sector—and to some extent in the service sector—means that we will be able to have more welfare and still consume more gadgets than ever before.

According to Baumol, it is actually the cheaper goods that is the major problem with prevailing social development. The richer we become, the more goods we will be able to buy, something that poses a threat to the environment.

But what if productivity does not continue to grow? Well, then we also get no cost disease, because the *disease* only *affects* societies that become richer and richer. If productivity increases were to stop, then welfare services will not become *increasingly expensive* over time.

Let us take a closer look at Baumol's theories and illustrate why the cost disease do not at all have the severe consequences that the advocates of the divided welfare state want it to have. With Baumol's own words, the famous *disease* instead gets a happy ending where we are increasingly able to finance the welfare in the future.

First, it is quite right that most services, including public and private welfare services such as healthcare, schooling and elderly care, become more expensive over time when compared to how the price of goods develops. This is because it is much easier to increase productivity in the private and public goods sector, than in the private and public service sectors.

The classic example is a concert by Beethoven performed by a string quartet a couple of hundred years ago. It still takes as long to play, and it still requires as many musicians. The musicians would of course be able to increase their productivity by playing twice as fast, but how would that sound? Productivity could also be increased by dismissing half the orchestra, but it would not the same concert as before. That is often (but not always) the case in the service sector. The string quartet is an extreme example, but the fact is that in many kinds of services it is difficult to increase productivity without making the quality suffer.

Measured in increase of productivity, nothing has thus happened with the concert since the eighteenth century. Albeit not as distinct, the same goes for many services in the service sector. Compared to the furious productivity growth in the goods sector, it still takes quite some time to get the haircut or see the dentist or be served in a restaurant.

The hairdresser could spend five minutes on each customer, but the question is how satisfied the customers would be. The restaurant could rationalize all the waiters and let the guests pick up the food themselves, in the kitchen, but then it would not be the same experience.

In the service sector, there is a large and important element of direct contact between producer and consumer. For those who buy a car, it doesn't matter how many hours it took to produce it, or how the car worker dressed, or how the contacts with the subcontractors worked, as long as it is a good car that is for sale. The consumer, as a consumer, has no interest in what happens in the factory. The consumer does not notice any rationalization nor any productivity growth that take place in the automotive industry.

The same goes for all goods manufacturing where the product's quality has nothing to do with the contact between producer and consumer, where the contact between producer and consumer is as superfluous as non-existent.

In addition, there is the fact that standardization is much more difficult in a number of service sectors. From the assembly line, thousands of exactly the same cars come out, but the hairdresser's customers all want their haircut in different ways.

At the same time, of course, it is quite possible find some productivity-enhancing measures in the service sector as well. This is done all the time. One of the most striking examples is the outstanding development in data and telecommunications, which has resulted in huge productivity gains and which has made many service jobs redundant in today's society.

Professor Baumol, for example, mentions that he did not need any secretary in the last decades of his professional career. Of course, all citizens notice this data revolution in hundreds of different ways, for example, when we pay our bills. There is certainly some kind of quality degradation compared to the personal contact with a bank assistant, but most people still perceive this do-it-yourself society (Baumol's term) as more modern and effective.

Speaking of modernity, it often happens that new and cheap goods can replace old services, which have become more expensive by the cost disease. In this context, Baumol mentions maids as one of the service professions rationalized by the entry of the vacuum cleaners, dishwashers and washing machines. Here, Baumol has obviously underestimated the Swedes' willingness to go back in time and, through tax subsidies, get the old society right back again.

Regardless of all the progress and setbacks, the cost disease is an obvious fact in large parts of the service sector, not least the welfare services. Productivity in these sectors is developing, quite naturally, at a much slower rate than in the goods sector. Some increases in productivity mean, as mentioned, poorer quality, while other such increases may be pure imagination. Baumol gives a funny example of the latter: the police increased their productivity when they started using police cars instead of horses. But at the same time, the thieves also started to use cars, so on the whole there were no productivity gains.

The remaining services are becoming more expensive while we have seen a tremendous productivity growth in the goods sector. The one who hesitates can think about how long it took to produce a car in the eighteenth century compared to how long it takes today. Joking aside, it is enough to go a few years back to see how production methods are getting better, a development that means that less human labour is needed for every car that is manufactured.

Services are becoming more expensive, and goods are becoming cheaper. The productivity growth in the goods sector means that less labour is needed in the same, but at the same time some services are also rationalized. In robotization, there is a tremendous potential to rationalize more service jobs. Just imagine what self-driving trucks, buses and cars would mean for all truck, bus and taxi drivers, and how all this human workforce could enter other service sectors—for example, the welfare sector.

As a result of productivity growth and subsequent rationalization, there is a continuous reduction in the number of jobs in large parts of the goods sector and also in certain service professions. As long as society develops, it is quite natural that jobs are passed over to the remaining service sector, not least to the welfare sector with its increasing need for labour.

Broadly speaking, this is exactly what has happened in all developed countries of the world. The development from an *agricultural society* to an *industrial society* to a *service society* has happened because productivity growth has been so huge in industry and agriculture. Of course, these sectors have not disappeared, far from it, but they have required less and less labour and will require even less labour in the future.

Part of this social development is thus that an increasing proportion of the total resources are directed to the welfare sector, such as healthcare. It has been called the first law of health economics (e.g. Kruk et al. 2016), and it seems to apply worldwide. In short, the law means that the richer a country becomes, the greater the share of GDP the country tends to spend on healthcare. Poor countries tend to spend a relatively small percentage of GDP on healthcare, while rich countries spend an increasing proportion of GDP on healthcare. When poor countries become richer, they undergo a transition in terms of healthcare expenditure.

Of course, there are many ways to make healthcare more efficient and to make the inevitable cost increases as small as possible. Baumol mentions everything from obsolete computer systems to costly negligence on the part of the staff. However, when he looks more closely at the statistics, it turns out that the computer systems have become better and the neglects fewer, but the costs have nevertheless increased since there is nothing that can cure the cost disease in a society that is developing.

In this context, it should be said that technological development enables great progress in all possible areas and levels in the health sector, and that there is also cost-saving potential in many of these advances. Joyia et al. (2017) provide an overview related to Internet of things (IoT) services and technologies in healthcare, services that can connect patients, doctors, nurses and hospitals in new ways and services that "enable the doctors and hospital staff to do their work more precisely and actively with less effort and intelligence". Elhayatmy et al. (2018) agree with the previous speaker. They believe that the new technology can be considered the "phase changer of the healthcare applications concerning the patient's health using low cost", and they further mean that "The foremost clue of relating IoT to healthcare is to join the physicians and patients through smart devices while each individual is roaming deprived of any limitations". Rahmani et al. (2018) also praise the IoT technology, which "provides a competent and structured approach to improve health and wellbeing of mankind". With reference to Koop et al. (2008), Rahmani et al. claim that the healthcare system through the new technology will develop from hospital-centred to hospital-home-centred and finally to home-centred as early as 2030. However, to achieve such a development, "new system architectures, technologies, and computing paradigms are required, particularly in the smart spaces and e-Health domains".

Similarly, there is enormous potential in the partially overlapping Artificial Intelligence (AI), where "The potential roles of AI techniques in healthcare delivery and medical research are becoming increasingly evident" (Reddy et al. 2019). There is great interest in AI-based healthcare solutions, and there also seem to be many who want to invest in these solutions. CB Insights lists over 100 companies that are

> applying machine learning algorithms and predictive analytics to reduce drug discovery times, provide virtual assistance to patients, and diagnose ailments by processing medical images, among other things.

For example, the company Sensely has developed a virtual nursing assistant, Molly, to follow-up with patients who are back home after a stay at the hospital. Similar chatbots have been developed for patient counselling via telephone or SMS. One example is British Babylon (e.g. Armstrong 2018; Iacobucci 2017) which is connected to a database containing all the symptoms and diseases in the world. Babylon asks follow-up questions and thus filters out the next step in the counselling. All steps require an average of twelve SMS back and forth and take about 1.5 minutes on average.

Reddy et al. (2019) point out four areas where AI will be of great importance in healthcare: healthcare administration, clinical decision support, patient monitoring and healthcare interventions. When it comes to administration, AI can free up time for doctors to engage in caring, for example, by doing "repetitive and routine tasks like patient data entry and automated review of laboratory data and imaging result". At the same time, AI, via machine learning, can be very helpful with scheduling and priorities, which can reduce waiting times in healthcare and make resources available more efficiently.

When it comes to clinical decision support, doctors will get more help from computers that have learned to diagnose and treat by studying lots of similar cases. This, in turn, can "can help to reduce medical errors and increase healthcare consistency and efficiency". When it comes to patient monitoring, smartphones and other devices have made it possible to collect lots of different types of data such as sleep patterns, blood pressure and heart rate. AI can also be used as surveillance in intensive care clinics and it can also be used after a hospital stay, where virtual assistants can "communicate appropriate health and medication information and schedule follow-up visits for patients". When it comes to healthcare interventions, there is already, for example, computer vision for automated analysis of 3D medical images, but AI is also used to assess a patient's condition through facial analysis. Another major area of application is elderly care, where robotic assistants can be used for example to remind elderly about regular activities and guiding them through unfamiliar environments.

In addition, there are a large number of potential uses for AI, not least in robotics where robots can be used, for example, in surgery (see, e.g., Diana and Marescaux 2015; Antoniou et al. 2015; Shademan et al. 2016). Development has already come a long way and it will go much longer in the future. The same goes for interpretation of X-ray images.

At Danderyd's hospital in Sweden, attempts are made in this area (Olczak et al. 2017) and it is said that AI is already as good as a senior physician in recognizing and interpreting fractures.[1]

Another example is Google Deepmind's collaboration with British Moorfield's Eye Hospital, which aims to read digitally scanned images with new AI algorithms in order to more effectively and more quickly detect different types of severe vision impairment. Some results have been published in Nature Medicine (De Fauw et al. 2018) and show that their AI's performance in making a referral recommendation "reaches or exceeds that of experts on a range of sight-threatening retinal diseases after training on only 14,884 scans".

Many breakthroughs within AI have not yet seen the light of day and others suffer from implementation lags (Brynjolfsson et al. 2018; Wachter and Howell 2018). Exactly where things like AI and IoT will lead us in terms of costs and productivity in the healthcare sector is impossible to say. For a long time, and also well into the future, the increase in healthcare costs—both in absolute and in relative terms—is a natural development that follows directly from the cost disease. Thanks to productivity growth, a country like Sweden has become much richer while the products in the goods sector have become much cheaper, which together means that we can afford more and more healthcare every year.

As long as productivity continues to grow, it is therefore quite natural that the share of healthcare as part of GDP increases. Baumol compares the years 2005 and 2015. If productivity were to continue to grow as of today, healthcare will then consume a larger—much larger—share of GDP than today. With continued productivity growth, however, GDP will be so much higher and commodity prices so much lower that we will be able to afford much more of everything.

With the above in mind, it is no wonder that Baumol puts a lot of energy into warning politicians for general budget cuts. Healthcare budgets should not be reduced through reduced taxes. On the contrary, health budgets should be increased through increased taxes. Politicians should not think that healthcare costs can be reduced over time, and journalists must understand the effects of the cost disease in order to pass this important knowledge on to the citizens.

Baumol's conclusions are simple but very important in the peculiar Swedish debate on the *future financing of welfare*. If we as a country become richer and richer, we will be able to afford more products than ever before, even though we gradually raise taxes to afford a better and more expensive welfare.

And what about public versus private? The question should be asked to the advocates of the divided welfare state, who make two erroneous claims in one and the same sentence: because we cannot afford welfare in the future, they argue, we must begin to privatize more and more of it.

Let's assume, for fun, that we will not be able to afford welfare in the future. If so, would it be cheaper if we privatize? Are private welfare services miraculously spared from the cost disease?

Of course not. The cost sickness strikes as hard against private as against public welfare services. For a society that gets richer and richer, there is no way to escape the price increases. Rather, privatization increases costs even further through a variety of factors and mechanisms mentioned in previous chapters. Moreover, such a system becomes very unequal. The classic example is the United States, which despite its unequal healthcare spends a very large percentage of GDP on the same.

Allowing citizens to pay privately or semi-privately is thus no way to escape the incurable cost disease. This common *misunderstanding* about public and private welfare costs is discussed on the page Ekonomistas.se, where Fredrik Andersson Carlö quite rightly states that:

> If welfare production becomes more expensive relative to other production because welfare production is very service-intensive and service production generally less efficient than production of goods, then it is quite reasonable that taxes should rise? If welfare production is to be carried out by the private sector instead of the public sector, it is exactly what would happen, through price increases instead of tax increases. The fact is that this is what happens when an increasing part of our private consumption goes to service consumption, partly because services become relatively more expensive goods, as product production is made more efficient. And who is complaining about it? Who is worried about how we can afford to go to a restaurant, buy a massage or hire craftsmen in the future? If one can raise prices, one can reasonably raise taxes. It is basically exactly the same thing.

In a report (Andersson 2019), an attempt is made to estimate what is needed to maintain the quality of welfare services in 2040. The report indicates that gradual tax increases will be necessary if the quality is to be maintained, and the increases will need to be even higher if one assumes that the welfare commitment should be restored to the level prevailing in 1990. In a third future scenario, with a maintained tax ratio, the report shows how the quality of welfare will gradually be eroded and how fewer welfare workers will be employed, that is, a reduced welfare commitment which would "probably reinforce the trend towards increased funding through private insurance". Similar reasoning can be found in SKL (2010) and the National Institute of Economic Research (Konjunkturinstitutet 2018).

The most important thing in the above reasoning, and throughout this chapter, is that relative costs will rise regardless of welfare model. Thus, we can choose between a costly, semi-privatized healthcare and a costly, tax-financed healthcare. The cost disease is a natural consequence of social development and a sign that we are better off than before. Which type of costs we choose—public or private—depends primarily on which society we want.

Note

1. https://ki.se/nyheter/ai-bedomer-rontgenbilder-lika-bra-som-lakare#-header-0.

References

Andersson, L. F. (2019). *Välfärdens framtid. Demografi, individuell välfärdskonsumtion och skatter i Sverige 2018 till 2040*. Stockholm: Arena ide.

Antoniou, S. A., Antoniou, G. A., Antoniou, A. I., & Granderath, F. A. (2015). Past, present, and future of minimally invasive abdominal surgery. *JSLS: Journal of the Society of Laparoendoscopic Surgeons, 19*(3), https://www.ncbi.nlm.nih.gov/pmc/articles/PMC4589904/.

Armstrong, S. (2018). The apps attempting to transfer NHS 111 online. *BMJ, 360,* k156.

Baumol, W. J. (2012). *The cost disease: Why computers get cheaper and health care doesn't.* New Haven, CT: Yale University Press.

Baumol, W. J., & Bowen, W. G. (1966). *Performing arts—The economic dilemma: A study of problems common to theatre, opera, music and dance.* Cambridge: MIT Press.

Brynjolfsson, E., Rock, D., & Syverson, C. (2018). Artificial intelligence and the modern productivity paradox: A clash of expectations and statistics. In *The economics of artificial intelligence: An agenda.* Chicago: University of Chicago Press.

De Fauw, J., Ledsam, J. R., Romera-Paredes, B., Nikolov, S., Tomasev, N., Blackwell, S., et al. (2018). Clinically applicable deep learning for diagnosis and referral in retinal disease. *Nature Medicine, 24*(9), 1342.

Diana, M., & Marescaux, J. (2015). Robotic surgery. *British Journal of Surgery, 102*(2), e15–e28.

Elhayatmy, G., Dey, N., & Ashour, A. S. (2018). Internet of things based wireless body area network in healthcare. In *Internet of things and big data analytics toward next-generation intelligence* (pp. 3–20). Cham: Springer.

Iacobucci, G. (2017). *London GP clinic sees big jump in patient registrations after Babylon app launch.*

Joyia, G. J., Liaqat, R. M., Farooq, A., & Rehman, S. (2017). Internet of Medical Things (IOMT): Applications, benefits and future challenges in healthcare domain. *Journal of Communications, 12*(4), 240–247.

Koop, C. E., Mosher, R., Kun, L., Geiling, J., Grigg, E., Long, S., et al. (2008). Future delivery of health care: Cybercare. *IEEE Engineering in Medicine and Biology Magazine, 27*(6), 29–38.

Konjunkturinstitutet. (2018). *Hållbarhetsrapport 2018 för de offentliga finanserna, inklusive tabell och figurunderlag.* KI-NR, 2.

Kruk, M. E., Yamey, G., Angell, S. Y., Beith, A., Cotlear, D., Guanais, F., et al. (2016). Transforming global health by improving the science of scale-up. *PLoS Biology, 14*(3), e1002360.

Nordhaus, W. D. (2008). Baumol's diseases: A macroeconomic perspective. *The BE Journal of Macroeconomics, 8*(1), 1–39.

Olczak, J., Fahlberg, N., Maki, A., Razavian, A. S., Jilert, A., Stark, A., et al. (2017). Artificial intelligence for analyzing orthopedic trauma radiographs: Deep learning algorithms—Are they on par with humans for diagnosing fractures? *Acta Orthopaedica, 88*(6), 581–586.

Rahmani, A. M., Gia, T. N., Negash, B., Anzanpour, A., Azimi, I., Jiang, M., et al. (2018). Exploiting smart e-Health gateways at the edge of healthcare Internet-of-Things: A fog computing approach. *Future Generation Computer Systems, 78,* 641–658.

Reddy, S., Fox, J., & Purohit, M. P. (2019). Artificial intelligence-enabled healthcare delivery. *Journal of the Royal Society of Medicine, 112*(1), 22–28.

Shademan, A., Decker, R. S., Opfermann, J. D., Leonard, S., Krieger, A., & Kim, P. C. (2016). Supervised autonomous robotic soft tissue surgery. *Science Translational Medicine, 8*(337), 337ra64–337ra64.

SKL. (2010). *Framtidens utmaning. Välfärdens långsiktiga finansiering.* Programberedningen för välfärdsfinansieringen.

Wachter, R. M., & Howell, M. D. (2018). Resolving the productivity paradox of health information technology: A time for optimism. *JAMA, 320*(1), 25–26.

17

A Choice Between Two Models

What to do with the Swedish welfare model? Right now, we are heading towards a divided welfare state, that is two very different welfare states in one and the same country. One of these welfare states, the hidden one, is emerging through state sponsoring of groups that have the economic opportunity and the formal right to take part in it. One example is the rapid emergence of *private* health insurance. Here, there has been a direct government sponsorship via favourable gross salary deductions. At the same time, there has been an indirect and even more hidden state sponsorship where private providers, insurance companies and policyholders freeride on the public welfare sector.

Large population groups are excluded from the hidden welfare. As far as private health insurance is concerned, you must not be a lemon who acidifies the market and raises premiums for the peaches, that is you should preferably be healthy to get an insurance policy. At the same time, you have had to have a willing employer in order make gross salary deductions, which means that the hidden welfare creates a new relationship employer–employee rather than state–citizen, this despite the fact that the state bears much of the costs.

J. Lapidus, *The Quest for a Divided Welfare State*,
https://doi.org/10.1007/978-3-030-24784-3_17

The hidden welfare state grows at the expense of the universal welfare state, which has traditionally been used by everyone. There are a number of factors that negatively affect the public welfare. Some of these are the direct and indirect sponsorships mentioned above but, moreover, the tax willingness of those who no longer benefit from public welfare decreases. Further, when the most vocal citizens leave the public system, they no longer have any reason to put pressure on politicians to fix the problems in the public health system.

The hidden welfare is dependent on the private welfare industry, which has also developed through state decisions and support measures. The dependency can be exemplified by private health insurance: without a nationwide network of private providers at all levels of care, insurance companies would not have anywhere to send their 650,000 policyholders, as publicly run healthcare facilities do not receive insurance patients.

At the same time, private healthcare providers tend to become increasingly dependent on insurance companies and their customers, in different ways. There is thus a mutual dependence between private provision and *private* funding or in other words between profits in welfare and the emergence of the hidden welfare state.

Much of the above is surprisingly unexplored areas in both Swedish and international context. Many researchers have contributed to increased knowledge about the part of the hidden welfare state that has to do with the direct and statutory sponsorships through various types of tax deductions and tax breaks. Few, however, have pointed out that the hidden welfare is a whole system of state sponsorship and semi-privatization at many different levels, a system that is efficient when it comes to eroding the universal welfare state.

The fact that profits in welfare create a new welfare model is something that has also been missed out in the Swedish debate. It could actually have been one of the strongest arguments against a profit-driven and increasingly powerful private welfare industry, whose directors are once again on the warpath. Today's battle for profits in welfare is compared to last century's struggle against wage-earner funds. The directors say it is the same as then and that they will demonstrate on the streets of Stockholm as happened on 4 October 1983.

It is a strange comparison. The wage-earner funds were the strong, reformist labour movement's attempt to take a first step towards economic democracy. The resistance to profits in welfare is the weak, fragmented, defensive effort of the labour movement to regain some of what was absolutely obvious at that time: a welfare sector beyond the logic and control of the market economy.

In that perspective, it becomes clear who has advanced their positions. An advancement that would have been impossible without the concessions of the reformist labour movement from the 1980s onwards. A process which, ironically, began when today's largest welfare companies were formed with capital from the discontinued wage-earner funds.

The advocates of a divided welfare state have wind in the sails, and more and more actors are boarding. Many of them confess to the ideas of liberalism. In this context, it is important to point out the illiberal nature of the divided welfare state, which is based on direct and indirect state sponsorship, but which is still considered a way forward by those who call themselves liberals. It's contradictory. It shows that today's liberals are not very interested in liberalism, but very interested in the widened gaps created by the hidden welfare state.

The gaps between people create inequality at all levels. The gaps are not only visible in the wallet but also in many other areas of life, not least when it comes to health where things such as longevity have begun to differ considerably between rich and poor areas. These gaps between people are at the same time a peculiar fertile ground for nationalism and neo-fascist parties of a kind and size that many believed to be a phenomenon of the past.

Shall we continue all the way to a divided welfare state? As with all major contemporary issues, a straightforward discussion is needed on the differences between different alternatives. The question deserves much better than tactical and slightly absurd reasoning that private and semi-private solutions are particularly favourable to the common and public health sector. Unfortunately, this kind of tactic can be effective. Opponents of the traditional welfare model know that it is popular in broad layers of the population. Therefore, semi-private welfare solutions are said to be fully in line with the Swedish welfare model, despite the fact that semi-private welfare solutions are the exact opposite of this model.

How to organize Swedish welfare is first and foremost a political issue. We can choose to have a progressive and ambitious tax system with high-quality welfare services according to Gustav Möller's statement that only the best is good enough for the people. Or, we can have low taxes and let people take individual responsibility for their welfare, combined with tax reliefs for the well-off.

Regardless of the welfare model we prefer, it is important to clarify what we are talking about and what is at stake. There are two models to choose from. One implies increased investment in tax-financed welfare services, and the other implies increased semi-private funding and reduced public commitment.

Many people want to continue towards a divided welfare state. They want to further reduce taxes on employment, entrepreneurship and ownership. At the same time, they want to stimulate the emergence of the hidden welfare, where things like the Rut deduction and no benefit taxation of health insurance policies mean that the state co-finances private solutions in the welfare area.

What is the alternative to this development? The alternative is to regain and further develop the traditional Swedish welfare model, to reconsider the expansion of the public sector as a process of democratization, where civic rights become more and stronger over time.

Such a model requires a slowly rising rather than falling tax ratio. Such a model requires that we once again withdraw healthcare, school and elderly care from the market's logic and control.

I would never take the term *Swedish values* in my mouth. But, if something was typically Swedish, and almost as world-famous as Borg and Stenmark, it was a universal welfare state as a result of public provision and funding of central welfare services.

Index

J. Lapidus, *The Quest for a Divided Welfare State*,
https://doi.org/10.1007/978-3-030-24784-3

W

The manufacturer's authorised representative in the EU is Springer Nature Customer Service Centre GmbH, Europaplatz 3, 69115 Heidelberg, Germany. If you have any concerns regarding our products, please contact ProductSafety@springernature.com

Printed and bound by CPI Group (UK) Ltd, Croydon, CR0 4YY

30/09/2026

02225656-0007